Frommer's

San ...isco

5th Edition

by Erika Lenkert

Here's what critics say about Frommer's:

"Amazingly easy to use. Very portable, very complete."

—*Booklist*

"Detailed, accurate, and easy-to-read information for all price ranges."

—*Glamour Magazine*

Wiley Publishing, Inc.

Published by:

WILEY PUBLISHING, INC.

111 River St.
Hoboken, NJ 07030-5774

ISBN 0-7645-7186-9

Editor: Kendra L. Falkenstein
Production Editor: Ian Skinnari
Photo Editor: Richard Fox
Cartographer: Nick Trotter
Production by Wiley Indianapolis Composition Services

For information on our other products and services or to obtain technical support, please contact our Customer Care Department within the U.S. at 800/762-2974, outside the U.S. at 317/572-3993 or fax 317/572-4002.

Wiley also publishes its books in a variety of electronic formats. Some content that appears in print may not be available in electronic formats.

Manufactured in the United States of America

5   4   3   2   1

Contents

List of Maps

ACKNOWLEDGMENTS

Huge thanks to expert researcher Michele Addey, who tirelessly helped ensure the most up-to-date accuracy of this book and also happens to be an excellent friend.

ABOUT THE AUTHOR

A native San Franciscan, **Erika Lenkert** resides in Napa Valley when she's not traipsing through San Francisco and across the globe in search of adventure and great food. She frequently writes *InStyle* magazine's entertaining guide and has contributed to *Travel + Leisure, Food & Wine, Bride's, Wine Country Living, San Francisco Magazine, Los Angeles Magazine,* and *Time Out*. Her latest achievement, an entertaining and cooking book called *The Last-Minute Party Girl: Fashionable, Fearless, Foolishly Simple Entertaining*, mixes fun, humor, and San Francisco dining experiences and recipes into one tasty and useful guide to living large, Bay Area style.

AN INVITATION TO THE READER

In researching this book, we discovered many wonderful places—hotels, restaurants, shops, and more. We're sure you'll find others. Please tell us about them, so we can share the information with your fellow travelers in upcoming editions. If you were disappointed with a recommendation, we'd love to know that, too. Please write to:

Frommer's Portable San Francisco, 5th Edition
Wiley Publishing, Inc. • 111 River St. • Hoboken, NJ 07030-5774

AN ADDITIONAL NOTE

Please be advised that travel information is subject to change at any time—and this is especially true of prices. We therefore suggest that you write or call ahead for confirmation when making your travel plans. The authors, editors, and publisher cannot be held responsible for the experiences of readers while traveling. Your safety is important to us, however, so we encourage you to stay alert and be aware of your surroundings. Keep a close eye on cameras, purses, and wallets, all favorite targets of thieves and pickpockets.

FROMMER'S STAR RATINGS, ICONS & ABBREVIATIONS

Every hotel, restaurant, and attraction listing in this guide has been ranked for quality, value, service, amenities, and special features using a **star-rating system.** In country, state, and regional guides, we also rate towns and regions to help you narrow down your choices and budget your time accordingly. Hotels and restaurants are rated on a scale of zero (recommended) to three stars (exceptional). Attractions, shopping, nightlife, towns, and regions are rated according to the following scale: zero stars (recommended), one star (highly recommended), two stars (very highly recommended), and three stars (must-see).

In addition to the star-rating system, we also use **seven feature icons** that point you to the great deals, in-the-know advice, and unique experiences that separate travelers from tourists. Throughout the book, look for:

Finds	Special finds—those places only insiders know about
Fun Fact	Fun facts—details that make travelers more informed and their trips more fun
Kids	Best bets for kids and advice for the whole family
Moments	Special moments—those experiences that memories are made of
Overrated	Places or experiences not worth your time or money
Tips	Insider tips—great ways to save time and money
Value	Great values—where to get the best deals

The following **abbreviations** are used for credit cards:

AE	American Express	DISC	Discover	V	Visa
DC	Diners Club	MC	MasterCard		

FROMMERS.COM

Now that you have the guidebook to a great trip, visit our website at **www.frommers.com** for travel information on more than 3,000 destinations. With features updated regularly, we give you instant access to the most current trip-planning information available. At Frommers.com, you'll also find the best prices on airfares, accommodations, and car rentals—and you can even book travel online through our travel booking partners. At Frommers.com, you'll also find the following:

- Online updates to our most popular guidebooks
- Vacation sweepstakes and contest giveaways
- Newsletter highlighting the hottest travel trends
- Online travel message boards with featured travel discussions

Planning Your Trip to San Francisco

1 Visitor Information

The **San Francisco Convention and Visitors Bureau,** 900 Market St. (at Powell St.), Hallidie Plaza, Lower Level, San Francisco, CA 94102 (*C* **415/391-2000;** www.sfvisitor.org), is the best source of specialized information about the city. Even if you don't have a specific question, you might want to request the free *Visitors Planning Guide* and the *San Francisco Visitors* kit. The kit includes a 6-month calendar of events, a city history, shopping and dining information, and several good, clear maps, plus lodging information. The bureau highlights only its members' establishments, so if it doesn't have what you're looking for, that doesn't mean it's nonexistent.

You can also get the latest on San Francisco at the following online addresses:

- The *Bay Guardian,* the city's free weekly paper: **www.sfbg.com**
- Hotel reservations: **www.hotelres.com**
- *SF Gate,* the city's *Chronicle* newspaper: **www.sfgate.com**
- CitySearch: **www.citysearch.com**

2 Money

ATMS

All over San Francisco, you'll find ATMs (automated teller machines) linked to a national network that most likely includes your bank at home. Withdrawing cash as you need it is the easiest way to deal with money while you're on the road. Be sure to find out your daily withdrawal limit before you depart. Also keep in mind that many banks impose a fee (approximately $3) every time a card is used at a different bank's ATM. On top of this, the bank from which you withdraw cash may charge its own fee. To compare banks' ATM fees within the U.S., use www.bankrate.com.

TRAVELER'S CHECKS

Traveler's checks are something of an anachronism from the days before the ATM made cash accessible at any time. Traveler's checks used to be the only sound alternative to traveling with dangerously large amounts of cash. These days, traveler's checks are less necessary because most cities have 24-hour ATMs that allow you to withdraw small amounts of cash as needed. If you choose to carry traveler's checks, be sure to keep a record of their serial numbers separate from your checks in the event that they are stolen or lost. You'll get a refund faster if you know the numbers.

CREDIT CARDS

Credit cards are a safe way to carry money: They also provide a convenient record of all your expenses, and they generally offer relatively good exchange rates.

3 When to Go

If you're dreaming of convertibles, Frisbee on the beach, and tank-topped evenings, change your reservations and head to Los Angeles. Contrary to California's sunshine-and-bikini image, San Francisco's weather is "mild" (to put it nicely) and can often be downright bone-chilling because of the common wet, foggy air and cool winds—it's nothing like that of Southern California. Summer, the most popular time to visit, is often characterized by damp, foggy days; cold, windy nights; and crowded tourist destinations. A good bet is to visit in spring or, better yet, autumn. Every September, right about the time San Franciscans mourn being cheated (or fogged) out of another summer, something wonderful happens: The thermometer rises, the skies clear, and the locals call in sick to work and head for the beach. It's what residents call "Indian summer." The city is also delightful during winter, when the opera and ballet seasons are in full swing; there are fewer tourists, many hotel prices are lower, and downtown bustles with holiday cheer.

CLIMATE

San Francisco's temperate, marine climate usually means relatively mild weather year-round. In summer, chilling fog rolls in most mornings and evenings, and if temperatures top 70°F (21°C), the city is ready to throw a celebration. Even when autumn's heat occasionally stretches into the 80s (upper 20s Celsius) and 90s (lower 30s Celsius), you should still dress in layers, or by early evening you'll learn firsthand why sweatshirt sales are a great business at Fisherman's

---

Tips **Travel Attire in San Francisco**

Even if it's sunny out, don't forget to bring a jacket; the weather can change almost instantly from sunny and warm to windy and cold.

Wharf. In winter, the mercury seldom falls below freezing and snow is almost unheard of, but that doesn't mean you won't be whimpering if you forget your coat. Still, compared to most of the states' weather conditions, San Francisco's is consistently pleasant.

San Francisco's Average Temperatures & Rainfall

	Jan	Feb	Mar	Apr	May	June	July	Aug	Sept	Oct	Nov	Dec
High °F	56	59	61	64	67	70	71	72	73	70	62	56
Low °F	43	46	47	48	51	53	55	56	55	52	48	43
High °C	13	15	16	18	19	21	22	22	23	21	17	13
Low °C	6	8	8	9	11	12	13	13	13	11	9	6
Rain (in.)	4.5	4.0	3.3	1.2	0.4	0.1	0.1	0.1	0.2	1.0	2.5	2.9
Rain (mm)	113.0	101.9	82.8	30.0	9.7	2.8	0.8	1.8	5.1	26.4	63.2	73.4

SAN FRANCISCO CALENDAR OF EVENTS

Also visit www.sfvisitor.org for an annual calendar of local events.

February

Chinese New Year, Chinatown. In 2005, public celebrations will again spill onto every street in Chinatown. Festivities begin with the "Miss Chinatown USA" pageant parade, and climax a week later with a celebratory parade of marching bands, rolling floats, barrages of fireworks, and a block-long dragon writhing in and out of the crowds. The revelry runs for several weeks and wraps up with a memorable parade through Chinatown that starts at Market and Second streets and ends at Kearny Street. Arrive early for a good viewing spot on Grant Avenue. For dates and information, call © **415/982-3000** or visit www.chineseparade.com.

March

St. Patrick's Day Parade, Union Square and Civic Center. Everyone's an honorary Irish person at this festive affair, which starts at 12:45pm at Market and Second streets and continues to City Hall. But the party doesn't stop there. Head down to the Civic Center for the post-party, or venture to The Embarcadero's Harrington's bar (245 Front St.) and celebrate with hundreds of the Irish-for-a-day yuppies as they gallivant around the closed-off streets and numerous pubs. No contact information. Sunday before March 17.

April

Cherry Blossom Festival, Japantown. Meander through the arts-and-crafts and food booths lining the blocked-off streets around Japan Center and watch traditional drumming, flower arranging, origami making, or a parade celebrating the cherry blossom and Japanese culture. Call © **415/563-2313** for information. Mid-to late April.

San Francisco International Film Festival, around San Francisco with screenings at the AMC Kabuki 8 Cinemas (Fillmore and Post sts.), and at many other locations. Begun in 1957, this is America's oldest film festival. It features more than 200 films and videos from more than 50 countries, as well as awards ceremonies in which renowned honorees join the festivities. Tickets are relatively inexpensive, and screenings are accessible to the public. Entries include new films by beginning and established directors. For a schedule or information, call © **415/931-FILM** or visit www.sffs.org. Mid-April to early May.

May

Cinco de Mayo Celebration, Mission District. This is when the Latino community celebrates the victory of the Mexicans over the French at Puebla in 1862; mariachi bands, dancers, food, and a parade fill the streets of the Mission. The parade starts at 10am at 24th and Bryant streets and ends at the Civic Center. No contact information. The Sunday before May 5.

Bay to Breakers Foot Race, The Embarcadero through Golden Gate Park to Ocean Beach. Even if you don't participate, you can't avoid this run from downtown to Ocean Beach, which stops morning traffic throughout the city. More than 60,000 entrants gather—many dressed in wacky, innovative, and sometimes X-rated costumes—for the approximately 7½-mile run. If you don't want to run, join the throng of spectators who line the route. Sidewalk parties, bands, and cheerleaders of all ages provide a good dose of true San Francisco fun. The *San Francisco Examiner* (© **415/359-2800;** www.examiner.com) sponsors the event. Third Sunday of May.

Carnival, Mission District, Mission Street between 14th and 24th streets, and Harrison Street between 16th and 21st streets. The Mission District's largest annual event is a day of festivities that culminates in a parade on Mission Street. For one of San Franciscans' favorite events, more than half a million spectators line the route, and samba musicians and dancers continue to entertain on 14th Street, near Harrison, at the end of the march. Call the hot line at ✆ **415/920-0125** for information. The Sunday of Memorial Day weekend.

June

Union Street Art Festival, Pacific Heights, along Union Street from Steiner to Gough streets. This outdoor fair celebrates San Francisco with themes, gourmet food booths, music, entertainment, and a juried art show featuring works by more than 350 artists. Call the **Union Street Association** (✆ **415/441-7055**) for more information or see www.unionstreetfestival.com. First weekend of June.

Haight Street Fair, Haight-Ashbury. A far cry from the froufrou Union Street Fair, this grittier fair features alternative crafts, ethnic foods, rock bands, and a healthy number of hippies and street kids whooping it up and slamming beers in front of the blaring rock-'n'-roll stage. The fair usually extends along Haight between Stanyan and Ashbury streets. For details and the exact date, call ✆ **415/661-8025.**

North Beach Festival, Grant Avenue, North Beach. In 2004, this party celebrated its 50th anniversary; organizers claim it's the oldest urban street fair in the country. Close to 100,000 city folk meander along Grant Avenue, between Vallejo and Union streets, to eat, drink, and browse the arts-and-crafts booths, poetry readings, swing-dancing venue, and *arte di gesso* (sidewalk chalk art). But the most enjoyable part of the event is listening to music and people-watching. Call ✆ **415/989-2220** for details. Usually Father's Day weekend, but call to confirm.

Stern Grove Midsummer Music Festival, Sunset District. Pack a picnic and head out early to join the thousands who come here to lie in the grass and enjoy classical, jazz, and ethnic music and dance in the grove, at 19th Avenue and Sloat Boulevard. The free concerts take place every Sunday at 2pm between mid-June and August. Show up with a lawn chair or blanket. There are food booths if you forget snacks, but you'll be dying to leave if you don't bring warm clothes—the Sunset District can be one of the coldest parts of the city. Call ✆ **415/252-6252** for listings. Sundays, mid-June through August.

San Francisco Lesbian, Gay, Bisexual, Transgender Pride Parade & Celebration, downtown's Market Street. This prideful event draws up to half a million participants who celebrate all of the above—and then some. The parade proceeds west on Market

Street until it gets to Market and Eighth Street, where hundreds of food, art, and information booths are set up around several soundstages. Call ⓒ **415/864-3733** or visit www.sfpride.org for information. Usually the third or last weekend of June.

July

Fillmore Street Jazz Festival, Pacific Heights. July starts with a bang, when the upscale portion of Fillmore closes to traffic and several blocks of arts and crafts, gourmet food, and live jazz fill the street. (The blocked-off section is changing, so call for details.) Call ⓒ **510/970-3217** for more information. First weekend in July.

Fourth of July Celebration & Fireworks, Fisherman's Wharf. This event can be something of a joke—more often than not, fog, like everyone else, comes into the city to join in the festivities. Sometimes it's almost impossible to view the million-dollar pyrotechnics from PIER 39 on the northern waterfront. Still, it's a party, and if the skies are clear, it's a darn good show. No contact information.

San Francisco Marathon, San Francisco and beyond. This is one of the largest marathons in the world. For entry information, contact West End Management, the event organizer (ⓒ **800/698-8699;** www.chroniclemarathon.com). Usually the second or third weekend in July.

September

A La Carte, A La Park, Sharon Meadow, Golden Gate Park. You probably won't get to go to all the restaurants you'd like while you're visiting the city, but you can get a good sampling at this annual event. More than 40 of the town's favorite restaurants, accompanied by 20 microbreweries and 20 wineries, offer tastings in San Francisco's favorite park. There's entertainment as well, and proceeds benefit the Friends of Recreation & Parks. Admission is around $10 adults in advance and $12 on-site, $8 seniors in advance and $10 on-site, free for children under 12. Call ⓒ **415/458-1988** for 2005 prices. Labor Day weekend.

Opera in the Park, usually in Sharon Meadow, Golden Gate Park. Each year the San Francisco Opera launches its season with a free concert featuring a selection of arias. Call ⓒ **415/861-4008** to confirm the location and date. Usually the Sunday after Labor Day.

San Francisco Blues Festival, on the grounds of Fort Mason, The Marina. The largest outdoor blues music event on the West Coast was 30 years old in 2002 and continues to feature local and national musicians performing back-to-back during the 3-day extravaganza. You can charge tickets by phone at © **415/421-8497** or online at www.ticketmaster.com. For schedule information, call © **415/826-6837;** for recorded information, call © **415/979-5588** or visit www.sfblues.com. Usually in late September.

Folsom Street Fair, along Folsom Street between 7th and 12th streets, SoMa. This is a local favorite for its kinky, outrageous, leather-and-skin gay-centric blowout celebration. It's hard-core, so only open-minded and adventurous types need head this way. Call © **415/861-3247** or visit www.folsomstreetfair.com for the date, which is usually at the end of September.

October

Castro Street Fair, The Castro. Celebrate life in the city's most famous gay neighborhood. Call © **415/841-1824** or visit www. castrostreetfair.org for information. First Sunday in October.

Reggae in the Park, Sharon Meadow, Golden Gate Park. This event draws thousands to the park to dance and celebrate the soulful sounds of reggae. Big-name reggae and world-beat bands play all weekend, and ethnic arts-and-crafts and food booths line the stage's periphery. Tickets are about $20 in advance, $25 onsite. Two-day discounted passes are available for $35. Free for children under 12. Call © **415/458-1988** for more details. First weekend in October.

Italian Heritage Parade, North Beach and Fisherman's Wharf. The city's Italian community leads the festivities around Fisherman's Wharf, celebrating Columbus's landing in America. The festival includes a parade along Columbus Avenue and sporting events, but for the most part, it's a great excuse to hang out in North Beach and people-watch. For information and the exact date, call © **415/434-1492** or visit www.sfcolumbusday.org. Sunday near October 12.

Halloween, The Castro. This is a huge night in San Francisco. A fantastical parade is organized at Market and Castro streets, and a mixed gay/straight crowd revels in costumes of extraordinary imagination. No contact information. October 31.

San Francisco Jazz Festival, various San Francisco locations. This festival presents eclectic programming in an array of fabulous jazz venues throughout the city. With close to 2 weeks of nightly entertainment and dozens of performers, the jazz festival is a hot ticket. Past events have featured Herbie Hancock, Dave Brubeck, the Modern Jazz Quartet, Wayne Shorter, and Bill Frisell. For information, call © **800/850-SFJF** or 415/788-7353;

or visit www.sfjazz.org. Also check the website for other events throughout the year. Late October and early November.

December

The Nutcracker, War Memorial Opera House, Civic Center. The **San Francisco Ballet** (© **415/865-2000**) performs this holiday classic annually. Order tickets to this Tchaikovsky tradition well in advance.

4 Specialized Travel Resources

TRAVELERS WITH DISABILITIES

Most disabilities shouldn't stop anyone from traveling. There are more options and resources out there than ever before.

The San Francisco Convention and Visitors Bureau (p. 1) should have the most up-to-date information on accessible options for travelers with disabilities.

Travelers in wheelchairs can request special ramped taxis by calling **Yellow Cab** (© **415/626-2345**), which charges regular rates for the service. Travelers with disabilities can also get a free copy of the *Muni Access Guide,* published by the San Francisco Municipal Railway, Accessible Services Program, 949 Presidio Ave. (© **415/923-6142**), which is staffed weekdays from 8am to 5pm. Many of the major car-rental companies offer hand-controlled cars for drivers with disabilities.

GAY & LESBIAN TRAVELERS

If you head down to the Castro—an area surrounding Castro Street near Market Street—you'll understand why the city is a mecca for gay and lesbian travelers. Since the 1970s, this unique part of town has remained a colorfully festive neighborhood, teeming with "outed" city folk who meander the streets shopping, eating, partying, or cruising. If anyone feels like an outsider in this part of town, it's heterosexuals, who, although warmly welcomed in the community, may feel uncomfortable or downright threatened if they harbor any homophobia or aversion to being "cruised." For many San Franciscans, it's just a fun area (especially on Halloween) with some wonderful shops.

Gays and lesbians make up a good deal of San Francisco's population, so it's no surprise that clubs and bars all over town cater to them. Although lesbian interests are concentrated primarily in the East Bay (especially Oakland), a significant community resides in the Mission District, around 16th and Valencia streets.

Several local publications concentrate on in-depth coverage of news, information, and listings of goings-on around town for gays and lesbians. The *Bay Area Reporter* has the most comprehensive listings, including a weekly calendar of events. Distributed free on Thursday, it can be found stacked at the corner of 18th and Castro streets and at Ninth and Harrison streets, as well as in bars, bookshops, and stores around town. It may also be available in gay and lesbian bookstores elsewhere in the country.

SENIOR TRAVEL

Mention the fact that you're a senior when you make your travel reservations. Although all of the major U.S. airlines except America West have canceled their senior discount and coupon book programs, many hotels still offer discounts for seniors. If you're a senior, don't be shy about asking for discounts; in most cities, people over the age of 60 qualify for reduced admission to theaters, museums, and other attractions, as well as discounted fares on public transportation. Always carry some kind of identification, such as a driver's license, that shows your date of birth.

The **Senior Citizen Information Line** (© 415/626-1033) offers advice, referrals, and information on city services. The **Friendship Line for the Elderly** (© 415/752-3778) is a support, referral, and crisis-intervention service.

Members of **AARP** (formerly known as the American Association of Retired Persons), 601 E St. NW, Washington, DC 20049 (© 888/687-2277; www.aarp.org), get discounts on hotels, airfares, and car rentals. AARP offers members a wide range of benefits, including *AARP: The Magazine* and a monthly newsletter. Anyone over 50 can join.

FAMILY TRAVEL

San Francisco is full of sightseeing opportunities and special activities geared toward children. You might also want to see *Frommer's San Francisco with Kids* (Wiley Publishing, Inc.), a good source of kid-specific information for your trip.

5 Getting There

BY PLANE

The Bay Area has two major airports: San Francisco International and Oakland International.

SAN FRANCISCO INTERNATIONAL AIRPORT Almost four dozen major scheduled carriers serve **San Francisco International**

Airport (© 650/821-8211; www.flysfo.com), 14 miles directly south of downtown on U.S. 101. Travel time to downtown during commuter rush hour is about 40 minutes; at other times, it's about 20 to 25 minutes.

The airport offers a **hot line** (© 415/817-1717) for information on ground transportation. It gives you a rundown of all your options for getting into the city from the airport (also see below for this information). Each of the three main terminals has a desk where you can get the same information.

GETTING INTO TOWN FROM SAN FRANCISCO INTERNATIONAL AIRPORT

Great news for the budget traveler! **BART** (Bay Area Rapid Transit; © 510/464-6000 or 415/989-2278; www.bart.gov) began running from SFO to numerous stops within downtown San Francisco in June 2003. This new route, which takes about 35 minutes, avoids gnarly traffic on the way and costs a heck of a lot less (around $6 each way, depending on exactly where you're going) than taxis or shuttles. Just jump on the airport's free shuttle bus to the International terminal, enter the BART station there, and you're on your way to San Francisco. Trains leave approximately every 15 minutes.

A **cab** from the airport to downtown costs $30 to $35, plus tip, and takes about 20 to 25 minutes, traffic permitting.

SFO Airporter buses (© 650/246-8942; www.sfoairporter.com) depart from outside the lower-level baggage-claim area for downtown San Francisco every 30 minutes from 5:35am to 9:05pm. Shuttles on the 30-minute circuit stop at several Union Square–area hotels, including the Westin St. Francis, Hilton, Nikko, Renaissance Parc 55, and downtown Marriott. A shuttle running every 60 minutes stops at the Palace Hotel, Crowne Plaza, Hyatt Regency, and Grand Hyatt. No reservations are needed. For the return trip, SFO Airporter picks up at hotels as early as 5:30am; make a reservation 24 hours in advance if possible. The cost per person is $14 one-way, $22 round-trip; children under 3 ride free.

Other private shuttle companies offer door-to-door airport service, in which you share a van with a few other passengers. **Super-Shuttle** (© 415/558-8500; www.supershuttle.com) takes you anywhere in the city, charging $14 to a residence or business. Add $8 for each additional person. It costs $65 plus $1 per each passenger to charter an entire van for up to seven people. The shuttle stops every 20 minutes or so and picks up passengers from the marked areas outside the terminals' upper levels. Reservations are required for the return trip to the airport only and should be made 1 day before departure. These shuttles often demand they pick you up 2 hours before your domestic flight and 3 hours before international flights and during holidays. Keep in mind that you could be the first one on and the last one off, so this trip could take a while; you might want to ask before getting in.

The San Mateo County Transit system, **SamTrans** (✆ **800/660-4287** in Northern California, or 650/508-6200; www.samtrans.com), runs two buses between the San Francisco Airport and the Transbay Terminal at First and Mission streets. Bus no. 292 costs $1.25 and makes the trip in about 55 minutes. The KX bus costs $3.50 and takes just 35 minutes but permits only one carry-on bag. Both buses run daily. The 292 starts at 5:27am and the KX starts at 6:03am. Both run frequently until 8pm, and then hourly until about midnight.

OAKLAND INTERNATIONAL AIRPORT   About 5 miles south of downtown Oakland, at the Hegenberger Road exit of Calif. 17 (U.S. 880), **Oakland International Airport** (✆ **510/563-3300;** www.oaklandairport.com) primarily serves passengers with East Bay destinations. Some San Franciscans prefer this less crowded, accessible airport during busy periods—especially because by car it takes around half an hour to get there from downtown San Francisco (traffic permitting). Also, the airport is accessible by BART, which is not influenced by traffic because it travels on its own tracks (see below for more information).

GETTING INTO TOWN FROM OAKLAND INTERNATIONAL AIRPORT

Taxis from the Oakland Airport to downtown San Francisco are expensive—approximately $50, plus tip.

Bayporter Express (✆ **877/467-1800** in the Bay Area, or 415/467-1800 elsewhere; www.bayporter.com) is a shuttle service that charges $26 for the first person and $12 for each additional person for the ride from the Oakland Airport to downtown San Francisco. Children under 12 pay $7. The fare for outer areas of San Francisco is higher. The service accepts advance reservations. To the right of the Oakland Airport exit, there are usually shuttles that take you to San Francisco for around $20 per person. The shuttles in this fleet are independently owned, and prices vary.

The cheapest way to reach downtown San Francisco is to take the shuttle bus from the Oakland Airport to **BART** (Bay Area Rapid Transit; ✆ **510/464-6000;** www.bart.gov). The AirBART shuttle bus runs about every 15 minutes Monday through Saturday from 6am to 11:30pm and Sunday from 8:30am to 11:30pm. It makes pickups in front of terminals 1 and 2 near the ground transportation signs. Tickets must be purchased at the Oakland Airport's vending machines prior to boarding. The cost is $2 for the 10-minute ride to BART's Coliseum station in Oakland. BART fares vary, depending on your destination; the trip to downtown San Francisco costs $2.75 and takes 20 minutes once you're on board. The entire excursion should take around 45 minutes.

BY CAR

San Francisco is easily accessible by major highways. **Interstate 5,** from the north, gets you close to San Francisco; connect with I-505 north of the city then I-80, which takes you straight into town. **U.S. 101** cuts south-north through the peninsula from San Jose and across the Golden Gate Bridge to points north. If you drive from Los Angeles, you can take the longer coastal route (437 miles and 11 hr.) or the inland route (389 miles and 8 hr.). From Mendocino, it's 156 miles and 4 hours; from Sacramento, 88 miles and 1½ hours; from Yosemite, 210 miles and 4 hours.

If you are driving and aren't already a member, it's worth joining the **American Automobile Association** (**AAA;** *C* **800/922-8228**). It charges $49 to $79 per year (with an additional one-time joining fee), depending on where you join, and provides roadside and other services to motorists. **Amoco Motor Club** (*C* **800/334-3300**) is another recommended choice.

For information about renting a car, see the "Car Rentals" section (beginning on p. 25) of chapter 2, "Getting to Know San Francisco."

2

Getting to Know San Francisco

This chapter offers useful information on how to become better acquainted with the city, even though half the fun of becoming familiar with San Francisco is wandering around and haphazardly stumbling upon great shops, restaurants, and vistas that even locals might not know about. You'll find that, although it's metropolitan, San Francisco is a small town, and you won't feel like a stranger for long. If you get disoriented, just remember that downtown is east and the Golden Gate Bridge is north—and even if you do get lost, you probably won't go too far, since water surrounds three sides of the city. The most difficult challenge you'll have, if you're traveling by car (which I suggest you avoid), is mastering the maze of one-way streets.

1 Orientation

VISITOR INFORMATION

The **San Francisco Visitor Information Center,** on the lower level of Hallidie Plaza, 900 Market St., at Powell Street (© **415/283-0177;** fax 415/362-7323), has information, brochures, discount coupons, and advice on restaurants, sights, and events in the city. The staff can provide answers in German, Japanese, French, Italian, and Spanish (as well as English, of course). To find the office, descend the escalator at the cable car turnaround. The office is open Monday through Friday from 8:30am to 5pm, Saturday and Sunday from 9am to 3pm. It's closed on January 1, Thanksgiving Day, and December 25.

Dial © **415/283-0177** any time, day or night, for a recorded message about current cultural events, theater, music, sports, and other special happenings. This information is also available in German, French, Japanese, and Spanish. Keep in mind that this service only recommends businesses that are members of the Convention and Visitors Bureau and is very tourist oriented. While there's tons of information, it's not representative of all that the city has to offer. You can get a fax with information anytime from the bureau's automated service if you call © **800/220-5747** and follow the prompts.

San Francisco Neighborhoods

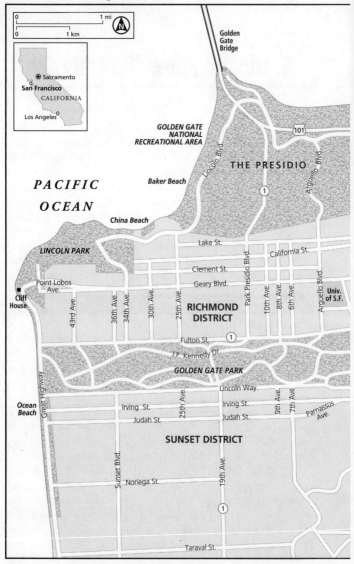

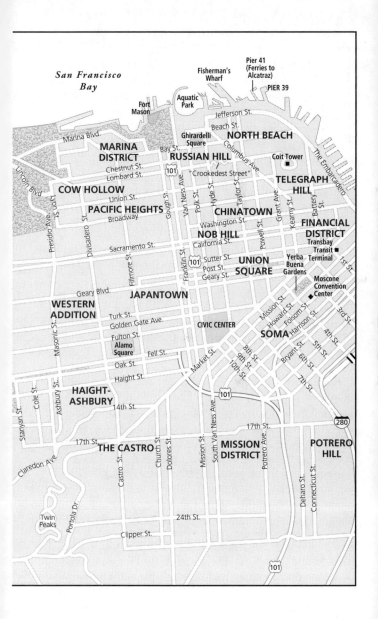

Pick up a copy of the *Bay Guardian* or the *S.F. Weekly,* the city's free alternative papers, to get listings of all city happenings. You'll find them in kiosks throughout the city and in most coffee shops.

For specialized information on Chinatown's shops and services, and on the city's Chinese community in general, contact the **Chinese Chamber of Commerce,** 730 Sacramento St. (© **415/982-3000**), open daily from 9am to 5pm.

CITY LAYOUT

San Francisco occupies the tip of a 32-mile peninsula between San Francisco Bay and the Pacific Ocean. Its land area measures about 46 square miles, although the city is often referred to as being 7 square miles. At more than 900 feet high, the towering Twin Peaks marks the geographic center of the city and is a killer place to take in a vista of San Francisco.

With lots of one-way streets and plenty of nooks and crannies, San Francisco might seem confusing at first, but it will quickly become easy to negotiate. The city's downtown streets are arranged in a simple grid pattern, with the exceptions of Market Street and Columbus Avenue, which cut across the grid at right angles to each other. Hills appear to distort this pattern, however, and can disorient you. As you learn your way around, the hills will become your landmarks and reference points. But even if you get lost, it's no big deal: San Francisco's a small town—so much so, in fact that I've run from one end to the other (during the Bay to Breakers Foot Race) in an hour flat.

MAIN ARTERIES & STREETS   Market Street is San Francisco's main thoroughfare. Most of the city's buses travel this route on their way to the Financial District from the outer neighborhoods to the west and south. The tall office buildings clustered downtown are at the northeast end of Market; 1 block beyond lies The Embarcadero and the bay.

The Embarcadero ⚡—an excellent strolling, skating, and biking route (thanks to recent renovations)—curves along San Francisco Bay from south of the Bay Bridge to the northeast perimeter of the city. It terminates at Fisherman's Wharf, the famous tourist-oriented pier. Aquatic Park, Fort Mason, and the Golden Gate National Recreation Area are on the northernmost point of the peninsula.

From the eastern perimeter of Fort Mason, **Van Ness Avenue** runs due south, back to Market Street. The area just described forms a rough triangle, with Market Street as its southeastern boundary, the waterfront as its northern boundary, and Van Ness Avenue as its western boundary. Within this triangle lie most of the city's main tourist sights.

FINDING AN ADDRESS   Since most of the city's streets are laid out in a grid pattern, finding an address is easy when you know the nearest cross street. Numbers start with 1 at the beginning of the street and proceed at the rate of 100 per block. When asking for directions, find out the nearest cross street and the neighborhood where your destination is located, but be careful not to confuse numerical avenues with numerical streets. Numerical avenues (Third Ave. and so on) are in the Richmond and Sunset Districts in the western part of the city. Numerical streets (Third St. and so on) are south of Market Street in the east and south parts of town.

NEIGHBORHOODS IN BRIEF

For further discussion of some of the below neighborhoods, see the "Neighborhoods Worth a Visit" section of chapter 5, beginning on p. 116.

Union Square   Union Square is the commercial hub of the city. Most major hotels and department stores are crammed into the area surrounding the actual square, which was named for a series of violent pro-union mass demonstrations staged here on the eve of the Civil War. A plethora of upscale boutiques, restaurants, and galleries occupy the spaces tucked between the larger buildings. A few blocks west is the **Tenderloin,** a patch of poverty and blight where you should keep your wits about you. The **Theater District** is 3 blocks west of Union Square.

The Financial District   East of Union Square, this area, bordered by The Embarcadero and by Market, Third, Kearny, and Washington streets, is the city's business district and the stomping grounds for many major corporations. The pointy TransAmerica Pyramid, at Montgomery and Clay streets, is one of the district's most conspicuous architectural features.

Nob Hill & Russian Hill   Bounded by Bush, Larkin, Pacific, and Stockton streets, Nob Hill is a genteel, well-heeled district, still occupied by the major power brokers and the neighborhood businesses they frequent. Russian Hill extends from Pacific to Bay and from Polk to Mason. It contains steep streets, lush gardens, and high-rises occupied by both the moneyed and the more bohemian.

Chinatown   A large red-and-green gate on Grant Avenue at Bush Street marks the official entrance to Chinatown. Beyond lies a 24-block labyrinth, bordered by Broadway, Bush, Kearny, and Stockton streets, filled with restaurants, markets, temples, shops—and, of course, a substantial percentage of San Francisco's

Chinese residents. Chinatown is a great place for exploration all along Stockton and Grant streets, Portsmouth Square, and the alleys that lead off them, like Ross and Waverly. This area is jam-packed, so don't even think about driving here.

North Beach The Italian quarter, which stretches from Montgomery and Jackson to Bay Street, is one of the best places in the city to grab a coffee, pull up a cafe chair, and do some serious people-watching. Nightlife is equally happening; restaurants, bars, and clubs along Columbus and Grant avenues attract folks from all over the Bay Area, who fight for a parking place and romp through the festive neighborhood. Down Columbus toward the Financial District are the remains of the city's Beat Generation landmarks, including Ferlinghetti's City Lights Bookstore and Vesuvio's Bar. Broadway—a short strip of sex joints—cuts through the heart of the district. **Telegraph Hill** looms over the east side of North Beach, topped by Coit Tower, one of San Francisco's best vantage points.

Fisherman's Wharf North Beach runs into Fisherman's Wharf, which was once the busy heart of the city's great harbor and waterfront industries. Today, it is a tacky but interesting tourist area with little, if any, authentic waterfront life, except for recreational boating and some friendly sea lions.

The Marina District Created on landfill for the Pan Pacific Exposition of 1915, the Marina District boasts some of the best views of the Golden Gate, as well as plenty of grassy fields alongside San Francisco Bay. Elegant Mediterranean-style homes and apartments, inhabited by the city's well-to-do singles and wealthy families, line the streets. Here, too, are the Palace of Fine Arts, the Exploratorium, and Fort Mason Center. The main street is Chestnut, between Franklin and Lyon, which abounds with shops, cafes, and boutiques. Because of its landfill foundation, the Marina was one of the hardest-hit districts in the 1989 quake.

Cow Hollow Located west of Van Ness Avenue, between Russian Hill and the Presidio, this flat, grazable area supported 30 dairy farms in 1861. Today, Cow Hollow is largely residential and largely yuppie. Its two primary commercial thoroughfares are Lombard Street, known for its many relatively inexpensive motels, and Union Street, a flourishing shopping sector filled with restaurants, pubs, cafes, and shops.

Pacific Heights The ultra-elite, such as the Gettys and Danielle Steel—and those lucky enough to buy before the real-estate boom—reside in the mansions and homes here. When the rich meander out of their fortresses, they wander down to Union Street and join the yuppies and the young who frequent the street's long stretch of chic boutiques and lively neighborhood restaurants, cafes, and bars.

Japantown Bounded by Octavia, Fillmore, California, and Geary, Japantown shelters only a small percentage of the city's Japanese population, but exploring these few square blocks and the shops and restaurants within them is still a cultural experience.

Civic Center Although millions of dollars have gone toward brick sidewalks, ornate lampposts, and elaborate street plantings, the southwestern section of Market Street remains somewhat dilapidated. The Civic Center, at the "bottom" of Market Street, is an exception. This large complex of buildings includes the domed and dapper City Hall, the Opera House, Davies Symphony Hall, and the Asian Art Museum. The landscaped plaza connecting the buildings is the staging area for San Francisco's frequent demonstrations for or against just about everything.

SoMa No part of San Francisco has been more affected by recent development than the area south of Market Street (dubbed "SoMa"). The area—until recently, a district of old warehouses and industrial spaces, with a few scattered underground nightclubs, restaurants, and shoddy residential areas—was the hub of dot-commercialization and half-million-dollar-plus lofts. Today, it's still alive with loft residents and surviving businesses. It also houses urban entertainment a la the Museum of Modern Art, Yerba Buena Gardens, Sony Metreon, and a slew of big-bucks hotels that make tons of money from businesspeople. The official boundaries are The Embarcadero, Highway 101, and Market Street, with the greatest concentrations of interest around Yerba Buena Center, along Folsom and Harrison streets between Steuart and Sixth, and at Brannan and Market. Along the waterfront are an array of restaurants and the absolutely fab SBC Park. Farther west, around Folsom, between 7th and 11th streets, much of the city's nightclubbing occurs.

Mission District This is another area that was greatly affected by the city's new wealth. The Mexican and Latin American populations here, with their cuisine, traditions, and art, make the Mission District a vibrant area to visit. Some parts of the neighborhood are still poor and sprinkled with the homeless, gangs, and drug addicts, but young urbanites have settled in the area, attracted by its "reasonably" (a relative term) priced rentals and endless oh-so-hot restaurants and bars that stretch from 16th and Valencia streets to 25th and Mission streets. Less adventurous tourists may just want to duck into Mission Dolores, cruise by a few of the 200-plus amazing murals, and head back downtown. But anyone who's interested in hanging with the hipsters and experiencing the hottest restaurant and bar nightlife should definitely beeline it here. Don't be afraid to visit this area, but do use caution at night.

The Castro One of the liveliest streets in town, the Castro is practically synonymous with San Francisco's gay community (even though it is technically a street in the Noe Valley District). Located at the very end of Market Street, between 17th and 18th streets, the Castro has dozens of shops, restaurants, and bars catering to the gay community. Open-minded straight people are welcome, too.

Haight-Ashbury Part trendy, part nostalgic, part funky, the Haight, as it's most commonly known, was the soul of the psychedelic, free-loving 1960s and the center of the counterculture movement. Today, the neighborhood straddling upper Haight Street on the eastern border of Golden Gate Park is more gentrified, but the commercial area still harbors all walks of life. Leftover aging hippies mingle with grungy, begging street kids outside Ben & Jerry's Ice Cream Store (where they might still be talking about Jerry Garcia), nondescript marijuana dealers whisper "Buds" as shoppers pass, and many people walking down the street have Day-Glo hair. But you don't need to be a freak or wear tie-dye to enjoy the Haight—the food, shops, and bars cover all tastes. From Haight Street, walk south on Cole Street for a more peaceful and quaint neighborhood experience.

Richmond & Sunset Districts San Francisco's suburbs of sorts, these are the city's largest and most populous neighborhoods, consisting mainly of small (but expensive) homes, shops, and neighborhood restaurants. Although they border Golden Gate Park and Ocean Beach, few tourists venture into "The Avenues," as these areas are referred to locally.

2 Getting Around
BY PUBLIC TRANSPORTATION

The **San Francisco Municipal Railway,** 401 Van Ness Ave., better known as "Muni" (© **415/673-6864;** www.sfmuni.com), operates the city's cable cars, buses, and streetcars. Together, these three services crisscross the entire city. Fares for buses and streetcars are $1.25 for adults, 35¢ for seniors over 65 and children 5 to 17. Cable cars,

Value Muni Discounts

Muni discount passes, called **Passports,** entitle holders to unlimited rides on buses, streetcars, and cable cars. A Passport costs $9 for 1 day, $15 for 3 days, and $20 for 7 consecutive days. Muni's **City Pass,** which costs $40 for adults, $31 for seniors 65 and older, and $24 for kids 5 to 17, entitles you to unlimited rides for 7 days, plus admission to the California Academy of Sciences, Palace of the Legion of Honor, Steinhart Aquarium, Museum of Modern Art, Exploratorium, and Blue & Gold Fleet Bay or Alcatraz cruises for 9 days. You can buy a Passport or City Pass at the San Francisco Visitor Information Center, Powell/Market cable car booth, Holiday Inn Civic Center, and TIX Bay Area booth at Union Square, among other outlets. But to include the Blue & Gold Fleet tour, you must purchase tickets through them by calling Blue & Gold Fleet at ✆ **415/705-5555.** A $2.25 fee applies when you get your tickets through this phone service.

which run from 6:30am to 1:30am, cost a whopping $3 for all people over 5 ($1 for seniors 6:30–7am and 9pm–midnight). Needless to say, they're packed primarily with tourists. Exact change is required on all vehicles except cable cars. Fares are subject to change.

For detailed route information, phone Muni or consult the bus map at the front of the San Francisco Yellow Pages. If you plan to use public transportation extensively, you might want to invest in a comprehensive transit and city map ($2), sold at the San Francisco Visitor Information Center (p. 13), Powell/Market cable car booth, and many downtown retail outlets. Also, see the "Muni Discounts" box for more information.

CABLE CAR   San Francisco's cable cars might not be the most practical means of transport, but the rolling historic landmarks are a fun ride. The three lines are concentrated in the downtown area. The most scenic, and exciting, is the **Powell-Hyde line,** which follows a zigzag route from the corner of Powell and Market streets, over both Nob Hill and Russian Hill, to a turntable at gaslit Victorian Square in front of Aquatic Park. The **Powell-Mason line** starts at the same intersection and climbs Nob Hill before descending to Bay Street, just 3 blocks from Fisherman's Wharf. The least scenic is the **California Street line,** which begins at the foot of Market Street and runs a straight course through Chinatown and over Nob Hill to

San Francisco Mass Transit

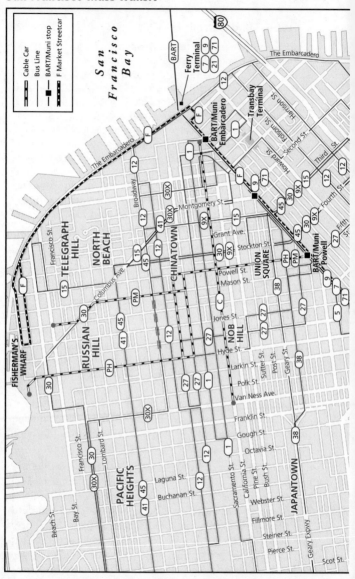

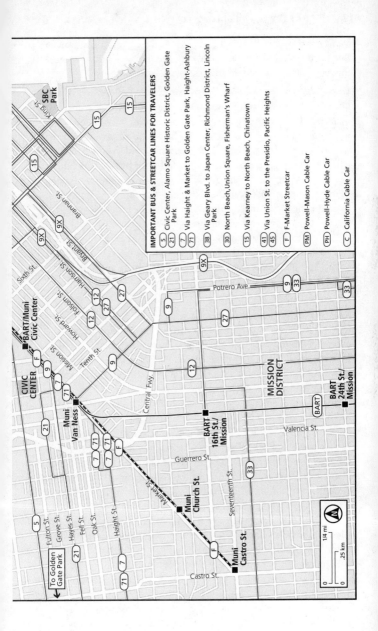

IMPORTANT BUS & STREETCAR LINES FOR TRAVELERS

(5) Civic Center, Alamo Square Historic District, Golden Gate Park

(21) Via Haight & Market to Golden Gate Park, Haight-Ashbury

(71)

(38) Via Geary Blvd. to Japan Center, Richmond District, Lincoln Park

(30) North Beach, Union Square, Fisherman's Wharf

(15) Via Kearney to North Beach, Chinatown

(41) Via Union St. to the Presidio, Pacific Heights

(45)

(F) F-Market Streetcar

(PM) Powell-Mason Cable Car

(PH) Powell-Hyde Cable Car

(C) California Cable Car

Van Ness Avenue. All riders must exit at the last stop and wait in line for the return trip. The cable car system operates from approximately 6:30am to 1:30am, and each ride costs $3.

BUS Buses reach almost every corner of San Francisco and beyond—they even travel over the bridges to Marin County and Oakland. Overhead electric cables power some buses; others use conventional gas engines. All are numbered and display their destinations on the front. Signs, curb markings, and yellow bands on adjacent utility poles designate stops, and most bus shelters exhibit Muni's transportation map and schedule. Many buses travel along Market Street or pass near Union Square and run from about 6am to midnight. After midnight, there is infrequent all-night "Owl" service. For safety, avoid taking buses late at night.

Popular tourist routes include bus nos. 5, 7, and 71, all of which run to Golden Gate Park; 41 and 45, which travel along Union Street; and 30, which runs between Union Square and Ghirardelli Square. A bus ride costs $1.25 for adults and 35¢ for seniors over 65 and children 5 to 17.

STREETCAR Five of Muni's six streetcar lines, designated J, K, L, M, and N, run underground downtown and on the streets in the outer neighborhoods. The sleek rail cars make the same stops as BART (see below) along Market Street, including Embarcadero Station (in the Financial District), Montgomery and Powell streets (both near Union Square), and the Civic Center (near City Hall). Past the Civic Center, the routes branch off: The J line takes you to Mission Dolores; the K, L, and M lines run to Castro Street; and the N line parallels Golden Gate Park and extends all the way to The Embarcadero and SBC Park. Streetcars run about every 15 minutes, more frequently during rush hours. They operate Monday through Friday from 5am to 12:45am, Saturday from 6am to 12:45am, and Sunday from 8am to 12:20am. The L and N lines operate 24 hours a day, 7 days a week, but late at night, regular buses trace the L and N routes, which are normally underground, from atop the city streets. Because the operation is part of Muni, the fares are the same as for buses, and passes are accepted.

A recent addition to this system is not a newcomer at all, but is, in fact, San Francisco's beloved rejuvenated 1930s streetcar. The beautiful multicolored F-Market line runs from 17th and Castro streets to Beach and Jones streets; every other streetcar continues to Jones and Beach streets in Fisherman's Wharf. This is a quick and charming way to get up- and downtown without any hassle.

BART   BART, an acronym for **Bay Area Rapid Transit** (© 415/ 989-2278; www.bart.gov), is a futuristic-looking, high-speed rail network that connects San Francisco with the East Bay—Oakland, Richmond, Concord, and Fremont. Four stations are on Market Street (see "Streetcar," above). Fares range from $1.25 to $7.10, depending on how far you go. Machines in the stations dispense tickets that are magnetically encoded with a dollar amount. Computerized exits automatically deduct the correct fare. Children 4 and under ride free. Trains run every 15 to 20 minutes, Monday through Friday from 4am to midnight, Saturday from 6am to midnight, and Sunday from 8am to midnight.

The 33-mile BART extension, which extends all the way to San Francisco International Airport, opened in June 2003.

BY TAXI

If you're downtown during rush hour or leaving a major hotel, it won't be hard to hail a cab; just look for the lighted sign on the roof that indicates the vehicle is free. Otherwise, it's a good idea to call one of the following companies to arrange a ride; even then, there's been more than one time when the cab never came for me. Don't expect prompt results on weekends, no matter how nicely you ask. The companies: **Veteran's Cab** (© 415/552-1300), **Luxor Cabs** (© 415/282-4141), and **Yellow Cab** (© 415/626-2345). Rates are approximately $2.85 for the first mile and $2.25 for each mile thereafter.

BY CAR

You don't need a car to explore downtown San Francisco. In fact, with the city becoming more crowded by the minute, a car can be your worst nightmare—you're likely to end up stuck in traffic with lots of aggressive and frustrated drivers, pay upward of $30 a day to park, and spend a good portion of your vacation looking for a parking space. Don't bother. However, if you want to venture outside the city, driving is the best way to go.

Before heading outside the city, especially in winter, call © 800/ 427-7623 for California **road conditions.**

CAR RENTALS   All the major rental companies operate in the city and have desks at the airports. When we last checked, you could get a compact car for a week for about $200, including all taxes and other charges, but prices change dramatically on a daily basis and depend on which company you rent from.

Some of the national car-rental companies operating in San Francisco include **Alamo** (© 800/327-9633; www.goalamo.com), **Avis** (© 800/331-1212; www.avis.com), **Budget** (© 800/527-0700; www.budget.com), **Dollar** (© 800/800-4000; www.dollar.com), **Enterprise** (© 800/325-8007; www.enterprise.com), **Hertz** (© 800/654-3131; www.hertz.com), **National** (© 800/227-7368; www.nationalcar.com), and **Thrifty** (© 800/367-2277; www.thrifty.com).

Car-rental rates vary even more than airline fares. Prices depend on the size of the car, where and when you pick it up and drop it off, the length of the rental period, where and how far you drive it, whether you buy insurance, and a host of other factors. A few key questions can save you hundreds of dollars, but you have to ask—reservations agents don't often volunteer money-saving information:

- Are weekend rates lower than weekday rates? Ask if the rate is the same for pickup Friday morning, for instance, as it is for Thursday night. Reservations agents won't volunteer this information, so don't be shy about asking.
- Does the agency assess a drop-off charge if you don't return the car to the same location where you picked it up?
- Are special promotional rates available? If you see an advertised price in your local newspaper, be sure to ask for that specific rate; otherwise, you could be charged the standard rate. Terms change constantly.
- Are discounts available for members of AARP, AAA, frequent-flier programs, or trade unions?
- How much tax will be added to the rental bill? Will there be local tax and state tax?
- How much does the rental company charge to refill your gas tank if you return with the tank less than full? Most rental companies claim their prices are "competitive," but fuel is almost always cheaper in town, so you should try to allow enough time to refuel the car before returning it.

Some companies offer "refueling packages," in which you pay for an entire tank of gas upfront. The cost is usually fairly competitive with local prices, but you don't get credit for any gas remaining in the tank. If a stop at a gas station on the way to the airport will make you miss your plane, then by all means take advantage of the fuel purchase option. Otherwise, skip it.

Make sure you're insured. Hasty assumptions about your personal auto insurance or a rental agency's additional coverage could end up costing you tens of thousands of dollars, even if you are involved in an accident that is clearly the fault of another driver.

If you already have your own car insurance, you are most likely covered in the United States for loss of or damage to a rental car and liability in case of injury to any other party involved in an accident. Be sure to check your policy before you spend extra money (usually $10 per day) on the **collision damage waiver (CDW),** offered by all agencies.

Most major credit cards (especially gold and platinum cards) provide some degree of coverage as well—if they were used to pay for the rental. Terms vary widely, however, so be sure to call your credit card company directly before you rent and rely on the card for coverage. If you are uninsured, your credit card may provide primary coverage as long as you decline the rental agency's insurance. If you already have insurance, your credit card may provide secondary coverage, which basically covers your deductible. However, note that *credit cards will not cover liability,* which is the cost of injury to an outside party and/or damage to an outside party's vehicle. If you do not hold an insurance policy, you should seriously consider buying additional liability insurance from your rental company, even if you decline the CDW.

PARKING   If you want to have a relaxing vacation, don't even attempt to find street parking on Nob Hill, in North Beach, in Chinatown, by Fisherman's Wharf, or on Telegraph Hill. Park in a garage or take a cab or a bus. If you do find street parking, pay attention to street signs that explain when you can park and for how long. Be especially careful not to park in zones that are tow areas during rush hours.

Curb colors also indicate parking regulations. *Red* means no stopping or parking; *blue* is reserved for drivers with disabilities who have a disabled plate or placard; *white* means there's a 5-minute limit; *green* indicates a 10-minute limit; and *yellow* and *yellow-and-black* curbs are for commercial vehicles only. Also, don't park at a bus stop or in front of a fire hydrant, and watch out for street-cleaning signs. If you violate the law, you might get a hefty ticket or your car might be towed; to get your car back, you'll have to get a release from the nearest district police department and then go to the towing company to pick up the vehicle.

When parking on a hill, apply the hand brake, put the car in gear, and *curb your wheels*—toward the curb when facing downhill, away from the curb when facing uphill. Curbing your wheels not only prevents a possible "runaway" but also keeps you from getting a ticket—an expensive fine that is aggressively enforced.

BY FERRY

TO/FROM SAUSALITO OR LARKSPUR   The **Golden Gate Ferry Service** fleet (© 415/923-2000) shuttles passengers daily between the San Francisco Ferry Building, at the foot of Market Street, and downtown Sausalito and Larkspur. Service is frequent, departing at reasonable intervals every day of the year except January 1, Thanksgiving Day, and December 25. Phone for an exact schedule. The ride takes half an hour, and one-way fares are $5.60 for adults and $4.20 for kids 6 to 12. Seniors and passengers with disabilities ride for $2.80. Up to two children under 6 with paying adults ride free on weekdays; on weekends, up to two children under 12 ride free with paying adults. Family rates are available on weekends.

Ferries of the **Blue & Gold Fleet** (© 415/773-1188 for recorded info, or 415/705-5555 for tickets) also provide round-trip service to downtown Sausalito and Larkspur, leaving from Fisherman's Wharf at Pier 41. The one-way cost is $7.25 for adults, $4 for kids 5 to 11. Boats run on a seasonal schedule; phone for departure information. Expect to pay an extra $3.50 per ticket for phone orders or skip the fee by buying in person at Pier 41.

FAST FACTS: San Francisco

American Express   For travel arrangements, traveler's checks, currency exchange, and other member services, an office is at 455 Market St., at First Street (© 415/536-2600), in the Financial District, open Monday through Friday from 9am to 5:30pm and Saturday from 10am to 2pm. To report lost or stolen traveler's checks, call © 800/221-7282. For American Express Global Assist, call © 800/554-2639.

Area Code   The area code for San Francisco is **415**; for Oakland, Berkeley, and much of the East Bay, **510**; for the peninsula, generally **650**. Most phone numbers in this book are in San Francisco's 415 area code, but there's no need to dial it if you're within city limits.

Business Hours   Most banks are open Monday through Friday from 9am to 5pm. Many banks also have ATMs for 24-hour banking (see the "Money" section, in chapter 1, beginning on p. 1).

Most stores are open Monday through Saturday from 10 or 11am to at least 6pm, with shorter hours on Sunday. But there are exceptions: Stores in Chinatown, Ghirardelli Square, and PIER 39 stay open much later during the tourist season, and large department stores, including Macy's and Nordstrom, keep late hours.

Most restaurants serve lunch from about 11:30am to 2:30pm and dinner from about 5:30 to 10pm. They sometimes serve later on weekends. Nightclubs and bars are usually open daily until 2am, when they are legally bound to stop serving alcohol.

Dentists In the event of a dental emergency, see your hotel concierge or contact the **San Francisco Dental Office,** 131 Steuart St. (© **415/777-5115**), between Mission and Howard streets, which offers emergency service and comprehensive dental care Monday and Tuesday from 8am to 4:30pm, Wednesday and Thursday from 10:30am to 6:30pm, and Friday 8am to 2pm.

Doctors **Saint Francis Memorial Hospital,** 900 Hyde St., between Bush and Pine streets on Nob Hill (© **415/353-6000**), provides emergency service 24 hours a day; no appointment is necessary. The hospital also operates a **physician-referral service** (© **800/333-1355** or 415/353-6566).

Drugstores **Walgreens** pharmacies are all over town, including one at 135 Powell St. (© **415/391-4433**). The store is open Monday through Friday from 7am to midnight and Saturday and Sunday from 8am to midnight; the pharmacy is open Monday through Friday from 8am to 9pm, Saturday from 9am to 5pm; it's closed on Sunday. The branch on Divisadero Street at Lombard (© **415/931-6415**) has a 24-hour pharmacy. **Merrill's** pharmacy and store, 1091 Market St. (© **415/431-5466**), smack in the middle of downtown tourist action, is open Monday through Friday from 9am to 6pm and is closed on weekends.

Earthquakes There will always be earthquakes in California, most of which you'll never notice. However, in case of a significant shaker, there are a few basic precautionary measures you should know. When you are inside a building, seek cover; do not run outside. Stand under a doorway or against a wall, and stay away from windows. If you exit a building after a substantial quake, use stairwells, not elevators. If you are in your car, pull over to the side of the road and stop—but not until you are away from bridges, overpasses, telephone poles, and power lines. Stay in your car. If you're out walking, stay outside and away from trees, power lines, and the sides of buildings. If you're in an area with tall buildings, find a doorway in which to stand.

Emergencies   Dial ℰ **911** for police, an ambulance, or the fire department; no coins are needed from a public phone.

Internet Access   Surprisingly, San Francisco has very few Internet cafes. However, there are locations around town where you can get online access, perhaps with a sandwich and a cup o' joe. You can do your laundry, listen to music, dine, and check your stocks online at SoMa's **Brainwash**, 1122 Folsom St., between Seventh and Eighth streets (ℰ **415/861-FOOD**). It's open Monday through Saturday from 7am to 11pm and Sunday from 8am to 11pm; rates are $1 per 5 minutes. For access without the ambience, try **Copy Central**, 110 Sutter St., at Montgomery Street (ℰ **415/392-6470**), which provides access cards costing $3 for 20 minutes, $5 for 40 minutes, and $7 for 60 minutes. Ditto **Kinko's**, 1967 Market St., near Gough Street (ℰ **415/252-0864**), which charges 20¢ per minute. Both of these companies have numerous locations around town.

Liquor Laws   Liquor stores and grocery stores, as well as some drugstores, can sell packaged alcoholic beverages between 6am and 2am daily. Most restaurants, nightclubs, and bars are licensed to serve alcoholic beverages during the same hours. The legal age for purchase and consumption of alcohol is 21; proof of age is required.

Newspapers & Magazines   The city's two main dailies are the *San Francisco Chronicle* and the *San Francisco Examiner;* both are distributed throughout the city. Check out the *Chronicle's* massive Sunday edition that includes a pink "Datebook" section—an excellent preview of the week's upcoming events. The free weekly *San Francisco Bay Guardian* and *San Francisco Weekly,* tabloids of news and listings, are indispensable for nightlife information; they're widely distributed through street-corner kiosks and at city cafes and restaurants.

Of the many free tourist-oriented publications, the most widely read are *Key, San Francisco Guide,* and *Where San*

Francisco. The first two are handbook-size weeklies contain maps and information on current events. The latter is a glossy regular format monthly magazine. You can find them in most hotels, shops, and restaurants in the major tourist areas.

Police For emergencies, dial © **911** from any phone; no coins are needed. For other matters, call © **415/553-0123.**

Post Office Dozens of post offices are located around the city. The closest to Union Square is inside the Macy's department store at 170 O'Farrell St. (© **800/275-8777**). You can pick up mail addressed to you and marked "General Delivery" (Poste Restante) at the **Civic Center Post Office Box Unit,** P.O. Box 429991, San Francisco, CA 94142-9991 (© **800/275-8777**). The street address is 101 Hyde St.

Safety San Francisco, like any other large city, has its fair share of crime, but most folks luckily don't have firsthand horror stories. In some areas, you need to exercise extra caution, particularly at night—notably the Tenderloin, the Western Addition (south of Japantown), the Mission District (especially around 16th and Mission sts.), the lower Fillmore area (also south of Japantown), around lower Haight Street, and around the Civic Center. In addition, there are a substantial number of homeless people throughout the city, with concentrations in and around Union Square, the Theater District (3 blocks west of Union Square), the Tenderloin, and Haight Street, so don't be alarmed if you're approached for spare change. Just use common sense.

For additional crime-prevention information, phone **San Francisco SAFE** (© **415/553-1984**).

Smoking If San Francisco is California's most European city in looks and style, the comparison stops when it comes to smoking in public. Each year, smoking laws in the city become stricter. Since 1998, smoking has been prohibited in restaurants and bars. Hotels are also offering more nonsmoking rooms, which often leaves those who like to puff out in the cold—sometimes literally.

Taxes An 8.5% sales tax is added at the register for all goods and services purchased in San Francisco. The city hotel tax is a whopping 14%. There is no airport tax.

Transit Information The San Francisco Municipal Railway, better known as **Muni,** operates the city's cable cars, buses, and streetcars. For customer service, call ⓒ **415/673-6864** weekdays from 7am to 5pm, weekends from 9am to 5pm. At other times, you can call this number to get recorded information.

Useful Telephone Numbers You might find the following numbers useful: **tourist information** (ⓒ **415/283-0177**); **highway conditions** (ⓒ **800/427-7623**); and **AOL Moviefone** (ⓒ **415/777-FILM**).

3

Where to Stay

Whether you want a room with a view or just a room, San Francisco is more than accommodating to its 14 million annual guests. Most of the city's 200-plus hotels cluster near Union Square, but some smaller independent gems are scattered around town.

When reading over your options, keep in mind that prices listed are "rack" (published) rates. At big, upscale hotels, almost no one actually pays them—and with the dramatic travel downturn over the past few years, there are still deals to be had. Therefore, you should always ask for special discounts or, even better, vacation packages. It's often possible to get the room you want for $100 less than what is quoted here, except when the hotels are packed (usually during summer and due to conventions) and bargaining is close to impossible. Use the rates listed here for the big hotels as guidelines for comparison only; prices for inexpensive choices and smaller B&Bs are closer to reality, though.

Hunting for hotels in San Francisco can be a tricky business, particularly if you're not a seasoned traveler. What you don't know—and the reservations agent may not tell you—could very well ruin your vacation, so keep the following pointers in mind when it comes time to book a room:

- Prices listed below do not include state and city taxes, which total 14%. Other hidden extras include parking fees, which can be up to $40 per day, and hefty surcharges—up to $1 per local call—for telephone use.
- San Francisco is Convention City, so if you want a room at a particular hotel during high season (summer, for example), book well in advance.
- Be sure to have a credit card in hand when making a reservation, and know that you may be asked to pay for at least 1 night in advance (this doesn't happen often, though).
- Hotels usually hold reservations until 6pm. If you don't tell the staff you're arriving late, you might lose your room.

- Almost every hotel in San Francisco requires a credit card imprint for "incidentals" (and to prevent walkouts). If you don't have a credit card, be sure to make special arrangements with the management before you hang up the phone, and make a note of the name of the person you spoke with.
- When you check in, if your room isn't up to snuff, politely inform the front desk of your dissatisfaction and ask for another. If the hotel can accommodate you, they almost always will—and sometimes will even upgrade you!

Read the below entries carefully: Many hotels also offer rooms at rates above and below the price category that applies to most of the units. If you like the sound of a place that's a bit over your budget, it never hurts to call and ask a few questions. Also note that we do not list single rates. Some hotels, particularly more affordable choices, do charge lower rates for singles, so inquire about them if you are traveling alone.

Other than the exceptional circumstances of the past few years, hotel rates in San Francisco don't vary much because the city is so popular year-round. Still, you should always ask about weekend discounts, corporate rates, and family plans; most larger hotels, and many smaller ones, offer them, but many reservations agents don't mention them unless you ask about them specifically.

You'll find nonsmoking rooms available in all larger hotels and many smaller hotels; reviews indicate establishments that are entirely nonsmoking. Nowadays, the best advice for smokers is to confirm a smoking-permitted room in advance.

While you'll find that most accommodations have an abundance of amenities (including phones, unless otherwise noted), don't be alarmed by the lack of air-conditioned guest rooms. San Francisco weather is so mild, you'll never miss them.

Pricing Categories

The accommodations listed below are classified first by area, then by price, using the following categories: **Very Expensive,** more than $250 per night; **Expensive,** $200 to $250 per night; **Moderate,** $150 to $200 per night; and **Inexpensive,** less than $150 per night. These categories reflect the rack rates for an average double room during the high season, which runs approximately from April to September.

> ### ⟨Value⟩ Dial Direct
>
> When booking a room in a chain hotel, call the hotel's local line and the toll-free number and see where you get the best deal. A hotel makes nothing on a room that stays empty. The clerk who runs the place is more likely to know about vacancies than someone from the toll-free number is and will often grant deep discounts in order to fill up rooms.

Most larger hotels can accommodate guests who use wheelchairs and those who have other special needs. Ask when you make a reservation to ensure that your hotel can accommodate your needs, especially if you are interested in a bed-and-breakfast.

Helping Hands Having reservations about your reservations? Leave it up to the pros:

San Francisco Reservations, 360 22nd St., Suite 300, Oakland, CA 94612 (📞 **800/677-1500** or 510/628-4450; www.hotelres.com), arranges reservations for more than 200 of San Francisco's hotels and often offers discounted rates. Their nifty website allows Internet users to make reservations online.

Other good online sites with discounted rates include **www. hotels.com** and **www.placestostay.com**.

1 Union Square

VERY EXPENSIVE

Campton Place Hotel 🟊🟊🟊   With a $15-million room renovation completed at the end of 2001, this already fabulous luxury boutique hotel offers some of the best accommodations in town—not to mention the most expensive. Rooms were completely gutted, old furnishings were replaced with limestone, pearwood, and more Italian-modern decor. The two executive suites and one luxury suite push the haute envelope to even more luxurious heights. Discriminating returning guests will still find superlative service, extralarge beds, exquisite bathrooms, bathrobes, top-notch toiletries, slippers, and every other necessity and extra that's made Campton Place a favored temporary address. Chef Daniel Humm delights diners with delicately prepared and very sculpted cuisine at the excellent Campton Place Restaurant, which underwent a glamorous face-lift in 2002.

340 Stockton St. (between Post and Sutter sts.), San Francisco, CA 94108. 📞 **800/ 235-4300** or 415/781-5555. Fax 415/955-5536. www.camptonplace.com. 110

units. $345–$475 double; from $550–$2,000 suite. American breakfast $17. AE, DC, MC, V. Valet parking $35. Cable car: Powell-Hyde and Powell-Mason lines (1 block west). Bus: 2, 3, 4, 30, or 45. **Amenities:** Restaurant; health club; concierge; courtesy car; secretarial services; 24-hr. room service; laundry service; same-day dry cleaning. *In room:* A/C, TV w/pay movies, T1 line, dataport, minibar, hair dryer, iron, safe.

Grand Hyatt San Francisco ✦

If the thought of a 10-second walk to Saks Fifth Avenue makes your pulse race, this high-rise luxury hotel is the place for you. The Grand Hyatt sits amid all the downtown shopping while also boasting some of the best views in the area. The lobby is indeed grand, with Chinese artifacts and enormous ceramic vases. Thankfully, the well-kept rooms were recently renovated; they're swankier than they used to be, but they still have an upscale corporate vibe. Each room has a lounge chair as well as a small desk and sitting area. Views from most of the 36 floors are truly spectacular.

Rates for concierge-level Regency Club rooms ($45 extra) include access to the lounge, honor bar, continental breakfast, and evening hors d'oeuvres. Three floors hold business-plan guest rooms, each of which has a private fax and special services; for the extra $20 cost of the room, you get 24-hour access to a printer, a photocopier, and office supplies; free local calls and credit card phone access; and a daily newspaper.

345 Stockton St. (between Post and Sutter sts.), San Francisco, CA 94108. ✆ **800/233-1234** or 415/398-1234. Fax 415/391-1780. www.sanfrancisco.grand.hyatt.com. 685 units. $159–$319 double; Regency Club $45 additional. AE, DC, DISC, MC, V. Valet parking $39. Cable car: Powell-Hyde and Powell-Mason lines (2 blocks west). Bus: 2, 3, 4, 30, 38, or 45. **Amenities:** Restaurant; bar; health club; concierge; business center; secretarial services; limited room service; laundry service; same-day dry cleaning. *In room:* A/C, TV w/pay movies, dataport, minibar, coffeemaker, hair dryer, iron, safe, high-speed Internet access, 2 phone lines with speaker capability.

Pan Pacific San Francisco ✦✦

The Pan Pacific—located conveniently close to Union Square—is artistically glitzy, enormous, and somehow romantic, all at the same time. If this were a Hollywood set, James Bond might hoodwink a villain here, magically drop down from the sky-rise's atrium, and disappear into the night. But all is quiet and intimate in the third-floor lobby, even though the skylight ceiling is another 18 floors up. The lobby's marble fountain with four dancing figures and its player piano set the mood for guests relaxing in front of the fireplace. Major room updating in 2004 means each rather large abode is now swathed in chic white-on-white decor and adorned with flatscreen TVs and Herman Miller chairs. The bathrooms remain regal and lavishly marble-clad with a mini-TV at the sink and cozy bathrobes.

Where to Stay near Union Square & Nob Hill

Alisa Hotel **20**
The Andrews Hotel **3**
The Argent Hotel **23**
Campton Place Hotel **21**
The Cartwright Hotel **13**
The Commodore Hotel **2**
The Fairmont Hotel & Tower **16**
Four Seasons Hotel San Francisco **24**
The Golden Gate Hotel **14**
Grand Hyatt San Francisco **22**
Handlery Union Square Hote. **7**
Hotel Bijou **28**
Hotel Palomar **26**
InterContinental Mark Hopkins **15**
The Juliana Hotel **19**
King George Hotel **6**
The Maxwell **9**
The Mosser **25**
The Nob Hill Inn **1**
Nob Hill Lambourne **18**
Pan Pacific San Francisco **11**
Prescott Hotel **10**
The Ritz-Carlton **17**
San Francisco Marriott **27**
The Savoy Hotel **4**
Sir Francis Drake **12**
The Warwick Regis **5**
Westin St. Francis **8**

500 Post St. (at Mason St.), San Francisco, CA 94102. © **800/533-6465** or 415/771-8600. Fax 415/398-0267. www.panpacific.com. 329 units. $340–$465 double; from $480 suite. AE, DC, DISC, MC, V. Valet parking $39. Cable car: Powell-Hyde and Powell-Mason lines. Bus: 2, 3, 4, 30, 38, or 45. Dogs under 25 lb. welcome for an additional $75 fee. **Amenities:** Restaurant; bar; exercise room; concierge; business center; 24-hr. room service; in-room massage; laundry service; same-day dry cleaning; butler service. *In room:* A/C, TV, fax, dataport, minibar, hair dryer, iron, safe.

Prescott Hotel 🎯🎯   It may be small and lack common areas, but the boutique Prescott Hotel has some big things going for it. The staff treats you like royalty, rooms are attractively unfrilly and masculine, the location (just a block from Union Square) is perfect, and limited room service is provided by one of the most popular downtown restaurants, Postrio. Ralph Lauren fabrics in dark tones of green, plum, and burgundy blend well with the cherrywood furnishings in each of the soundproof rooms; the view, alas, isn't so pleasant. The very small bathrooms contain terry robes and Aveda products, and the suites have Jacuzzi bathtubs. Concierge-level guests are pampered with a free continental breakfast, evening cocktails and hors d'oeuvres, and even 3 days per week head-and-shoulders massages.

545 Post St. (between Mason and Taylor sts.), San Francisco, CA 94102. © **800/283-7322** or 415/563-0303. Fax 415/563-6831. www.prescotthotel.com. 164 units. $275–$340 double; $300 concierge-level double (including breakfast and evening cocktail reception); from $365 suite. AE, DC, DISC, MC, V. Valet parking $35. Cable car: Powell-Hyde and Powell-Mason lines (1 block east). Bus: 2, 3, 4, 30, 38, or 45. **Amenities:** Restaurant; bar; small exercise room; concierge; limited courtesy car; limited room service. *In room:* TV w/pay movies, fax/printer, dataport, minibar, hair dryer, iron, safe, high-speed Internet access, video games.

Westin St. Francis 🎯🎯 *Kids*   At the turn of the 20th century, Charles T. Crocker and a few of his wealthy buddies decided that San Francisco needed a world-class hotel, and up went the St. Francis. Since then, hordes of VIPs have hung their hats and hosiery here, including Emperor Hirohito of Japan, Queen Elizabeth II of England, Mother Teresa, King Juan Carlos of Spain, the shah of Iran, and all the U.S. presidents since Taft. In 1972, the hotel gained the 32-story Tower, doubling its capacity and adding banquet and conference centers. The older rooms of the main building vary in size and have more old-world charm than the newer rooms, but the Tower is remarkable for its great views of the city from above the 18th floor.

Although the St. Francis is too massive to offer the personal service you get at the smaller deluxe hotels on Nob Hill, few other hotels in San Francisco can match its majestic aura. Stroll through the vast, ornate lobby, and you can feel 100 years of history oozing from its

---

Fun Fact **Hotel Rendezvous**

For nearly a century, the most popular place for visitors to rendezvous in San Francisco has been under the magnificent hand-carved grandfather clock in the lobby of the Westin St. Francis hotel.

---

hand-carved redwood paneling. The hotel has done massive renovations costing $185 million over the past decade, replacing the carpeting, furniture, and bedding in every main-building guest room; gussying up the lobby; and restoring the facade.

The Westin makes kids feel right at home, too, with a goody bag upon check-in. The tower's Grandview Rooms, which were renovated in 2001, today evoke a contemporary design along the lines of the W Hotel. The historic main building accentuates its history with traditional, more elegant ambience, high ceilings, and crown molding. Alas, the venerable Compass Rose tearoom is no longer, but in its place is a new (debuted in August of 2004) fancy restaurant, Michael Mina, by the famed chef of Aqua.

335 Powell St. (between Geary and Post sts.), San Francisco, CA 94102. (C) **800/ WESTIN-1** or 415/397-7000. Fax 415/774-0124. www.westin.com. 1,195 units. Main building: $199–$499 double; Tower (Grand View): $219–$549 double; from $550 suite (in either building). Extra person $30. Continental breakfast $15–$18. AE, DC, DISC, MC, V. Valet parking $42. Cable car: Powell-Hyde and Powell-Mason lines (direct stop). Bus: 2, 3, 4, 30, 38, 45, or 76. Pets under 40 lb. accepted (dog beds available on request). **Amenities:** 2 restaurants; bar with pianist nightly; elaborate health club and spa; concierge; car-rental desk; business center; 24-hr. room service. *In room:* A/C, TV, dataport, minibar, fridge, hair dryer, iron, high-speed Internet access, cordless phones.

EXPENSIVE

Handlery Union Square Hotel 🎿 *Kids*   A mere half block from Union Square, the Handlery was already a good deal frequented by European travelers before the 1908 building underwent a complete overhaul in 2002. Now you'll find every amenity you could possibly need, plus lots of extras, in the extremely tasteful and modern (although sedate and a little dark) rooms. Rooms range from coral and gray in the historic building to taupe and tan in the newer club-level building. In between is a clean heated outdoor pool. Literally everything was replaced here: mattresses, alarm radios, refrigerators, light fixtures, paint, carpets, and furnishings. Perks include adjoining L.A.-based chain restaurant The Daily Grill (which is unfortunately not as tasty as its sister restaurants down south) and club-level options (all in the newer building) that include larger rooms, a complimentary morning newspaper, a bathroom scale, robes, two two-line phones, and adjoining doors that make the units great choices for families. Downsides? Not a lot of direct light, no grand feeling in the lobby, and lots of trekking if you want to go to and from the adjoining buildings that make up the hotel. All in all, it's a good value for downtown. Personally, this would be a choice second to the less expensive The Warwick Regis or Savoy.

351 Geary St. (between Mason and Powell sts.), San Francisco, CA 94102. © 800/843-4343 or 415/781-7800. Fax 415/781-0269. www.handlery.com. 377 units. $189 double. Club section from $289 double, from $280 suite. Extra person $10. AE, DC, DISC, MC, V. Parking $28. Cable car: Powell-Hyde and Powell-Mason lines (direct stop). Bus: 2, 3, 4, 30, 38, or 45. **Amenities:** Restaurant; heated outdoor swimming pool; access to nearby health club ($10 per day); sauna; barber shop; room service (7am–10pm); babysitting; same-day laundry. *In room:* A/C, TV w/Nintendo and pay movies, dataport, fridge, complimentary coffee/tea-making facilities, hair dryer, iron, safe, wireless Internet access, voice mail.

Sir Francis Drake 🐦🐦   It took a change of ownership and a multimillion-dollar restoration to revive the Sir Francis Drake, but the stately old queen is again housing guests with old–San Francisco aplomb. Granted, the venerable septuagenarian is still showing signs of age despite the fact that the owners continue to throw millions toward renovations. But the price of imperfection certainly shows in the room rate: a good $100 less per night than its Nob Hill cousins. The hotel is perfect for people who are willing to trade a chipped bathroom tile or oddly matched furniture for the opportunity to vacation in pseudo-grand fashion. Allow Tom Sweeny, the ebullient (and legendary) Beefeater doorman, to handle your bags as you enter the elegant, captivating lobby and live like the king or queen of Union Square without all the pomp, circumstance, and credit card bills.

Scala's Bistro (p. 70), one of the most festive restaurants downtown, serves good Italian cuisine in a stylish setting; the Parisian-style Café Expresso does an equally commendable job serving coffees, pastries, and

---

Fun Fact A Living Legend

Tom Sweeny, the head doorman at the Sir Francis Drake hotel, is San Francisco's living historical monument. Dressed in traditional Beefeaters attire (you can't miss those $1,400 duds), he's been the subject of countless snapshots—an average 200 per day for the past 20 years—and has shaken hands with every president since Gerry Ford.

sandwiches daily. The superchic Starlight Room, on the 21st floor, offers cocktails, entertainment, and dancing nightly with a panoramic view of the city.

450 Powell St. (at Sutter St.), San Francisco, CA 94102. © **800/227-5480** or 415/392-7755. Fax 415/391-8719. www.sirfrancisdrake.com. 417 units. $219–$259 double; $500–$700 suite. AE, DC, DISC, MC, V. Valet parking $35. Cable car: Powell-Hyde and Powell-Mason lines (direct stop). Bus: 2, 3, 4, 45, or 76. **Amenities:** 2 restaurants; bar; exercise room; concierge; limited room service; same-day laundry service/dry cleaning. *In room:* A/C, TV w/pay movies, dataport, minibar, hair dryer, iron, Nintendo.

MODERATE

A few worthy hotel companies operate many properties throughout the city. **Holiday Inn** (© **800/465-4329;** www.holiday-inn.com) has several strategic locations, including pretty properties in Fisherman's Wharf and Cow Hollow. **Personality Hotels** (© **800/553-1900;** www.personalityhotels.com) spiffs up older buildings in central locales, and **Joie de Vivre** (© **800/SF-TRIPS;** www.jdvhospitality. com) has lots of festive options scattered around town.

The Commodore Hotel ✦   If you're looking to pump a little fun and fantasy into your vacation, this six-story downtown Art Deco building is the place to go. San Francisco hotelier Chip Conley of Joie de Vivre Hospitality is behind this groovy revamped hotel frequented by an eclectic mix of 20-somethings and everyday folks in search of reasonably priced accommodations. Stealing the show is the Red Room, a small New York–slick bar and lounge that reflects no other color of the spectrum but ruby red (you gotta see this one). The stylish lobby, which was renovated in 2000, comes in a close second, followed by the adjoining Titanic Café, a cute little diner that serves American fare for breakfast and lunch. The "Neo-Deco" rooms, all of which underwent upgrades through 2001, are simple but lively with bright colors, whimsical furnishings, pretty artwork, and small bathrooms refurbished in 1998.

825 Sutter St. (at Jones St.), San Francisco, CA 94109. © **800/338-6848** or 415/923-6800. Fax 415/923-6804. www.thecommodorehotel.com. 110 units. $125–$169 double. AE, DC, DISC, MC, V. Parking $25. Bus: 2, 3, 4, 27, 19, 47, 49. **Amenities:** Diner; bar; access to nearby health club ($15 per day); concierge; Internet access in lobby. *In room:* TV w/pay movies, dataport, coffeemaker, fridge, hair dryer, iron.

The Juliana Hotel ✦✦ *(Value* A European-style boutique hotel in the best possible way, the Juliana is hard not to like. Completely renovated in 1996 and again in 2001, rooms are trendy-French, with yellow and pale-blue-striped wallpaper, and candy-striped yellow-and-red upholstered chairs. It's vibrant and cheery, for sure, but not the kind of place where you'd want to nurse a wicked hangover. With coffee available in the lobby in the morning and wine at night (included in the room rate), there's no real reason to leave. Guest rooms and bathrooms can be on the small side, but the junior suites have plenty of space and lovely homey touches.

590 Bush St. (at Stockton St.), San Francisco, CA 94108. © 800/328-3880 or 415/392-2540. Fax 415/391-8447. www.julianahotel.com. 107 units. $129–$205 double; $159–$235 junior suite; $189–$265 executive suite. Special winter packages available. AE, DC, MC, V. Valet parking $32; self-parking $24. Cable car: Powell-Hyde and Powell-Mason lines (1 block west). Bus: 2, 3, 4, 30, 38, or 45. **Amenities:** Exercise room; high-speed Internet access in lobby; same-day laundry service/dry cleaning. *In room:* A/C, TV, dataport, minibar, coffeemaker, hair dryer, iron.

The Warwick Regis ★★ Ⓥⁿᵃˡᵘᵉ   Louis XVI might have been a rotten monarch, but he certainly had taste. Fashioned in the style of pre-Revolutionary France, the Warwick is awash with pristine French and English antiques, Italian marble, chandeliers, four-poster beds, hand-carved headboards, and the like. The result is an expensive-looking hotel that, for all its pleasantries and perks, is surprisingly affordable when compared to its Union Square contemporaries—especially considering that all rooms underwent a renovation in 2002. Rooms can be on the small side; nonetheless, they're some of the city's most charming. Honeymooners should splurge on the fireplace rooms with canopy beds—ooh la la! Adjoining the lobby is La Scene Café, a beautiful place to start your day with a latte and end it with a nightcap.

490 Geary St. (between Mason and Taylor sts.), San Francisco, CA 94102. © 800/827-3447 or 415/928-7900. Fax 415/441-8788. www.warwicksf.com. 80 units. $119–$159 double; $159–$269 suite. AE, DC, DISC, MC, V. Parking $28. Cable car: Powell-Hyde and Powell-Mason lines. Bus: 2, 3, 4, 27, or 38. **Amenities:** Restaurant; access to nearby health club ($15 per day); concierge; business center; secretarial services; 24-hr. room service; babysitting; laundry service; dry cleaning. *In room:* TV, dataport, minibar, hair dryer, iron, safe, wireless Internet access.

INEXPENSIVE

Alisa Hotel ★★ Ⓥⁿᵃˡᵘᵉ   The five-story Alisa Hotel is definitely a budget gem. While it has standard characteristics of discount European-style hotels—small lobby, narrow hallways, cramped rooms—the owners here have distanced themselves from the competition by including a very pleasing dose of artistry. The lobby, for example, hosts rotating art exhibits and contains groovy furnishings, while the guest rooms are soothingly outfitted with quality Pan-Asian furnishings and tasteful accouterments such as Japanese fans, framed prints, and your very own personal "Moon Frog," the Chinese symbol of peace and harmony. You'll love the lively location as well: right across the street from the entrance to Chinatown and 2 blocks from Union Square. Considering the price (rooms with a very clean shared bathroom start at $49), quality, and location, it's quite possibly the best budget hotel in the city. Don't sweat it if they're booked: Their sister property, The Olympic Hotel (call the 800 number or see www.olympichotelsf.com), acquired in December 2003, is nearby and equally priced and hospitable.

447 Bush St. (at Grant St.), San Francisco, CA 94108. ⓒ **800/956-4322** or 415/956-3232. Fax 415/956-0399. www.alisahotel.com. 51 units, 26 with private bathroom. $69–$119 double with bathroom; $49–$69 double without bathroom. Rates include continental breakfast. AE, DC, MC, V. Nearby parking $20. Bus: All Market St. buses. Cable car: Powell-Hyde and Powell-Mason lines. **Amenities:** 24-hour concierge; fax and copy services. *In room:* TV, 2-line direct dial telephone w/dataport and voice mail, hair dryer, iron/ironing board, wireless Internet, small fridge and microwave in some rooms.

The Andrews Hotel 🍴

For the location and price, the Andrews is a safe bet for an enjoyable stay. Two blocks west of Union Square, the Andrews was a Turkish bath before its conversion in 1981. As is typical in Euro-style hotels, the rooms are small but well maintained and comfortable, with nice touches like white lace curtains and fresh flowers. Upgrades in 2002 included new mattresses and carpets. And even though the bathrooms were painted in 2003, they will remain tiny no matter how lovely the face-lift may be. A bonus is the adjoining Fino Bar and Ristorante, which offers respectable Italian fare and free wine to hotel guests in the evening.

624 Post St. (between Jones and Taylor sts.), San Francisco, CA 94109. ⓒ **800/926-3739** or 415/563-6877. Fax 415/928-6919. www.andrewshotel.com. 48 units (some with shower only). $99–$145 double; $149–$159 superior rooms. Rates include continental breakfast and evening wine. AE, DC, MC, V. Valet parking $28. Cable car: Powell-Hyde and Powell-Mason lines (3 blocks east). Bus: 2, 3, 4, 30, 38, or 45. **Amenities:** Restaurant; access to nearby health club; concierge; room service (5:30–10pm); babysitting; coffee in lobby; nearby self-service laundromat; laundry service; dry cleaning. *In room:* TV/VCR w/video library, dataport, fridge in suites only, hair dryer on request, iron, high-speed Internet access ($10 per day).

The Cartwright Hotel 🍴🍴

Diametrically opposed to the hip-hop, happenin' Hotel Triton down the street, the Cartwright Hotel is geared toward the more mature traveler. Management takes pride in its reputation for offering comfortable rooms at fair prices, which explains why most guests have been repeat customers for a long time. Remarkably quiet, despite its convenient location near one of the busiest downtown corners, the eight-story hotel looks not unlike it did when it opened some 80 years ago. High-quality antiques collected during its decades of faithful service furnish the lobby and the individually decorated rooms, all of which were blessed with new carpets, mattresses, wallpaper, phones, and window treatments in 2001 and underwent a complete restoration in 2004 (think new paint and new furniture finishes). A nice perk usually reserved for fancier hotels is the fully equipped bathrooms, all of which have tubs, massaging showers, terry robes, and thick fluffy towels. *Tip:* Request a room with a view of the backyard; they're the quietest. Complimentary wine is served in the small library each night, and afternoon tea and cookies are a daily treat, as are the apples and hot beverages in the lobby. A breakfast room added in 2004 serves a complimentary expanded continental breakfast.

524 Sutter St. (at Powell St.), San Francisco, CA 94102. ✆ **800/227-3844** or 415/421-2865. Fax 415/398-6345. www.cartwrighthotel.com. 114 units. $89–$159 double; $139–$189 family/business suite (sleeps 4). Rates include 24-hr. tea, coffee, and apples in the lobby, continental breakfast, nightly wine hour, weekday newspapers, and afternoon cookies. AE, DC, DISC, MC, V. Valet parking $30; self-parking $22. Cable car: Powell-Hyde and Powell-Mason lines (direct stop). Bus: 2, 3, 4, 30, or 45. **Amenities:** Access to nearby health club; concierge; pay-for-use Internet access. *In room:* TV, dataport, minibar, fridge, hair dryer, iron.

The Golden Gate Hotel ★★ (Value)   San Francisco's stock of small hotels in historic turn-of-the-20th-century buildings includes some real gems, and the Golden Gate Hotel is one of them. It's 2 blocks north of Union Square and 2 blocks down (literally) from the crest of Nob Hill, with cable car stops at the corner for easy access to Fisherman's Wharf and Chinatown. The city's theaters and best restaurants are also within walking distance. But the best thing about the 1913 Edwardian hotel is that it's family run: John and Renate Kenaston and daughter Gabriele are hospitable innkeepers who take obvious pleasure in making their guests comfortable. Each individually decorated room has handsome antique furnishings (plenty of wicker) from the early 1900s, quilted bedspreads, fresh flowers, and recently updated carpeting. Request a room with a claw-foot tub if you enjoy a good, hot soak. Afternoon tea is served daily from 4 to 7pm, and guests are welcome to use the house fax and computer with wireless DSL free of charge.

775 Bush St. (between Powell and Mason sts.), San Francisco, CA 94108. ✆ **800/835-1118** or 415/392-3702. Fax 415/392-6202. www.goldengatehotel.com. 25 units, 14 with bathroom. $85 double without bathroom; $130 double with bathroom. Rates include continental breakfast and afternoon tea. AE, DC, MC, V. Self-parking $15. Cable car: Powell-Hyde and Powell-Mason lines (1 block east). Bus: 2, 4, 30, 38, or 45. BART: Powell and Market. **Amenities:** Access to health club 1 block away; activities desk; office equipment available; laundry service/dry cleaning next door. *In room:* TV, dataport, hair dryer and iron upon request, wireless Internet access.

Hotel Bijou ★ (Value)   Three words sum up this hotel: clean, colorful, and cheap. Although it's on the periphery of the gritty Tenderloin

(just 3 blocks off Union Square), once inside this gussied-up 1911 hotel, all's cheery, bright, and perfect for the budget traveler who wants a little style with your savings. Joie de Vivre hotel group disguised the hotel's age with lively decor, a Deco theater theme, and a heck of a lot of vibrant paint. To the left of the small lobby is a "theater" where guests can watch San Francisco–based movies nightly (cute old-fashioned theater seating, though it's just a basic TV showing videos). Upstairs, rooms named after locally made films are small, clean, and colorful (think buttercup, burgundy, and purple), and have all the basics from clock radios, dressers, and small desks to tiny bathrooms (one of which is so small you have to close the door to access the toilet). Alas, a few mattresses could be firmer, and there's only one small and slow elevator. But considering the price, and perks like the continental breakfast and friendly service, you can't go wrong here.

111 Mason St., San Francisco, CA 94102. ℂ 800/771-1022 or 415/771-1200. www.hotelbijou.com. 65 units. $95–$139 double. Rates include continental breakfast. AE, DC, DISC, MC, V. Valet parking $21. Streetcar: Powell St. station. Bus: All Market St. buses. **Amenities:** Concierge; limited room service, same-day laundry service/dry cleaning. *In room:* TV, dataport, hair dryer, iron.

King George Hotel ⟨⟨ ⟨Value⟩ Built in 1914 for the Panama-Pacific Exhibition (when rooms went for $1 per night), the delightful boutique King George has fared well over the years with its mostly European clientele. The location—surrounded by cable car lines, the Theater District, Union Square, and dozens of restaurants—is superb, and the rooms, all of which were renovated in 1999 and received new textiles in 2002, are surprisingly quiet for such a busy spot. Although rooms can be small, the hotel makes the most of the space; and truth be told, with affordable prices, spiffy bathrooms, firm mattresses, desks, and a handsome studylike ambience, the smaller quarters come off pretty darned well. A big hit since it started a few years back is the hotel's English afternoon tea, served in the Windsor Tea Room Saturday, Sunday, and holidays from 2 to 5 pm. Recent additions include a pub and 24-hour business center.

334 Mason St. (between Geary and O'Farrell sts.), San Francisco, CA 94102. ℂ 800/ 288-6005 or 415/781-5050. Fax 415/835-5991. www.kinggeorge.com. 153 units. $140 double; $240 suite. Breakfast $6.50–$8. Special-value packages available seasonally. AE, DC, DISC, MC, V. Valet parking $25; self-parking $22. Cable car: Powell-Hyde and Powell-Mason lines (1 block west). Bus: 1, 2, 3, 4, 5, 7, 30, 38, 45, 70, or 71. **Amenities:** Tearoom; evening lounge/bar; access to health club ½ block away; concierge; 24-hr. business center; secretarial services; 24-hr. room service; same-day laundry service/dry cleaning; wireless Internet access in lobby. *In room:* TV w/pay movies and Nintendo, dataport, hair dryer, iron, safe, complimentary high-speed Internet access.

The Savoy Hotel 🏨🏨 *Value*   A European-style hotel through and through, the Savoy is one of my favorite moderately priced downtown hotels (The Warwick Regis, see below, is my other top pick). With a nice cozy apartment-like feel to each guest room, old well-cleaned bathrooms with original tiles, 18th-century period furnishings, fluffy featherbeds, and goose-down pillows, it's easy to relax here. Not all rooms are alike—they can be small, but each has beautiful white wood shutters, full-length mirrors, and two-line telephones. Guests also enjoy access to the newly relocated Millennium (p. 70), San Francisco's only gourmet vegan restaurant, which moved here from the Civic Center in 2003.

580 Geary St. (between Taylor and Jones sts.), San Francisco, CA 94102. © 800/ 227-4223 or 415/441-2700. Fax 415/441-0124. www.thesavoyhotel.com. 83 units. $119–$139 double; $149–$169 junior suite. Complimentary wine and cheese 4:30–6pm daily. Ask about package (like an extra $30 for parking and continental breakfast), government, senior, and corporate rates. AE, DC, DISC, MC, V. Parking $26. Bus: 2, 3, 4, 27, or 38. **Amenities:** Restaurant; bar; concierge; laundry service; dry cleaning. *In room:* TV, dataport, hair dryer, iron, safe.

2 Nob Hill

VERY EXPENSIVE

The Fairmont Hotel & Tower 🏨🏨   The granddaddy of Nob Hill's elite cadre of ritzy hotels, the Fairmont wins high honors for an incredibly jaw-dropping lobby. Even if you're not a guest, it's worth a side trip to gape at its massive marble Corinthian columns, vaulted ceilings, velvet chairs, gilded mirrors, and spectacular wraparound staircase. In previous years, we've warned that the rooms fell short, but thanks to an $85-million renovation completed in 2001, the glamour carries to guest rooms where everything is new and in good taste. In addition to the expected luxuries, guests will appreciate such details as goose-down pillows, electric shoe buffers, bathroom scales, and large walk-in closets. Spectacular views from the top floors remain the showstoppers, but nuances such as a 24-hour on-call dentist and doctor, high-speed Internet access, a notary public, a travel agency, and in-room PlayStations and dual phone lines enhance every guest's stay. Whatever you do, make a point of getting to the Tonga Room, a fantastically kitsch Disneylandlike tropical bar and restaurant where happy hour hops and "rain" falls every 20 minutes.

950 Mason St. (at California St.), San Francisco, CA 94108. © 800/441-1414 or 415/772-5000. Fax 415/391-4833. www.fairmont.com. 591 units. Main building $289–$409 double; from $500 suite. Tower $269–$359 double; from $800 suite. Extra person $30. AE, DC, DISC, MC, V. Parking $39. Cable car: California St. line (direct stop). **Amenities:** 3 restaurants; bar; health club ($15 daily); concierge; tour

desk; car-rental desk; wireless Internet in lobby; business center; shopping arcade; salon; 24-hr. room service; massage; babysitting; same-day laundry service/dry cleaning. *In room:* A/C, TV w/pay movies and PlayStation, fax, dataport, kitchenette in some units, minibar, coffeemaker, hair dryer, iron, safe, high-speed Internet access.

InterContinental Mark Hopkins ★★★   Built in 1926 on the spot where railroad millionaire Mark Hopkins's turreted mansion once stood, the 19-story Mark Hopkins gained global fame during World War II when it was de rigueur for Pacific-bound servicemen to toast their good-bye to the States in the Top of the Mark cocktail lounge. Nowadays, this great hotel, which renovated its rooms in 2000, caters mostly to convention-bound corporate executives, since its prices often require corporate charge accounts. Each neo-classical room is exceedingly comfortable and comes with all the fancy amenities you'd expect from a world-class hotel, including custom furniture, plush fabrics, sumptuous bathrooms, Frette bathrobes, and extraordinary views of the city. Luxury suites, renovated in early 2001, are twice the size of most San Francisco apartments and cost close to a month's rent per night. A minor caveat: The hotel has only three guest elevators, making a quick trip to your room difficult during busy periods.

The Top of the Mark (p. 167), a fantastic bar/lounge, offers dancing to live jazz or swing, Sunday brunch, and cocktails in swank, old-fashioned style. (Romantics, this place is for you, but keep in mind that there's a $10 cover fee on Fri and Sat after 8:30pm for the live nightly entertainment.) The Top of the Mark serves cocktails Monday through Saturday. The formal Nob Hill Restaurant offers California cuisine on Sundays only.

1 Nob Hill (at California and Mason sts.), San Francisco, CA 94108. ℂ **800/327-0200** or 415/392-3434. Fax 415/421-3302. www.markhopkins.net. 380 units. $395–$525 double; from $650 suite; from $3,000 luxury suite. Continental breakfast $20; breakfast buffet $35. AE, DC, DISC, MC, V. Valet parking $35, some oversize vehicles prohibited. Cable car: California St. and Powell lines (direct stop). Bus: 1. **Amenities:** 2 restaurants; bar; exercise room; concierge; car-rental desk; business center; secretarial services; 24-hr. room service; massage; babysitting; laundry service/dry cleaning; concierge-level floors. *In room:* A/C, TV w/pay movies, VCR in suites only, dataport, minibar, coffeemaker, hair dryer, iron, safe.

The Ritz-Carlton ★★★   Ranked among the top hotels in the world, the Ritz-Carlton has been the benchmark for San Francisco's luxury hotels since it opened in 1991. A Nob Hill landmark, the former Metropolitan Insurance headquarters stood vacant for years until the Ritz-Carlton company acquired it and embarked on a $100-million, 4-year renovation. The interior was completely gutted and restored with fine furnishings, fabrics, and artwork, including a pair

---

Fun Fact **I'll Have a Scotch**

The Ritz-Carlton's bar holds claim to one of the country's largest collection of single-malt scotches. Prices range from $7.25 to $66 per glass.

---

of Louis XVI blue marble urns with gilt mountings, and 19th-century Waterford candelabras. The Italian marble bathrooms offer every possible amenity: double sinks, telephone, name-brand toiletries, and plush terry robes. The more expensive rooms take advantage of the hotel's location—the south slope of Nob Hill—and have good views of the city. Club rooms, on the top floors, have a dedicated concierge, separate elevator-key access, and complimentary meals throughout the day. No restaurant in town has more formal service than this hotel's Dining Room, which is a fine place but is not included in this book's dining chapter, because, while excellent, others in its price range are more exciting. The less formal Terrace Restaurant offers contemporary Mediterranean cuisine and the city's best Sunday brunch. The lobby lounge serves afternoon tea and cocktails, daily, and sushi twice a week, with low-key live entertainment from 3pm to 1am.

600 Stockton St. (between Pine and California sts.), San Francisco, CA 94108. © 800/241-3333 or 415/296-7465. Fax 415/986-1268. www.ritzcarlton.com. 336 units. $395–$695 double; $475–$695 club-level double; from $695 suite. Buffet breakfast $27; Sun champagne brunch $65. Weekend discounts and packages available. AE, DC, DISC, MC, V. Parking $45. Cable car: Powell-Hyde and Powell-Mason lines (direct stop). **Amenities:** 2 restaurants; bar; indoor heated pool; outstanding health club; Jacuzzi; sauna; concierge; courtesy car; business center; secretarial services; 24-hr. room service; in-room massage and manicure; babysitting; same-day laundry service/dry cleaning. *In room:* A/C, TV w/pay movies, dataport, minibar, hair dryer, iron, safe, Internet access.

MODERATE

The Nob Hill Inn *Value*   Although most of the rooms at the luxurious Nob Hill Inn are well out of budget range, the three Gramercy rooms are among the most opulent you will find in the city for $125. Built in 1907 as a private home, the four-story inn has been masterfully refurbished with Louis XV antiques, expensive fabrics, reproduction artwork, and a magnificent etched-glass European-style lift. Even the lowest-priced rooms receive equal attention: large bathrooms with marble sinks and claw-foot tubs, antique furnishings, faux-antique phones and discreetly placed televisions, and a comfortable full-size bed. Granted, the Gramercy rooms are small. But they're so utterly charming that it's tough to complain, especially when you consider that rates include continental breakfast, after-noon tea and sherry, and the distinction of staying at one of the city's most prestigious hotels.

1000 Pine St. (at Taylor St.), San Francisco, CA 94109. (C) **415/673-6080.** Fax 415/673-6098. www.nobhillinn.com. 21 units. $125–$195 double; $245–$275 suite. Rates include continental breakfast, afternoon tea, and sherry. AE, DC, DISC, MC, V. Valet parking $30 per day (7:30am–10:30pm); self-parking 2 blocks away $20 per day. Cable car: California St. line. Bus: 1. **Amenities:** Concierge. *In room:* TV, kitch-enette in some, hair dryer, iron.

Nob Hill Lambourne ★★   One of San Francisco's top "business boutique" hotels, the Nob Hill Lambourne bills itself as an urban health spa, offering massages, aromatherapy, and yoga tapes to ease corporate-level stress. Even without this hook, the Lambourne deserves a top-of-the-class rating. Sporting one of San Francisco's most stylish interiors, the hotel flaunts the comfort and quality of its contemporary French design, made even better with its renovation in early 2003. Top-quality, hand-sewn mattresses and goose-down com-forters complement a host of thoughtful in-room accouterments that include umbrellas and CD player/stereos. Bathrooms have oversize

---

(*Value* **Free Parking in the City by the Bay**

With parking fees averaging $20 to $30 a night at most hotels (talk about a monopoly), you might consider staying at one of the lodgings listed below if you're crazy enough to drive the sinister streets of San Francisco. (As one seasoned driver put it, "We separate pedestrians between the quick and the dead.") All offer free parking—some even offer free covered parking—and are moderate to low priced.

- **Beck's Motor Lodge,** 2222 Market St. (at 15th St.); (C) **800/227-4360** or 415/621-8212.
- **Cow Hollow Motor Inn & Suites,** 2190 Lombard St. (between Steiner and Fillmore sts.); (C) **415/921-5800.** See p. 61.
- **Laurel Inn,** 444 Presidio Ave. (at California St.); (C) **800/552-8735** or 415/567-8467. See p. 61.
- **The Phoenix Hotel,** 601 Eddy St. (at Larkin St.); (C) **800/248-9466** or 415/776-1380. See p. 55.
- **The Wharf Inn,** 2601 Mason St. (at Beach St.); (C) **800/548-9918** or 415/673-7411. See p. 60.

tubs. Suites include an additional sitting room. The wine hour starts at 6pm. Smokers should seek a room elsewhere: This place prohibits puffing.

725 Pine St. (between Powell and Stockton sts.), San Francisco, CA 94108. (C) 800/ 274-8466 or 415/433-2287. Fax 415/433-0975. www.nobhilllambourne.com. 20 units. From $175 double; $299 suite. Rates include continental breakfast and evening wine hour. AE, DC, DISC, MC, V. Valet parking $30. Cable car: Powell-Mason, Powell-Hyde, and California St. lines (1 block north). **Amenities:** Access to nearby health club; spa treatments; concierge; in-room massage; laundry service; same-day dry cleaning. *In room:* TV/VCR, dataport, kitchenette, minibar, coffeemaker, hair dryer, iron, free high-speed Internet access, CD player.

3 SoMa

VERY EXPENSIVE

The Argent Hotel ✸✸ The large number of rooms and fine location—just a block south of Market Street, and a block from the Moscone Convention Center—make the Argent attractive to both groups and business travelers. Rooms, which are decorated with warm, modern, and surprisingly attractive furnishings (surprising considering what a corporate hotel it is) and textiles, have floor-to-ceiling windows and are well outfitted with three telephones (with voice mail). Corner suites look across the Bay Bridge and to SBC (formerly Candlestick) Park. But then again, so long as you're on an upper story, you're bound to get a good view of the city. Rooms are available for visitors with disabilities.

50 Third St. (between Market and Mission sts.), San Francisco, CA 94103. (C) 800/ 505-9039 or 415/974-6400. Fax 415/495-6152. www.argenthotel.com. 667 units. $245–$265 double; from $449 suite. $40 extra for executive-level rooms. AE, DC, DISC, MC, V. Valet parking $37. Streetcar: All Market St. streetcars. Bus: All Market St. buses. **Amenities:** Restaurant; bar; fitness center; concierge; business center; secretarial services; limited room service; in-room massage; babysitting; same-day laundry service/dry cleaning. *In room:* A/C, TV w/pay movies, dataport, kitchenettes in some rooms, minibar, coffeemaker, hair dryer, iron, safe, high-speed Internet access (deluxe rooms).

Four Seasons Hotel San Francisco ✸✸✸ What makes this überluxury hotel that opened in late 2001 one of my favorites in the city is its perfect combination of elegance, trendiness, and modern luxury. The entrance, either off Market or through a narrow alley off Third Street, is deceptively underwhelming, although it does tip you off to the hotel's overall discreetness. Take the elevators up to the lobby and you're instantly surrounded by calm, cool, and collected hotel perfection. I have yet to get familiar with the confusing lobby-level elevators, some of which go to luxury apartments and others to hotel guest quarters. But I quickly adopted the sexy cocktail lounge as my second home. After all, what's not to love about dark mood lighting, comfy leather chairs, bottomless bowls of olives and spicy wasabi-covered peanuts, a great wine and cocktail list, and a pianist playing jazz standards intermingled with Pink Floyd and No Doubt? Many of the oversize rooms (starting at 460 sq. ft. and including 46 suites) overlook Yerba Buena Gardens. Not too trendy, not too traditional, they're just right, with custom-made mattresses and pillows that guarantee the all-time best night's sleep, beautiful works of art, and huge luxury marble bathrooms with deep tubs and L'Occitane toiletries. Hues of taupe, beige, and green are almost as soothing as the superfluous service. Adding to the perks are free access to the building's huge Sports Club L.A., round-the-clock business services, a 2-block walk to Union Square and the Moscone Convention Center, and a vibe that combines sophistication with a hipness far more refined than the W or the Clift.

757 Market St. (between Third and Fourth sts.), San Francisco, CA 94103. (C) 800/332-3442 or 415/633-3000. Fax 415/633-3001. www.fourseasons.com. 277 units. $469–$600 double; $800 executive suite. AE, DC, DISC, MC, V. Parking $39. Streetcar: F, and all underground streetcars. BART: All trains. Bus: All Market St. buses. **Amenities:** Restaurant; bar; huge fitness center; spa; 24-hr. multilingual concierge; high-tech business center; secretarial services; salon; 24-hr. room service; in-room massage; overnight dry-cleaning and laundry service. *In room:* AC, TV w/pay movies, fax, minibar, hair dryer, safe.

Hotel Palomar 🐦🐦   The Kimpton Boutique Hotels' most luxurious downtown property occupies the top five floors of a refurbished 1907 landmark office building. As the group's most refined boutique property, the French-inspired interior designed by Cheryl Rowley features rooms with an updated twist on 1930s modern design, with artful, understated textural elements such as emerald-tone velvets, fine woods, and raffia. Tailored lines and rich textures throughout lend a sophisticated, fresh aspect to the overall air of elegance. Rooms, however, can range from very cozy (read: small) to ultracool and spacious (try for a corner room overlooking Market St.). There's not much in the way of public spaces, but the hotel makes up for it with its rooms' fab-factor, homey luxuries like CD players and 27-inch televisions, and its dining room, the Fifth Floor Restaurant (p. 77), which is one of the hottest (and most expensive) restaurants in town. That said, if you want the full-blown luxury hotel experience, you're better off with one of the Nob Hill or Union Square big boys.

12 Fourth St. (at Market St.), San Francisco, CA 94103. (C) 877/294-9711 or 415/348-1111. Fax 415/348-0302. www.hotelpalomar.com. 198 units. From $349 double; from $449 suite. Continental breakfast $18. AE, DC, DISC, MC, V. Parking

Where to Stay Around Town

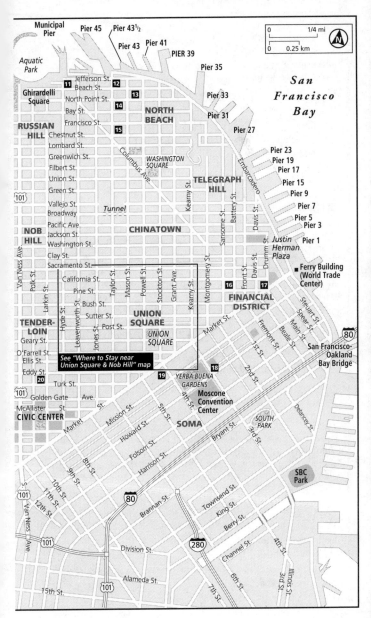

Municipal Pier

Pier 45   Pier 43½

Pier 43   Pier 41

PIER 39

Pier 35

Aquatic Park

San Francisco Bay

Jefferson St. Beach St.

North Point St.

Bay St.

Ghirardelli Square

11

12

13

14

Pier 33

Pier 31

NORTH BEACH

Francisco St.

RUSSIAN HILL

Chestnut St.

15

Pier 27

Lombard St.

Greenwich St.

Filbert St.

Union St.

Green St.

WASHINGTON SQUARE

Pier 23

Pier 19

Pier 17

Pier 15

TELEGRAPH HILL

Columbus Ave.

Kearny St.

Embarcadero

Vallejo St.

Broadway

Tunnel

Pier 9

Pier 7

Pier 5

Pier 3

NOB HILL

Pacific Ave.

Jackson St.

Washington St.

CHINATOWN

Sansome St.

Battery St.

Davis St.

Pier 1

Clay St.

Sacramento St.

Justin Herman Plaza

Van Ness Ave.

California St.

Pine St.

Drumm St.

Ferry Building (World Trade Center)

{101}

Polk St.

Larkin St.

Bush St.

Hyde St.

Leavenworth St.

Jones St.

Taylor St.

Mason St.

Powell St.

Stockton St.

Grant Ave.

Kearny St.

Montgomery St.

Front St.

Davis St.

16

17

FINANCIAL DISTRICT

TENDER-LOIN

Sutter St.

Post St.

UNION SQUARE

UNION SQUARE

Market St.

Steuart St.

Spear St.

Main St.

Beale St.

Geary St.

O'Farrell St.

Ellis St.

Eddy St.

Fremont St.

1st St.

San Francisco-Oakland Bay Bridge

20

See "Where to Stay near Union Square & Nob Hill" map

{101}

Turk St.

Golden Gate Ave.

McAllister St.

CIVIC CENTER

Market St.

19

18

YERBA BUENA GARDENS

Moscone Convention Center

2nd St.

{80}

Mission St.

4th St.

3rd St.

SOMA

Delancey St.

Howard St.

5th St.

Bryant St.

SOUTH PARK

Folsom St.

Harrison St.

9th St.

8th St.

Van Ness Ave.

10th St.

11th St.

12th St.

{80}

Brannan St.

Townsend St.

King St.

Berry St.

SBC Park

{101}

{280}

Division St.

Channel St.

4th St.

6th St.

Alameda St.

7th St.

3rd St.

Illinois St.

15th St.

0   ¼ mi

0   0.25 km

Kids The Best Family-Friendly Hotels

Argonaut Hotel (p. 59)   Not only is it near all the funky kid fun of Fisherman's Wharf and the National Maritime Museum, but this bayside hotel, a winner for the whole family, also has kid-friendly perks like the opportunity for each child to grab a gift from the hotel's "treasure chest."

Comfort Suites (121 E. Grand Ave.; ✆ 800/293-1794 or 650/589-7100; www.csusfo.com)   A Nintendo in each room, enough pay cable channels to keep you and your kids glued to the TV set for an entire day, and a pull-out sleeper sofa in addition to a king-size bed make this an attractive option for families.

Cow Hollow Motor Inn & Suites (p. 61)   Two-bedroom suites allow kids to shack up in style instead of camping on the pull-out couch.

Handlery Union Square Hotel (p. 39)   Never mind that it's been completely renovated. The real kid-friendly kickers here are the adjoining rooms in the "newer" addition; a heated, clean, outdoor pool; and the adjoining restaurant, The Daily Grill, which offers the gamut of American favorites.

Hotel Del Sol (p. 60)   It's colorful enough to represent a Crayola selection, but tots are more likely to be impressed

$36. Streetcar: F, and all underground streetcars. BART: All trains. Dogs welcome. **Amenities:** Restaurant; fitness center; concierge; courtesy car; business center; secretarial services; room service; in-room massage; babysitting; same-day laundry service/dry cleaning. *In room:* A/C, TV, fax/copier, dataport, minibar, fridge, hair dryer, iron, safe, complimentary high-speed Internet, CD player.

W San Francisco Hotel 🏨🏨   Starwood Hotels & Resorts' 31-story property is as modern and hip as its fashionable clientele. Sophisticated, slick, and stylish, it suits its neighbors, which include the Museum of Modern Art, the Moscone Center, and the Metreon Sony entertainment center. The striking gray granite facade, piped with polished black stone, complements the octagonal three-story glass entrance and lobby. The hip, urban style extends to the guest rooms, which have a residential feel. Each contains a "luxury" feather bed by the in-room CD player and VCR and the toys available at the courtyard pool.

The Maxwell Hotel (386 Geary St.; ✆ **888/734-6299** or 415/986-2000; www.maxwellhotel.com)   The colorful environs of this "theater Deco meets Victorian" style hotel are only half the reason kids will get a kick out of a stay here. Added bonuses are a VIP kids program, which includes a second, adjoining room at half the regular price.

The Phoenix Hotel (p. 49)   If you want to up your cool factor with the little ones, check them into this ultra-hip hotel. Kids will love the funky retro vibe and the courtyard pool.

San Francisco Airport North Travelodge (p. 65)   It's nothing fancy, but if you've got an early flight out, want to stay near the airport, and don't want to rent an extra room to accommodate the little ones, this place (with pull-out couches in every room) is a good bet.

Stanyan Park Hotel (750 Stanyan St.; ✆ **415/751-1000;** www.stanyanpark.com)   Plenty of elbow room and a half-block walk to Golden Gate Park's Children's Playground make this a prime spot for shacking up family style.

Westin St. Francis (p. 38)   A classic San Francisco hotel down to its hospitality, the Westin welcomes the little ones with fun gifts and free drink refills at their restaurants.

with a goose-down comforter and pillows, Waterworks linens, an oversize dark-wood desk, an upholstered chaise longue, and louvered blinds that open to (usually) great city views. Each room also contains a compact media wall complete with a Sony CD and videocassette player, an extensive CD library, and a 27-inch color TV with Internet service (and an infrared keyboard). Bathrooms are supersleek and stocked with Aveda products. Furthering the supercool vibe is a bi-level bar and XYZ restaurant, which serves fresh and bold American fare within a zippy white-on-white interior. All in all, since 2000, this has been one of the top places to be.

181 Third St. (between Mission and Howard sts.), San Francisco, CA 94103. ✆ **800/877-WHOTEL** or 415/777-5300. Fax 415/817-7823. www.whotels.com/sanfrancisco. 423 units. From $469 double; from $1,000 suite. AE, DC, DISC, MC, V. Valet parking

$40. Streetcar: J, K, L, or M to Montgomery. Bus: 15, 30, or 45. **Amenities:** Restaurant; 2 bars; heated atrium pool and Jacuzzi; fitness center; spa; concierge; business center; Wi-Fi in public spaces; secretarial services; 24-hr. room service; same-day laundry service/dry cleaning. *In room:* A/C, TV/VCR w/pay movies and Internet access, fax, dataport, minibar, coffeemaker, hair dryer, iron, safe, CD player.

EXPENSIVE

San Francisco Marriott 🎭🎭   Some call it a masterpiece; others liken it to the world's biggest parking meter. In either case, the Marriott is one of the largest buildings in the city, making it a popular stop for convention-goers and those looking for a room with a view. Fortunately, the controversy does not extend to the rooms, which were renovated to the tune of $34 million in 2003; expect a pleasant place to crash with large bathrooms and exceptional city vistas. *Tip:* Upon arrival, enter from Fourth Street, between Market and Mission, to avoid a long trek to the registration area.

55 Fourth St. (between Market and Mission sts.), San Francisco, CA 94103. ✆ 800/228-9290 or 415/896-1600. Fax 415/486-8101. www.sfmarriott.com. 1,500 units. $199–$349 double; $499–$3,250 suite. AE, DC, DISC, MC, V. Parking $38. Cable car: Powell-Hyde and Powell-Mason lines (3 blocks west). Streetcar: All Market St. streetcars. Bus: All Market St. buses. **Amenities:** 2 restaurants; 2 bars; indoor pool; health club; tour desk; car rental; business center; laundry service; dry cleaning. *In room:* A/C, TV w/pay movies, dataport, hair dryer, iron.

MODERATE

The Mosser 🎭🎭 *Value*   "Hip on the Cheap" might best sum up The Mosser, a highly atypical budget hotel that incorporates Victorian architecture with modern interior design. It originally opened in 1913 as a luxury hotel only to be dwarfed by far more modern sky rise hotels that surround it. But a major multimillion-dollar renovation in the fall of 2001 transformed this aging charmer into a sophisticated, stylish, and surprisingly affordable SoMa lodging. Guest rooms are replete with original Victorian flourishes—bay windows, high ceilings, hand-carved moldings—that juxtapose well with the contemporary custom-designed furnishings, granite showers, stainless steel fixtures, ceiling fans, Frette linens, and modern electronics. The least expensive rooms share a bathroom but are an incredible deal with rates starting at $60. The hotel's restaurant, Annabelle's Bar and Bistro, serves lunch and dinner, and The Mosser even houses Studio Paradiso, a state-of-the-art recording studio. The location is excellent as well—3 blocks from Union Square, 2 blocks from the MOMA and Moscone Convention Center, and half a block from the cable car turnaround.

54 Fourth St. (at Market St.), San Francisco, CA 94103. ✆ 800/227-3804 or 415/986-4400. Fax 415/495-4091. www.themosser.com. 166 units, 112 with bathroom. $109–$179 double with bathroom; $59–$89 double without bathroom. Rates

include safe deposit boxes, fax, and mail services. AE, DC, MC, V. Parking $27. Streetcar: F, and all underground Muni and BART. **Amenities:** Restaurant; bar; 24-hr. concierge; same-day laundry service/dry cleaning. *In room:* TV, dataport, hair dryer, iron/ironing board, ceiling fan, AM/FM stereo with CD player, voice mail.

4 The Financial District

VERY EXPENSIVE

The Mandarin Oriental ✿✿✿ *(Finds)*   No hotel boasts better ultra-luxury digs with incredible views than this gem. The only reason to pause in the lobby or mezzanine is for the recommended Asian tea service (complete with bento box of incredible bite-size delicacies) or cocktails. Otherwise, heaven begins after a rocketing ride on the elevators to the rooms, all of which are located between the 38th and 48th floors of a high-rise. Each of the very roomy accommodations offers extraordinary panoramic views of the bay and city. Not all rooms have tub-side views (incredible and standard with the signature rooms!), but every one does have a luxurious marble bathroom stocked with a natural loofah, a large selection of name-brand toiletries, terry and cotton cloth robes, a makeup mirror, and silk slippers. Guest rooms are equally opulent, with beautiful Asian-influenced decor, handsome furnishings, and all-around comfort and accouterments that make it difficult to leave your room.

222 Sansome St. (between Pine and California sts.), San Francisco, CA 94104. ✆ 800/622-0404 or 415/276-9888. Fax 415/433-0289. www.mandarinoriental.com. 158 units. $470–$655 double; $675–$725 signature rooms; from $1,400 suite. Continental breakfast $21; American breakfast $32. AE, DC, DISC, MC, V. Valet parking $36. Streetcar: J, K, L, or M to Montgomery. Bus: All Market St. buses. **Amenities:** Restaurant; bar; fitness center; concierge; car rental; business center; 24-hr. room service; in-room massage; laundry service; same-day dry cleaning. *In room:* A/C, TV w/pay movies, fax, dataport, minibar, hair dryer, iron, safe, high-speed Internet access, CD player.

EXPENSIVE

Hyatt Regency San Francisco ✿   The Hyatt Regency, a convention favorite, rises from the edge of the Embarcadero Center at the foot of Market Street. The gray concrete structure, with a 1970s, bunkerlike facade, is shaped like a vertical triangle, serrated with long rows of jutting balconies. The 17-story atrium lobby, illuminated by museum-quality theater lighting, features flowing water and a simulated environment of California grasslands and wildflowers.

Rooms, most of which were part of an $50-million renovation in 2000, are comfortably furnished in "contemporary decor" a la corporate hotel fashion. Bonuses include new ergonomic workstation chairs, and all new textiles in shades of gold, charcoal gray, and celadon. Upgraded digs for Gold Passport members, which, along with the suites, underwent a textiles renovation in 1999, have extra perks like tea- and coffeemaking facilities and private fax machines on request. The hotel's 16th and 17th floors house the Regency Club, with 102 larger guest rooms, complimentary continental breakfast, and after-dinner cordials.

The Eclipse Café serves breakfast and lunch daily; during evenings it becomes A Cut Above steakhouse. Thirteen-Views Bar serves cocktails and bar food for dinner. The Equinox, a revolving rooftop restaurant and bar that's open for dinner and Sunday brunch, has 360-degree city views.

5 Embarcadero Center, San Francisco, CA 94111. © **800/233-1234** or 415/788-1234. Fax 415/398-2567. www.hyatt.com. 805 units. $159–$315 double; extra $50 for executive suite. Continental breakfast $15. AE, DC, DISC, MC, V. Valet parking $38. Streetcar: All Market St. streetcars. Bus: All Market St. buses. **Amenities:** Restaurant; cafe; bar; access to health club; concierge; business center; laundry; dry cleaning. *In room:* A/C, TV, dataport, minibar, high-speed Internet access.

5 North Beach/Fisherman's Wharf

EXPENSIVE

Best Western Tuscan Inn at Fisherman's Wharf 𝕮𝕮   The Best Western Tuscan Inn is one of the best midrange hotels at Fisherman's Wharf. Like an island of respectability in a sea of touristy schlock, it exudes a level of style and comfort far beyond those of its neighboring competitors. Splurge on hotel parking—which is actually cheaper than the wharf's outrageously priced garages—and then saunter toward the plush lobby, warmed by a grand fireplace. Even the rooms are a definite cut above competing Fisherman's Wharf hotels. Most have writing desks and armchairs. The only caveat is the lack of scenic views—a small price to pay for a good hotel in a great location. This hotel also offers seven wheelchair-accessible rooms.

425 North Point St. (at Mason St.), San Francisco, CA 94133. © **800/648-4626** or 415/561-1100. Fax 415/561-1199. www.tuscaninn.com. 221 units. $189–$269 double; $229–$369 suite. Rates include coffee, tea, and evening fireside wine reception. AE, DC, DISC, MC, V. Parking $26. Cable car: Powell-Mason line. Bus: 10, 15, or 47. Pets welcome for $50 fee. **Amenities:** Access to nearby gym; concierge; courtesy car; secretarial services; limited room service; same-day laundry service/dry cleaning. *In room:* A/C, TV w/pay movies, dataport, minibar, coffeemaker, hair dryer, iron, Nintendo.

Sheraton Fisherman's Wharf Hotel 𝕮   Built in the mid-1970s, this contemporary, four-story hotel offers the reliable comforts of a Sheraton in San Francisco's most popular tourist area. In other words, the clean, modern rooms are comfortable and well equipped but nothing unique to the city. A corporate floor caters exclusively to business travelers.

2500 Mason St. (between Beach and North Point sts.), San Francisco, CA 94133. ℭ **800/325-3535** or 415/362-5500. Fax 415/956-5275. www.sheratonatthewharf. com. 529 units. $239–$274 double; $550–$1,000 suite. Extra person $20. Continental breakfast $11. AE, DC, DISC, MC, V. Valet parking $30. Cable car: Powell-Mason line (1 block east, 2 blocks south). Streetcar: F. Bus: 10 or 49. **Amenities:** Restaurant; bar; outdoor heated pool; exercise room; concierge; car-rental desk; business center; limited room service; laundry; dry cleaning. *In room:* A/C, TV, fax (in suites only), dataport, coffeemaker, hair dryer, high-speed Internet access.

MODERATE

Argonaut Hotel ★★ *Kids*   The Kimpton Hotel Group gives visitors a new reason to stay at Fisherman's Wharf with this boutique gem, which opened in 2003 at the very cool San Francisco Maritime National Historic Park. Half a block from the bay (though miraculously quiet), the four-story timber and brick landmark building, originally built in 1909 as a warehouse for the California Fruit Canners Association (and later used by William Randolph Hearst to store items that eventually ended up inside his Hearst Castle in San Simeon), is your best choice in this category at the wharf. Its 239 rooms and 13 suites are whimsically decorated to emulate a luxury cruise ship in cheerful nautical colors of blue, white, red, and yellow (though evidence of its modest past appears in original brick walls, large timbers, and steel warehouse doors). Luxurious touches include flat-screen TVs, DVD and CD players, Aveda toiletries, and—get this—leopard-spotted bathrobes along with all the standard hotel amenities. All guests are welcome at nightly weekday wine receptions and can use the lobby's two very popular (and free) Internet terminals. Suites have killer views and come fully loaded with telescopes and spa tubs. Get a "view" room, which peers onto the wharf or bay (some rooms offer fabulous views of Alcatraz). If you're bringing the kids, know that the Argonaut's friendly staff goes out of their way to make little ones feel at home and allows each pint-size guest to pick a new plaything from the hotel's "treasure chest." *Tip:* The concierge seems to be able to work wonders when you need tickets to Alcatraz—even when the trips are officially sold out.

495 Jefferson St. (at Hyde St.), San Francisco, CA 94109. ℭ **866/415-0704** or 415/ 563-0800. Fax 415/345-5513. www.argonauthotel.com. 252 units. $159–$339 double; $249–$599 suite. Rates include evening wine in the lobby, daily newspaper, and kid-friendly perks like cribs and strollers. AE, DC, DISC, MC, V. Parking $32. Bus: 10, 30, or 47. Streetcar: F. Cable car: Powell-Hyde line. **Amenities:** Restaurant; bar; fitness center; concierge; laundry service; dry cleaning; yoga video and mats. *In room:* TV w/pay movies, minibar, coffeemaker, hair dryer, iron, safe, high-speed Internet access, DVD player, Nintendo, Web TV.

The Wharf Inn ★★ (Value)   My top choice for good-value lodging at Fisherman's Wharf, the Wharf Inn offers above-average accommodations at one of the most popular tourist attractions in the world. The recently refurbished rooms, done in handsome tones of forest green, burgundy, and pale yellow, come well stocked. But more important, they are well situated smack-dab in the middle of the wharf, 2 blocks from PIER 39 and the cable car turnaround, and they're within walking distance of The Embarcadero and North Beach. The inn is ideal for car-bound families because parking is free (that saves $25 a day right off the bat).

2601 Mason St. (at Beach St.), San Francisco, CA 94133. (C) 800/548-9918 or 415/673-7411. Fax 415/776-2181. www.wharfinn.com. 51 units. $95–$199 double; $299–$425 penthouse. AE, DC, DISC, MC, V. Free parking. Cable car: Powell-Mason line. Streetcar: F. Bus: 10, 15, 39, or 47. **Amenities:** Access to nearby health club ($10 per day); concierge; tour desk; car-rental desk; complimentary coffee/tea and newspapers. *In room:* TV, dataport, coffeemaker, hair dryer, iron on request.

INEXPENSIVE

The San Remo Hotel ★★ (Value)   This small, European-style *pensione* is one of the best budget hotels in San Francisco. In a quiet North Beach neighborhood, within walking distance of Fisherman's Wharf, the Italianate Victorian structure originally served as a boardinghouse for dockworkers displaced by the great fire of 1906. As a result, the rooms are small and bathrooms are shared, but all is forgiven when it comes time to pay the bill. Rooms are decorated in cozy country style, with brass and iron beds; oak, maple, or pine armoires; and wicker furnishings. The immaculate shared bathrooms feature tubs and brass pull-chain toilets with oak tanks and brass fixtures. If the penthouse is available, book it: You won't find a more romantic place to stay in San Francisco for so little money. It has its own bathroom, TV, fridge, and patio.

2237 Mason St. (at Chestnut St.), San Francisco, CA 94133. (C) 800/352-REMO or 415/776-8688. Fax 415/776-2811. www.sanremohotel.com. 62 units, 61 with shared bathroom. $55–$95 double; $155–$175 penthouse suite. AE, DC, MC, V. Self-parking $10–$14. Cable car: Powell-Mason line. Streetcar: F. Bus: 10, 15, 30, or 47. **Amenities:** Access to nearby health club; self-service laundry; TV room. *In room:* Ceiling fan.

6 The Marina/Pacific Heights/Cow Hollow

MODERATE

Hotel Del Sol ★★ (Kids) (Value)   The cheeriest motel in town is located just 2 blocks off the Marina District's bustling section of Lombard. Three-level Hotel del Sol is all about festive flair and luxury touches. The sunshine theme extends from the Miami

Beach–style use of vibrant color, as in the yellow, red, orange, and blue exterior, to the heated courtyard pool, which beckons the youngish clientele as they head for their cars parked (for free!) in cabana-like spaces. (The great pool with pool toys can keep the tots busy all day.) Fair-weather fun doesn't stop at the front door of the hotel, which boasts 57 spacious rooms with equally cheery interior decor (read: loud and very colorful) as well as unexpected extras like CD players, Aveda products, and tips on the town's happenings and shopping meccas. Sorry, smokers: You'll have to step outside to puff.

3100 Webster St. (at Greenwich St.), San Francisco, CA 94123. © 877/433-5765 or 415/921-5520. Fax 415/931-4137. www.thehoteldelsol.com. 57 units. $119–$165 double; $160–$235 suite. Rates include continental breakfast. AE, DC, DISC, MC, V. Free parking. Bus: 22, 28, 41, 43, 45, or 76. **Amenities:** Heated outdoor pool; dry cleaning. *In room:* TV/VCR, dataport, kitchenettes in some units, iron, wireless high-speed Internet access ($10 per day), CD player.

Laurel Inn ⚘⚘ *Value*   If you don't mind being out of the downtown area, this lovely hotel, renovated in 1999, is one of the most tranquil, affordable places to rest your head. Tucked just beyond the southernmost tip of the Presidio and Pacific Heights, the outside is nothing impressive—just another motor inn. And that's what it was until the hotel group Joie de Vivre breathed new life into the place. Now decor is *très* chic and modern, with Zen-like influences (think W Hotel at half the price). Some rooms have excellent city views; all have spiffy bathrooms. The continental breakfast is fine, but why bother when you're across the street from Ella's, which serves San Francisco's best breakfast? Other thoughtful touches: 24-hour coffee and tea service, pet-friendly rooms, and free parking! Add the great shopping 1 block away at Sacramento Street and the new and very hip bar, G, which serves libations and a surprisingly active slice of glamorous young Pacific Heights–style revelry, and there are plenty of reasons to stay here.

444 Presidio Ave. (at California Ave.), San Francisco, CA 94115. © 800/552-8735 or 415/567-8467. Fax 415/928-1866. www.thelaurelinn.com. 49 units. $155–$190 double. Rates include continental breakfast and afternoon lemonade and cookies. AE, DC, DISC, MC, V. Free parking. Bus: 1, 3, 4, or 43. Pets accepted. **Amenities:** Adjoining bar; concierge; valet service; access to great new JCC gym across the street at $10 per day. *In room:* TV/VCR, dataport, kitchenette in some units, hair dryer, iron, CD player.

INEXPENSIVE

Cow Hollow Motor Inn & Suites ⚘ *Kids*   If you're less interested in being downtown than in playing in and around the beautiful bayfront Marina, check out this modest brick hotel on busy Lombard

Street. There's no fancy theme, but each room, which was completely renovated in 2004, has cable TV, free local phone calls, free covered parking, and a coffeemaker. Families will appreciate the one- and two-bedroom suites, which have full kitchens and dining areas as well as antique furnishings and surprisingly tasteful decor.

2190 Lombard St. (between Steiner and Fillmore sts.), San Francisco, CA 94123. ℂ 415/921-5800. Fax 415/922-8515. www.cowhollowmotorinn.com. 129 units. $86–$125 double; from $225 suite. Extra person $10. AE, DC, MC, V. Free parking. Bus: 28, 30, 43, or 76. **Amenities:** Car-rental desk; laundry and dry cleaning within a block. *In room:* A/C, TV, dataport, kitchenettes in suites only, coffeemaker, hair dryer.

Marina Inn 🏠🏠 *Value*   Marina Inn is one of the best low-priced hotels in San Francisco. How it offers so much for so little is mystifying. Each guest room in the 1924 four-story Victorian looks like something from a country furnishings catalog, complete with rustic pinewood furniture, a four-poster bed with silky-soft comforter, pretty wallpaper, and soothing tones of rose, hunter green, and pale yellow. You also get remote-control televisions discreetly hidden in pine cabinetry—all for as little as *$65 a night!* Combine that with continental breakfast, friendly service, and an armada of shops and restaurants within easy walking distance, and there you have it: the top choice for best overall value. (**Note:** Traffic can be a bit noisy here, so the hotel added double panes on windows facing the street.)

3110 Octavia St. (at Lombard St.), San Francisco, CA 94123. ℂ 800/274-1420 or 415/928-1000. Fax 415/928-5909. www.marinainn.com. 40 units. Nov–Feb $65–$105 double; Mar–May $75–$125 double; June–Oct $85–$135 double. Rates include continental breakfast. AE, DC, MC, V. Bus: 28, 30, 43, or 76. *In room:* TV, hair dryer and iron on request.

7 Japantown & Environs

EXPENSIVE

Radisson Miyako Hotel 🏠   Japantown's Miyako is a tranquil alternative to staying downtown, which is only about 12 blocks away. The 16-story tower and five-story Garden Wing overlook the Japan Center, the city's largest complex of Japanese shops and restaurants (as well as a huge movie complex). The hotel, which underwent a $3-million renovation in 2002, manages to maintain a feeling of peace and quiet you'd expect somewhere much more remote. Rooms are Zen-like with East-meets-West decor. The Western-style (don't think cowboy) rooms are fine, but romantics and adventurers should opt for the traditional-style Japanese rooms with tatami mats and futons, a *tokonoma* (alcove for displaying art), and shoji screens that slide away to frame views of the city. Two futon luxury suites have Japanese rock gardens and deep-tub Japanese bathrooms. A bonus: Fillmore Street's upscale boutiques are just a few blocks away.

1625 Post St. (at Laguna St.), San Francisco, CA 94115. ℭ 800/333-3333 or 415/922-3200. Fax 415/921-0417. www.miyakohotel.com. 218 units. $149–$229 double; from $269 suite. Children under 18 stay free in parent's room. AE, DC, DISC, MC, V. Valet parking $20; self-parking $13. Bus: 2, 3, 4, or 38. **Amenities:** Limited exercise room; business center; limited room service; in-room massage; same-day laundry service/dry cleaning. *In room:* TV w/pay movies, dataport, coffeemaker; hair dryer, iron.

INEXPENSIVE

The Hotel Majestic ⭐⭐ ⓥ*alue*   Both tourists and business travelers adore the all-nonsmoking Majestic because it covers every professional need while retaining the ambience of a luxurious old-world hotel. It was built in 1902, and the lobby alone sweeps guests into another era, with an overabundance of tapestries, tasseled brocades, Corinthian columns, and intricate, lavish detail. Guest rooms are just as opulent, with French and English antiques; the centerpiece of many rooms is a large four-poster canopy bed. You'll also find custom-made, mirrored armoires and antique reproductions. All drapes, fabrics, and carpets were replaced in 1997. Beds got new spreads in 2002, and half the bathrooms and guest rooms underwent a $2-million renovation in 1999.

Perks go beyond the usual. As well as bathrobes, two phones (one of which is portable), and umbrellas, the hotel offers complimentary faxes sent and received by the office (a nice touch!), fresh-baked cookies with turndown service, and well-lit desks. Some rooms have fireplaces. Their intimate and very atmospheric Avalon cocktail lounge has a beautiful French mahogany bar topped with marble and a collection of African butterflies.

1500 Sutter St. (between Octavia and Gough sts.), San Francisco, CA 94109. ℭ 800/869-8966 or 415/441-1100. Fax 415/673-7331. www.thehotelmajestic.com. 58 units. $135–$150 double; from $250 suite. Rates include complimentary continental breakfast in lobby 7–10am, and wine and appetizers 4–6pm. Group, government, corporate, and relocation rates available. AE, DC, DISC, MC, V. Valet parking $19. Bus: 2, 4, 47, or 49. **Amenities:** Bar; access to nearby health club ($10 per day); concierge; 24-hr. room service; in-room massage; babysitting; same-day laundry/dry-cleaning service. *In room:* TV, dataport, fridge in some rooms, hair dryer, iron, wireless Internet access.

8 The Castro

Though most accommodations (mostly converted homes) in the Castro cater to a gay and lesbian clientele, everyone is welcome. Unfortunately, there are few choices, and their amenities don't really compare to those at most of the better (and much larger) hotels throughout San Francisco.

MODERATE

The Parker Guest House 🐾🐾   This is the best B&B option in the Castro, and one of the best in the entire city. In fact, even some of the better hotels could learn a thing or two from this fashionable, gay-friendly, 5,000-square-foot, 1909 beautifully restored Edwardian home and new adjacent annex a few blocks from the heart of the Castro's action. Within the bright, cheery urban compound, period antiques abound. But thankfully, the spacious guest rooms are wonderfully updated with smart patterned furnishings, voice mail, robes, and spotless private bathrooms (plus amenities) en suite or, in two cases, across the hall. A fire burns nightly in the cozy living room, and guests are also welcome to make themselves at home in the wood-paneled common library (with fireplace and piano), sunny breakfast room overlooking the garden, and spacious garden with fountains and a steam room. Animal lovers will appreciate the companionship of the house pug named Parker.

520 Church St. (between 17th and 18th sts.), San Francisco, CA 94114. ℂ **888/ 520-7275** or 415/621-3222. Fax 415/621-4139. www.parkerguesthouse.com. 21 units. $119–$200 double; $200 junior suite. Rates include extended continental breakfast and evening wine and cheese. AE, DISC, MC, V. Self-parking $15. Streetcar: J Church. Bus: 22 or 33. **Amenities:** Access to nearby health club; steam room; concierge; wireless Internet access. *In room:* TV, dataport, hair dryer, iron.

9 Near San Francisco International Airport
MODERATE

Embassy Suites 🐾   If you've stayed at an Embassy Suites before, you know the drill. But this hotel is one of the best airport options, if only for the fact that every room is a suite. But there is more: The property has an indoor pool, whirlpool, courtyard with fountain, palm trees, and a bar/restaurant. Plus, each tastefully decorated two-room suite has nice additions such as two TVs. Additionally, a complimentary breakfast of your choice is available before you're whisked to the airport on the free shuttle—all that and the price is still right.

250 Gateway Blvd., South San Francisco, CA 94080. ℂ **800/362-2779** or 650/589-3400. Fax 650/589-1183. www.embassysf.com. 312 units. $109–$199 double. Rates include breakfast and complimentary evening beverages. AE, DC, MC, V. **Amenities:** Restaurant; bar; indoor pool; Jacuzzi; airport shuttle. *In room:* A/C, TV, fridge, coffeemaker, hair dryer, iron, wireless high-speed Internet access, microwave.

INEXPENSIVE

San Francisco Airport North Travelodge *Kids*   The Travelodge is a good choice for families, mainly because of the hotel's large heated pool. Although new carpets and bedspreads were added in 2001, the rooms are as ordinary as you'd expect from a Travelodge. Still they're comfortable and come with plenty of perks like Showtime and free toll-free and credit card calls. Each junior suite has a microwave and refrigerator. The clincher is the 24-hour complimentary shuttle, which makes the 2-mile trip to the airport in 5 minutes.

326 S. Airport Blvd. (off Hwy. 101), South San Francisco, CA 94080. © **800/578-7878** or 650/583-9600. Fax 650/873-9392. www.sfotravelodge.com. 199 units. $79–$129 double. AE, DC, DISC, MC, V. Free parking. **Amenities:** Restaurant; heated outdoor pool; courtesy shuttle to airport; fax and copier services; dry cleaning. *In room:* A/C, TV w/pay movies, coffeemaker, hair dryer, iron, safe, microwaves available.

4

Where to Dine

San Francisco's restaurants are so renowned that many people visit the city just to eat—and with good reason. The city's brilliant chefs, combined with California's abundance of organic produce, seafood, free-range meats, and Northern California wine, guarantee some of the world's finest dining, and fierce competition means slackers need not apply to any local kitchen.

Unfortunately, over the past few years, kitchen talent and quality ingredients have cost more and more (and higher gas prices aren't helping, since delivery expenses are also on the rise). Add to that the new San Francisco $8.50 minimum wage, which is threatening the already struggling livelihood of strapped restaurants (especially since it applies even to waiters, who don't need a raise as much as kitchen staff).

But on the bright side, "small plate" menus—or snacking through a meal on cheaper, smaller dishes—are more popular than ever, as are cheaper, more affordable, and casual newcomer destinations. Thus, though there are plenty of bargains to be found, the costlier spots included in this book can be so good, you might not mind spending $25 to $35 per entree.

Though trendy, much of San Francisco dining is *not only* about trendy fare. As one of the world's cultural crossroads, the city is blessed with a cornucopia of cuisines. Afghan, Cajun, Burmese, Jewish, Moroccan, Persian, Cambodian, vegan—whatever you're in the mood for, this town has it covered. So book your reservations and break out the credit cards, because half the fun of visiting San Francisco is the

Pricing Categories

The restaurants listed below are classified first by area, then by price, using the following categories: **Very Expensive,** dinner from $75 per person; **Expensive,** dinner from $50 per person; **Moderate,** dinner from $35 per person; and **Inexpensive,** dinner less than $35 per person. These categories reflect prices for an appetizer, main course, dessert, and glass of wine.

Tips **E-Reservations**

Want to book your reservations online? Go to **www.opentable. com**, where you can save seats in San Francisco and the rest of the Bay Area in real time.

rare opportunity to sample most of the flavors of the world in one fell swoop.

As you join the locals in their most beloved pastime, there are a few things you should keep in mind:

- If you want a table at the restaurants with the best reputations, you probably need to book 6 to 8 weeks in advance for weekends, and a couple of weeks ahead for weekdays.
- If there's a long wait for a table, ask if you can order at the bar, which is often faster and more fun.
- Don't leave *anything* valuable in your car while dining, particularly in or near high-crime areas such as the Mission, downtown, or—believe it or not—Fisherman's Wharf (thieves know tourists with nice cameras and a trunkful of mementos are headed there). Also, it's best to give the parking valet only the key to your car, *not* your hotel room or house key.
- ***Remember:*** It is against the law to smoke in any restaurant in San Francisco, even if it has a separate bar or lounge area. You're welcome to smoke outside, however.
- This ain't New York: Plan on dining early. Most restaurants close their kitchens around 10pm.

1 Union Square
VERY EXPENSIVE

Fleur de Lys ⍟ FRENCH   Fleur de Lys is the city's most traditional and formal classic French affair. Draped in 700 yards of rich patterned fabric mood-lit with dim French candelabras, and accented with an extraordinary sculptural floral centerpiece, this restaurant is a romantic spot, so long as your way of wooing includes donning a dinner jacket. Equally formal is the cuisine of chef Hubert Keller (former President Clinton's first guest chef at the White House), who is usually in the kitchen preparing the menus (and watching a closed-circuit TV of the dining room to ensure all goes smoothly). Diners in favor of grazing should start with the "Symphony" appetizer, a culinary medley with bite-size samplings of foie gras terrine, sea scallop cake, and lobster gelée. Other sure things include radicchio-wrapped salmon with canellini beans and Banyuls vinegar and olive oil; and lamb loin with spiced honey, caramelized cumin-seed sauce, and mint oil. The selection of around 700 French and California wines is also impressive.

777 Sutter St. (at Jones St.). © **415/673-7779.** www.fleurdelyssf.com. Reservations required. 3-course menu $68, 4-course $76, 5-course $88; vegetarian and vegan options available. AE, DC, MC, V. Mon–Thurs 6–9:30pm; Fri–Sat 5:30–10:30pm. Valet parking $12. Bus: 2, 3, 4, 27, or 38.

EXPENSIVE

Le Colonial ⋇ *Finds* VIETNAMESE   Sexy environs and decent— albeit pricey—French Vietnamese food make this an excellent choice for folks who enjoy bar snacking. I'm sorry to say that a chef change in 2002 knocked the food down a few notches since previous visits. But the vibrant flavors of tender wok-seared beef tenderloin with watercress onion salad still do the trick. The upstairs lounge (which opens at 4:30pm) is where romance reigns, with cozy couches, seductive surroundings, and a kicked-back cocktail crowd of swank professionals. My advice: Skip the dining room, head upstairs, and nosh your way through the appetizer menu.

20 Cosmo Place (off Taylor St., between Post and Sutter sts.). © **415/931-3600.** Reservations recommended. Main courses $18–$33. AE, DC, MC, V. Sun–Wed 5:30–10pm; Thurs–Sat 5:30–11pm. Valet parking $5 1st hr., $2 each additional ½ hr. Bus: 2, 3, 4, or 27.

MODERATE

Kuleto's ⋇ ITALIAN   After systematic retrofitting and a face-lift in spring 2002, Kuleto's is back in business as one of downtown's Italian darlings. Muscle a seat at the antipasto bar, and fill up on Italian specialties and selections from the wine list featuring 40 by-the-glass options. Or partake in the likes of penne pasta drenched in tangy lamb-sausage marinara sauce, clam linguine (generously overloaded with fresh clams), or any of the fresh-fish specials grilled over

---

Tips Multicourse Dining

Ordering a "fixed-price," "prix-fixe," or "tasting" menu can be a good bargain as well as a great way to sample lots of dishes at one sitting. Many dining rooms in town offer these multicourse menus, which tend to cost around $75 for four courses, including dessert.

Where to Dine in Union Square & the Financial District

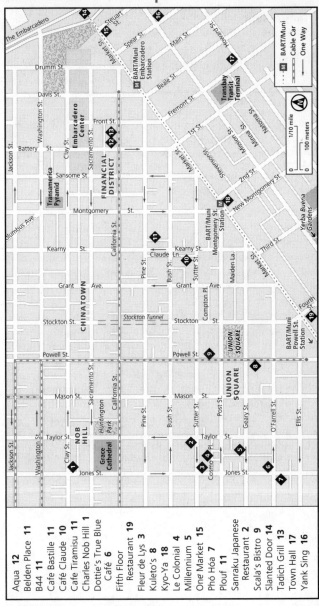

Impressions

[San Francisco is] the city that knows how.
— Pres. William Howard Taft

[San Francisco is] the city that knows chow.
— Trader Vic, restaurateur

---

hardwoods in the casually refined dining room. If you don't arrive by 6pm, expect to wait—this place fills up fast.

In the Villa Florence Hotel, 221 Powell St. (between Geary and O'Farrell sts.). ℰ **415/ 397-7720.** Reservations recommended. Breakfast $5–$10; main courses $10–$20. AE, DC, MC, V. Mon–Fri 7–10:30am; Sat–Sun 8–10:30am; daily 11:30am–11pm. Cable car: Powell-Mason and Powell-Hyde lines. Streetcar: Powell. Bus: 2, 3, 4, or 38.

Millennium ℱ VEGAN   Banking on the trend toward lighter, healthier cooking, chef Eric Tucker and his band of merry waiters set out to prove that a meatless menu doesn't mean you have to sacrifice taste. In a narrow, handsome, Parisian-style dining room with checkered tile flooring, French windows, and sponge-painted walls, Millennium has had nothing but favorable reviews for its egg-, butter-, and dairy-free creations since the day it opened. Favorites include sweet-and-spicy plantain torte served over a wonderful papaya and black-bean salsa appetizer, and main courses such as the phyllo purse stuffed with mushrooms, root vegetables, and almond-baked tofu with creamy garlic and corn pudding, or pan-seared black rice risotto cakes stuffed with black Himalayan truffle "butter" over a sherried parsnip and parsley root purée with roasted winter squash, sweet peppers, exotic mushrooms, and sorrel coulis. No need to divert from PC dining with your wine choice—all the selections here are organic.

In the Savoy Hotel, 580 Geary St. (between Taylor and Jones sts.). ℰ **415/487-9800.** www.millenniumrestaurant.com. Reservations recommended. Main courses $13–$19. AE, DC, MC, V. Daily 5–10pm. Valet parking $11. Bus: 38.

Scala's Bistro ℱ FRENCH/ITALIAN   Firmly entrenched at the base of the refurbished Sir Francis Drake hotel, this downtown favorite blends Parisian-bistro and old-world atmosphere with jovial and bustling results. With just the right balance of elegance and informality, it's a perfect place to have some fun (and apparently most people do).

Of the lovely array of Italian and French dishes, it's worth starting with the "Earth and Surf" calamari appetizer or grilled portobello mushrooms. Golden beet salad and Anchor Steam mussels are also good bets. Generous portions of moist, rich duck-leg confit will satisfy hungry appetites, but if you can order only one thing, make it Scala's signature dish: seared salmon. Resting on a bed of creamy buttermilk mashed potatoes and accented with a tomato, chive, and white-wine sauce, it's downright delicious. Finish with Bostini cream pie, a dreamy combo of vanilla custard and orange chiffon cake with a warm chocolate glaze.

In the Sir Francis Drake hotel, 432 Powell St. (at Sutter St.). ℭ **415/395-8555.** Reservations recommended. Breakfast $7–$10; main courses $12–$24 lunch and dinner. AE, DC, DISC, MC, V. Mon–Sun 8am–midnight. Cable car: Powell-Hyde line. Bus: 2, 3, 4, 30, 45, or 76.

INEXPENSIVE

Café Claude ⋒⋒ FRENCH   Euro transplants love Café Claude, a crowded and lively restaurant tucked into a narrow (and very European feeling) side street near Union Square. Seemingly everything—every table, spoon, saltshaker, and waiter—is imported from France. With prices topping out at about $18 on the menu featuring classics like steak tartare, steamed mussels, duck confit salad, escargot, New York steak with spinach gratin and crisp potatoes, and lamb chops with braised baby fennel, leeks, and red-wine garlic jus, Café Claude offers an affordable slice of Paris without leaving the city. There is live jazz on Saturdays from 7:30 to 10:30pm, and atmospheric sidewalk seating is available when the weather permits.

7 Claude Lane (off Sutter St.). ℭ **415/392-3515.** www.cafeclaude.com. Reservations recommended. Main courses $12–$18. AE, DC, DISC, MC, V. Mon 11:30am–5:30pm; Tues–Wed 11:30am–10:30pm; Thurs–Fri 11:30am–10:30pm; Sat 11:30am–10pm. Cable car: Powell-Mason and Powell-Hyde lines.

Pho Hóa ⋒ (Value) VIETNAMESE   Although it's only a few blocks off of Union Square, the walk to this simple Vietnamese restaurant in the downtrodden Tenderloin District is quite an adventure, often characterized by crack-smoking loiterers (literally) and plenty of people down on their luck. Thing is, the folks along the way are usually friendly enough and the arrival promises huge, killer bowls of Vietnamese soup with all the classic fixings (basil, bean sprouts, and so on) at absurdly low prices. Any of the dozens of selections is a meal in itself, be it my favorite—the seafood soup with rice noodles—or those with beef, chicken, shrimp, or flank steak. There are also plenty of rice dishes—with beef, vegetables, deep-fried egg rolls, or barbecued pork, and intensely strong iced coffee. For a cheap, hearty, but light meal, this is my favorite downtown option, and could be yours, too, provided you can overlook the fact that they use MSG and that the atmosphere is nothing more than clean cafeteria-style.

431 Jones St. (between O'Farrell and Ellis sts.). ℂ **415/673-3163.** Reservations not accepted. Soups and main courses $5.50–$9. No credit cards. Daily 8am–7pm. Bus: 27 or 38.

Sanraku Japanese Restaurant 🖈 *Value* JAPANESE/SUSHI   A perfect combination of great cooked dishes and sushi at bargain prices makes this straightforward, bright, and busy restaurant the best choice for folks hankering for Japanese food. The friendly, hardworking staff does their best to keep up with diners' demands, but the restaurant gets quite busy during lunch when a special box lunch of the likes of a California roll, soup, seaweed salad, deep-fried salmon roll, and beef with noodles with steamed rice comes at a very digestible $8.50. The main menu, which is always available, features truly irresistible sesame chicken with teriyaki sauce and rice; tempura; a vast selection of *nigiri* (raw fish sushi) and rolls; and delicious combination plates of sushi, sashimi, and teriyaki. Dinner sees brisk business, too, but magically, there always seems to be an available table.

704 Sutter St. (at Taylor St.). ℂ **415/771-0803.** www.sanraku.com. Main courses $6.25–$11 lunch, $10–$21 dinner. AE, DISC, MC, V. Mon–Sat lunch 11am–4pm, dinner 4–10pm; Sun 4–10pm. Cable car: Powell-Mason line. Bus: 2, 3, 4, 27, or 38.

2 Financial District

VERY EXPENSIVE

Aqua 🖈🖈 SEAFOOD   Without question, Aqua remains San Francisco's finest seafood restaurant, light years beyond the genre of shrimp cocktails and lemon-butter sauce. In 2003, heralded chef Laurent Manrique arrived from Campton Place to preside over the tasty traditions of previous chefs Michael Mina and George Marrone, and he continues to dazzle customers with a bewildering juxtaposition of earth and sea. The ahi tartare—my favorite all-time rendition, period—is mixed tableside with pears, pine nuts, quail egg, and spices. Sculptural grilled medallions of ahi tuna with foie gras in Pinot sauce are beyond decadent. Desserts are equally impressive. The large dining room with high ceilings, one big floral arrangement, and otherwise stark decor can be seriously loud, but that doesn't stop power-lunchers from powwowing by day and well-dressed gourmands from feasting in style at night. Steep prices prevent most people from making a regular appearance, but for special occasions or billable lunches, Aqua is on my top-10 list. Keep in mind that there's no valet or street parking at lunch, so you'll have to pull into one of The Embarcadero lots 2 blocks away.

252 California St. (near Battery). ℂ **415/956-9662.** Reservations recommended. Main courses $29–$39; 5-course tasting menu $90 or $100; vegetarian tasting

menu $55. AE, DC, MC, V. Mon–Fri 11:30am–2pm; Mon–Sat 5:30–10:30pm; Sun 5:30–9:30pm. Bus: All Market St. buses.

EXPENSIVE

Kyo-Ya 𝕽 JAPANESE/SUSHI   It's anything but cheap, but this restaurant offers an authentic Japanese experience, from the decor to the service to (most assuredly) the tasty sushi (skip the less impressive box lunch). Specialties include the freshest sushi, sashimi, and their elegant fixed-price menu. To start, try any of the appetizers, and move on to the grilled butterfish with miso sauce. Complete dinners include *kobachi* (tiny appetizer of chef's choice), soup, rice, pickles, and dessert. Kyo-Ya gets extra points for serving fresh wasabi, which puts the powdered stuff to shame. Many consider this—along with Kabuto (p. 103)—among the top five sushi restaurants in the city. (Unfortunately—and surprisingly—San Francisco is dreadfully lacking in truly great sushi spots.)

⟨Finds⟩ The Sun on Your Face at Belden Place

San Francisco has always been woefully lacking in the alfresco dining department. One exception is **Belden Place,** an adorable little brick alley in the heart of the Financial District that is open only to foot traffic. When the weather is agreeable, the restaurants that line the alley break out the big umbrellas, tables, and chairs, and voilà—a bit of Paris just off Pine Street.

A handful of adorable cafes line Belden Place and offer a variety of cuisines all at a moderate price. There's **Cafe Bastille,** 22 Belden Place (© 415/986-5673), a classic French bistro and fun speakeasy basement serving excellent crepes, mussels, and French onion soup; it schedules live jazz on Fridays. **Cafe Tiramisu,** 28 Belden Place (© 415/421-7044), is a stylish Italian hot spot serving addictive risottos and gnocchi. **Plouf,** 40 Belden Place (© 415/986-6491), specializes in big bowls of mussels slathered in a choice of seven sauces, as well as fresh seafood. **B44,** 44 Belden Place (© 415/986-6287), serves up a side order of Spain alongside its revered paella and other seriously zesty Spanish dishes.

Conversely, come at night for a Euro-speakeasy vibe with your dinner.

In the Palace Hotel, 2 New Montgomery St. (at Market St.). © 415/546-5090. www.kyo-ya-restaurant.com. Reservations recommended. Sushi $5–$20; main courses $25–$50 lunch and dinner; 7-course fixed-price menu $75. AE, DC, DISC, MC, V. Mon–Fri 11:30am–2pm; Tues–Sat 6–10pm. Streetcar: All Market St. streetcars. Bus: All Market St. buses.

One Market ✦✦ CALIFORNIA

If you don't mind enormous restaurants, this one, which features a farm-fresh menu, is outstanding thanks to executive chef Adrian Hoffman, who is undoubtedly one of the city's most talented and creative chefs. Amid the airy dining room of banquettes, mahogany, slate floors, seating for 220, and a bar that displays a prominent colorful mural of a market scene, a sea of diners feasts on delights from the ever-changing menu of fresh salads, fish, meat, and game, which manage to be fresh, far more inventive than most dishes around town, and outstanding in flavor. Go headfirst into decadence with the excellent shaved foie gras and hazelnut salad, in which cherries and duck liver brioche create an exciting combination of texture and flavor. Swoon over grilled Sonoma quail with bitter chicory glaze. Or take it over the top with osso buco for two with poached pears, apples, potatoes, and mustard greens. Arrive early to mingle with the corporate crowd that convenes from 4:30 to 7pm for happy hour.

1 Market St. (at Steuart St., across from Justin Herman Plaza). © 415/777-5577. www.onemarket.com. Reservations recommended. Main courses $19–$31. AE, DC, MC, V. Mon–Fri 11:30am–2pm; Mon–Thurs 5:30–9pm; Fri–Sat 5:30–9pm. Valet parking $10. Bus: All Market St. buses, streetcar, and BART.

The Slanted Door ✦✦ Finds VIETNAMESE

This restaurant is so popular that Mick Jagger and former President Clinton made stopovers when they hit town. Why? Despite the sometimes can't-be-bothered staff, the restaurant serves incredibly fresh and flavorful (albeit relatively expensive) Vietnamese food. No doubt it's even more of a hot spot since its April 2004 relocation to its beautiful bay-inspired custom-designed space in the Ferry Building Marketplace. But no matter. This is the place to be. Pull up a chair and order anything from clay-pot catfish or amazing green papaya salad to one of the lunch rice dishes, which come in a large ceramic bowl and are topped with such options as grilled shrimp and stir-fried eggplant. Dinner items, which change seasonally, might include beef with garlic and organic onions, grapefruit, and jicama salad. Whatever you order, it's bound to be wholesome, flavorful, and outstanding. There's also an eclectic collection of teas, which come by the pot for $3 to $5.

1 Ferry Plaza (at The Embarcadero and Market). © 415/861-8032. Reservations recommended. Lunch main courses $8.50–$16; most dinner dishes $9–$27. AE,

MC, V. Mon–Sun 11:30am–2:30pm; Sun–Thurs 5:30–10pm; Fri–Sat 5:30–10:30pm. Bus: All Market Street buses. Streetcar: F, N-Judah line.

MODERATE

Tadich Grill 🌟🌟 *Finds* SEAFOOD   Not that the veteran restaurant needed more reason to be beloved, but the city's ongoing loss of local institutions makes 156-year-old Tadich the last of a long-revered dying breed. This business began as a coffee stand during the 1849 gold rush and claims to be the very first to broil seafood over mesquite charcoal, in the early 1920s. An old-fashioned power-dining restaurant to the core, Tadich boasts its original mahogany bar, which extends the length of the restaurant, and seven curtained booths for private powwows. Big plates of sourdough bread top the tables.

You won't find fancy California cuisine here. The novella-like menu features a slew of classic salads, such as sliced tomato with Dungeness crab or prawn Louis; daily specials; meats and fish from the charcoal broiler; grilled items; and casseroles. Hot dishes include baked avocado with shrimp Diablo; baked casserole of stuffed turbot with crab and shrimp a la Newburg; charcoal-broiled steaks; and petrale sole with butter sauce, a local favorite. Plus, almost everyone orders a side of big, tasty french fries.

240 California St. (between Battery and Front sts.). ✆ 415/391-1849. Reservations not accepted. Main courses $14–$20. MC, V. Mon–Fri 11am–9:30pm; Sat 11:30am–9:30pm. Streetcar: All Market St. streetcars. BART: Embarcadero. Bus: All Market St. buses.

Yank Sing 🌟🌟 CHINESE/DIM SUM   Loosely translated as "a delight of the heart," cavernous Yank Sing is the best dim sum restaurant in the downtown area. Confident, experienced servers take the nervousness out of novices—they're good at guessing your gastric threshold as they wheel carts carrying small plates of exotic dishes past each table. Most dim sum dishes are dumplings, filled with tasty concoctions of pork, beef, fish, or vegetables. *Congees* (porridges), spare ribs, stuffed crab claws, scallion pancakes, shrimp balls, pork buns, and other palate-pleasers complete the menu. While the food is delicious, the location makes this the most popular tourist spot and weekday lunch spot; at other times, residents generally head to Ton Kiang (p. 104), the undisputed top choice for these Chinese delicacies. A second location, open during weekdays for lunch only, is at 49 Stevenson St., off First Street (✆ **415/541-4949**).

101 Spear St. (at Mission St. at Rincon Center). ✆ **415/957-9300.** Dim sum $2.80–$4.50 for 2–4 pieces. AE, DC, MC, V. Mon–Fri 11am–3pm; Sat–Sun 10am–4pm. Free validated parking in Rincon Center Garage on weekends. Cable car: California St. line. Streetcar: F. Bus: 1, 12, 14, or 41; BART.

3 SoMa

For a map of restaurants in this section, see the "Where to Dine Around Town" map on p. 78.

VERY EXPENSIVE

bacar 🎔🎔 AMERICAN BRASSERIE   No other dining room makes wine as integral to the meal as popular bacar. Up to 250 eclectic, fashionable diners pack into this warehouse-restaurant's three distinct areas—the casual (loud) downstairs salon, the bustling bar and loud mezzanine, or the more quiet upstairs, which looks down on the mezzanine's action—for chef Arnold Eric Wong's "American Brasserie" (that is, French bistro with a California twist) cuisine. I'm a fan of the creamy salt-cod and crab *brandade* (purée) and zesty roasted mussels with a chile-and-garlic sauce that begs to be soaked up by the accompanying grilled bread. Ditto the braised beef short ribs. Just as much fun is the wine selection, which gives you 1,300 choices. Around 100 come by the glass, 2-ounce pour, or 250- or 500-milliliter decanter, and wine director Debbie Zachareas is often available to introduce you to new and exciting options. (She also periodically offers half off on every bottle on Mondays, during which restaurant staff from around the city converge to splurge.) If you want a festive night out, this is the place to come—especially when jazz is playing Monday through Saturday evenings.

448 Brannan St. (at Third St.). ✆ **415/904-4100**. www.bacarsf.com. Reservations recommended. Main courses lunch $14–$17, dinner $22–$38. AE, DC, DISC, MC, V. Sun 5:30–11pm; Mon–Thurs and Sat 5:30pm–midnight; Fri 11:30am–2:30pm and 5:30pm–midnight. Valet parking (Mon–Sat beginning at 6pm) $10. Bus: 15, 30, 45, 76, or 81.

Boulevard 🎔🎔 *Finds* AMERICAN   Master restaurant designer Pat Kuleto and chef Nancy Oaks teamed up to create one of San Francisco's most revered restaurants, and although it made its debut in 1993, it's still one of my—and the city's—all-time favorites.

The dramatically artistic Belle Epoque interior, with vaulted brick ceilings, floral banquettes, a mosaic floor, and tulip-shaped lamps, is the setting for Oaks's equally impressive sculptural and mouthwatering dishes. Starters alone could make a perfect meal, especially if you indulge in sweetbreads wrapped in prosciutto on watercress and Lola Rose lettuce, with garlic croutons and whole-grain mustard vinaigrette; Sonoma foie gras with elderberry syrup, toast, and Bosc pear salad; or Maine sea scallops on garlic mashed potato croustade with truffle and portobello mushroom relish. The nine or so main courses are equally creative and might include pan-roasted miso-glazed sea bass with asparagus salad, Japanese rice, and shiitake mushroom broth; or spit-roasted cider-cured pork loin with sweet potato–swirled mashed potatoes and sautéed baby red chard. Vegetarian items, such as wild-mushroom risotto with fresh chanterelles and Parmesan, are also offered. Three levels of formality—bar, open kitchen, and main dining room—keep things from getting too snobby. Although steep prices prevent most from making Boulevard a regular gig, you'd be hard-pressed to find a better place for a special, fun-filled occasion. Cocktailers: Do ask the bartender about the special martinis—they're some of the best in town.

1 Mission St. (between The Embarcadero and Steuart sts.). ℂ **415/543-6084.** Reservations recommended. Main courses $9–$17 lunch, $24–$32 dinner. AE, DC, DISC, MC, V. Mon–Fri 11:30am–2:15pm; Sun–Thurs 5:30–10pm; Fri–Sat 5:30–10:30pm. Valet parking $12 lunch, $10 dinner. Bus: 15, 30, 32, or 45.

Fifth Floor Restaurant ✿✿✿ FRENCH   Executive chef Laurent Gras made his way through Michelin-star restaurants in France, spent 5 years as chef de cuisine at Restaurant Alain Ducasse, and forged his own ground at the Waldorf=Astoria's Peacock Alley before wowing diners at this swank French spot. Like the decor—rich colors and fabrics, red leather and velvet banquettes, Frette linens, zebra-striped carpeting, and a clublike atmosphere—Gras's menu is luxurious. But it's his creativity and attention to detail that makes this place one of the city's top restaurants. Here nearly everything is original and incredibly well executed—from an avocado dome hiding a mound of crabmeat brought to life with jalapeño and basil to "Lobster cappuccino," a lobster broth emulsified with chestnuts, prawns, and sautéed lobster. Main courses, like veal tournedos caramelized with sweetbread, black-pepper *jus,* and braised potato; or slow-baked lamb with truffle, pistachio, and olives with steamed cabbage, are also precisely prepared. The wine program also reigns, with one of the most prestigious and expensive lists around and a professional team to serve it. To see where this restaurant falls on a map, see the "Where to Dine in Union Square & the Financial District" map on p. 69.

In the Hotel Palomar, 12 Fourth St. (at Market St.). ℂ **415/348-1555.** www.fifth floor.citysearch.com. Reservations required. Main courses $31–$65; tasting menu $95. AE, DC, DISC, MC, V. Mon–Wed 5:30–9:30pm; Thurs–Sat 5:30–10pm. Valet parking $12. Bus: All Market St. buses.

EXPENSIVE

Town Hall ✿ AMERICAN   Mitchell and Steven Rosenthal (Postrio) and front man Doug Washington (One, Vertigo, Jardiniere, and Postrio) are behind this SoMa warehouse hot spot, which opened at the end of 2003, featuring an attractive and rustically

Where to Dine Around Town

GOLDEN GATE NAT'L REC. AREA

MARINA DISTRICT

Bay St.
Francisco St.
Chestnut St.
Lombard St.
Greenwich St.

PACIFIC HEIGHTS

Divisadero St.
Scott St.
Pierce St.
Steiner St.
Fillmore St.
Webster St.
Buchanan St.
Laguna St.
Octavia St.
Gough St.
Franklin St.

ALTA PLAZA PARK
Washington St.
Clay St.
Sacramento St.
California St.
Pine St.
Bush St.
Sutter St.
Post St.
Geary St.

Pacific Medical Center

LAFAYETTE PARK

Pacific Ave.
Jackson St.

Japan Center

JAPANTOWN

O'Farrell St.
Ellis St.
Eddy St.
Turk St.
Golden Gate Ave.
McAllister St.

St. Fulton St.
Grove St.
Ivy St.
Hayes St.
Fell St.
Oak St.
Page St.
Haight St.
Waller St.
Hermann St.
Duboce Ave.

ALAMO SQUARE

To Haight-Ashbury (see inset at left)

14th St.
15th St.
16th St.

Castro St.
Noe St.
Sanchez St.
Church St.
Market St.
Dolores St.
Guerrero St.
Valencia St.
Mission St.

McCoppin

MISSION DISTRICT

To Airport
17th St.

Haight-Ashbury

Conservatory Dr.
McLaren Lodge
Fulton St.
Grove St.
Hayes St.
Fell St.
Oak St.
Page St.
Haight St.
Waller St.
Frederick St.
Carl St.
Parnassus Ave.

John F. Kennedy Dr.
Stanyan St.
Shrader St.
Cole St.
Clayton St.
Belvedere St.
Downey St.
Ashbury St.
Masonic Ave.
Delmar St.

PANHANDLE

GOLDEN GATE PARK

Kezar
Pavilion
Beulah St.
Kezar Stadium

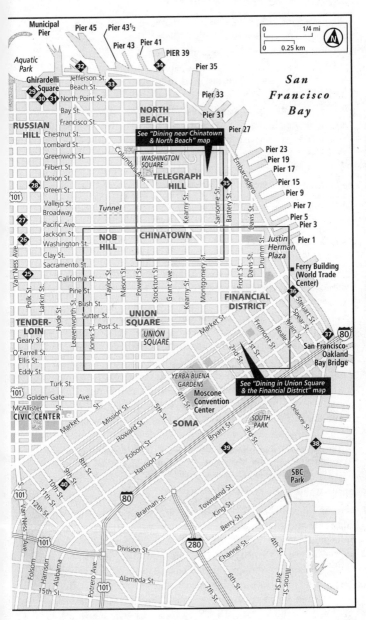

glitzy interior (brick, windows, airy, communal tables) and huge portions of hearty American regional cuisine. The homey food's good, but during my visits the menu tended to play it safe (think cioppino; grilled chicken with caramelized shallot mashed potatoes, banger sausage, and mustard herb jus; wild mushroom lasagna with salsa verde; and grilled rib-eye with hash brown potatoes, creamed leeks, and brown-butter garlic sauce). That said, everything was well done and butterscotch and the chocolate pot de crème by Janet Rikala Dalton astounded. There's definitely a scene here, so if you want a side of schmoozing with your dinner, this is your place. *Note:* A light menu is served between lunch and dinner.

342 Howard St. (at Fremont St.). ✆ 415/908-3900. www.townhallsf.com. Reservations recommended. Main courses $10–$17 lunch, $16–$25 dinner. AE, MC, V. Mon–Thurs 11:30am–10pm; Fri 11:30am–11pm; Sat 5:30–11pm; Sun 5:30–10pm. Bus: 10 or 76.

MODERATE

Gordon Biersch Brewery Restaurant CALIFORNIA   Popular with the young Republican crowd (loose ties and tight skirts predominate), this modern, two-tiered brewery and restaurant eschews traditional brewpub fare—no spicy chicken wings on this menu—in an attempt to attract a more upscale clientele. And it works. Goat cheese ravioli is a bestseller, followed by the herb-roasted half-chicken with garlic mashed potatoes. Start with the delicate and crunchy calamari *fritti* appetizer or, if you're a garlic hound, the tangy Caesar salad. Most dishes can be paired with one of the brewery's lagers. Couples bent on a quiet, romantic dinner can skip this place; when the lower-level bar fills up, you practically have to shout to be heard. Beer-lovers who want to pair their suds with decent grub will be quite content.

2 Harrison St. (on The Embarcadero). ✆ 415/243-8246. www.gordonbiersch.com. Reservations recommended. Main courses $9.50–$20. AE, DC, DISC, MC, V. Sun–Tues 11:30am–11pm; Wed–Thurs 11:30am–midnight; Fri–Sat 11am–2am. Bus: 32.

INEXPENSIVE

AsiaSF ⋆ ASIAN/CALIFORNIA   Part restaurant, part gender-illusionist musical revue, AsiaSF manages to be completely entertaining and extremely high-quality. As you're entertained by Asian men—dressed as women—who lip-sync show tunes, you can nibble on excellent grilled shrimp and herb salad; baby-back pork ribs with honey tamarind glaze, pickled carrots, and sweet-potato crisps; or filet mignon with Korean dipping sauce, miso eggplant, and fried potato stars. The full bar, *Wine Spectator* award–winning wine list,

and sake list add to the festivities. Fortunately, the food and the atmosphere are as colorful as the staff, which means a night here is more than a meal—it's a very happening event.

201 Ninth St. (at Howard St.). ℂ 415/255-2742. www.asiasf.com. Reservations recommended. Main courses $9–$19. AE, DISC, MC, V ($25 minimum). Sun–Thurs 6–10pm; Fri–Sat 5–10pm. Streetcar: Civic Center on underground streetcar. BART: Civic Center. Bus: 9, 12, or 47.

4 Nob Hill/Russian Hill

For a map of restaurants in this section, see the "Where to Dine Around Town" map on p. 78.

VERY EXPENSIVE

La Folie ☆☆ *Finds* FRENCH   My mother and I call this unintimidating, cozy, intimate French restaurant "the house of foie gras." Why? Because on our first visit, virtually every dish overflowed with the ultrarich delicacy. But in truth, there's more to chef Roland Passot's fantastic three-, four-, and five-course menus. Like what? Melt-in-your-mouth starters such as roast quail and—drum roll, please—foie gras with salad, wild mushrooms, and roasted garlic. Generous main courses include rôti of quail and squab stuffed with wild mushrooms and wrapped in crispy potato strings; and roast venison with vegetables, quince, and huckleberry sauce. The country-French decor is undergoing a remodel as this book goes to press, but no doubt the room will remain tasteful but not too serious. The staff is friendly, knowledgeable, and accommodating, and the food is outstanding. Best of all, the environment is relaxed, comfortable, and very neighborhoody. Finish with any of the delectable desserts. If you're not into the tasting menu, don't be deterred; the restaurant tells me they'll happily price out individual items.

2316 Polk St. (between Green and Union sts.). ℂ 415/776-5577. www.lafolie.com. Reservations recommended. 3-course tasting menu $60; 4-course tasting menu $75; 5-course chef's tasting menu $85; vegetarian tasting menu $60. AE, DC, DISC, MC, V. Mon–Sat 5:30–10pm. Bus: 19, 41, 45, 47, 49, or 76.

EXPENSIVE

House of Prime Rib ☆☆ STEAKHOUSE   Anyone who loves a huge slab of meat and old-school–style dining will feel right at home at this shrine to prime (rib). It's a fun and ever-packed affair within the men's clublike dining rooms (fireplaces included), where drinks are stiff, waiters are loose, and all the beef is roasted in rock salt, sliced tableside, and served with salad dramatically tossed tableside, followed by creamed spinach and either a baked potato and York-shire pudding, which accompany the entree. To placate the occasional non-meat eater, they offer a fish-of-the-day special. Another bonus: kids' prime rib dinners are a paltry $8.95.

1906 Van Ness Ave. (near Washington St.). ℂ **415/885-4605.** Reservations recommended. Complete dinners $24–$30. AE, DC, MC, V. Mon–Thurs 5:30–10pm; Fri–Sat 5–10pm; Sun 4–10pm. Valet parking: $6. Bus: 47 or 49.

MODERATE

Swan Oyster Depot 𝆎𝆎 *Finds* SEAFOOD   Turning 93 years old in 2005, Swan Oyster Depot is a classic San Francisco dining experience you shouldn't miss. Opened in 1912, this tiny hole-in-the-wall, run by the city's friendliest servers, is little more than a narrow fish market that decided to slap down some bar stools. There are only 20 or so seats here, jammed cheek-by-jowl along a long marble bar. Most patrons come for a quick cup of chowder or a plate of oysters on the half shell that arrive chilling on crushed ice. The menu is limited to fresh crab, shrimp, oyster, clam cocktails, Maine lobster, and Boston-style clam chowder, all of which are exceedingly fresh. *Note:* Don't let the lunchtime line dissuade you—it moves fast.

1517 Polk St. (between California and Sacramento sts.). ℂ **415/673-1101.** Reservations not accepted. Seafood cocktails $7–$15; clams and oysters on the half shell $7–$7.50 per half-dozen. No credit cards. Mon–Sat 8am–5:30pm. Bus: 19.

5 Chinatown

For a map of restaurants in this section, see the "Where to Dine near Chinatown & North Beach" map on p. 83.

INEXPENSIVE

R&G Lounge 𝆎𝆎 CHINESE   It's tempting to take your chances and duck into any of the exotic restaurants in Chinatown, but if you want a sure thing, go directly to the two-story R&G Lounge. During lunch, both recently modernized floors are packed with hungry neighborhood workers who go straight for the $5 rice-plate specials. Even then, you can order from the dinner menu, which features legendary deep-fried salt-and-pepper crab (a little too greasy and rich for my taste); and delicious chicken with black-bean sauce. A personal favorite is melt-in-your-mouth R&G Special Beef, which explodes with the tangy flavor of the accompanying sauce. I was less excited by the tired chicken salad, house specialty noodles, and bland spring rolls. But that was just fine since I saved room for generous and savory seafood in a clay pot and delicious classic roast duck.

Where to Dine near Chinatown & North Beach

Bix **7**
Brandy Ho's Hunan Food **5**
Caffè Macaroni **6**
L'Osteria del Forno **2**

Mo's Gourmet Burgers **3**
Pasta Pomodoro **1**
R & G Lounge **8**
Tommaso's **4**

Cable Car ====

0   1/10 mile
0   100 meters

(Kids) The Best of San Francisco's Family-Friendly Restaurants

Andalé Taqueria (p. 93)   So casual, so inexpensive, and offering lots of options, you can feed the whole clan here—and fit them comfortably in the dining room or on the patio.

Beach Chalet Brewery & Restaurant (p. 101)   You can relax and enjoy house-made beers and snacks while the kids peer at the ocean through picture windows or check out the Beach Chalet historic displays downstairs.

Cliff House (p. 102)   The folks at this oceanfront multiplex of restaurants are used to churning out fast meals for tourists with kids in tow.

Mel's Diner (p. 94)   A 1950s-style diner with all the trappings (think shakes, burgers, fries, and 25¢ jukeboxes), this family-friendly spot gives tots Crayons and coloring-book pages.

Pane e Vino (p. 93)   It's the accommodating staff at this neighborhood Italian restaurant that makes it a good spot to take the kids. Plus their menu is classic Italian, which means there are plenty of inoffensive offerings for the tots in tow.

Pasta Pomodoro (p. 86)   Cheap, fast, and informal is the perfect recipe for a tasty Italian dining experience.

Tommaso's (p. 87)   You can satisfy the kids' (and your) pizza craving at this small North Beach joint, which is known to serve the best brick-oven baked pies in town in a very casual, cramped, and old-school authentic atmosphere.

Ton Kiang (p. 104)   Chinese families head here every weekend to gather around large round tables and indulge in dim sum small-plate feasts. Decor is minimal, which makes the folks feel that much better when the soy sauce hits the plate or a few bites of rice hit the floor.

631 Kearny St. (at Clay St.). ✆ **415/982-7877.** Reservations recommended. Main courses $9–$30. AE, DC, DISC, MC, V. Mon–Thurs 11am–9:30pm; Fri 11am–10pm; Sat 11:30am–10pm; Sun 11:30am–9:30pm. Parking validated across the street at Portsmouth Sq. garage 24 hr. or Holiday Inn after 5pm. Bus: 1, 9AX, 9BX, 12, or 15.

6 North Beach/Telegraph Hill

For a map of restaurants in this section, see the "Where to Dine near Chinatown & North Beach" map on p. 83.

EXPENSIVE

Bix *Moments* AMERICAN/CALIFORNIA   The martini lifestyle may now be *en vogue,* but it was never out of style in this sexy and glamorous retro supper club. Bix is utterly stylish, with curving mahogany paneling, giant silver pillars, and dramatic lighting, all of which sets the stage for live music and plenty of hobnobbing. While the ultrasleek setting has overshadowed the food in the past, the legions of diners entranced by the Bix experience don't seem to care—and it seems as of late Bix is "on" again. Chicken hash has been a menu favorite for the past 17 years, but newer luxury comfort-food dishes—such as caviar service, marrow bones with toast and shallot confit, steak tartare, and pan-roasted seasonal fish dishes—are developing their own fan clubs. ***Bargain tip:*** At lunch there's a three-course prix-fixe menu for $20.

56 Gold St. (between Sansome and Montgomery sts.). © **415/433-6300.** Reservations recommended. Main courses $12–$15 lunch, $16–$32 dinner. AE, DC, DISC, MC, V. Mon–Fri 11:30am–3:30pm; Mon–Thurs 5:30–11pm; Fri–Sat 5:30pm–midnight; Sun 5:30–10pm. Valet parking $10. Bus: 15, 30, 41, or 45.

MODERATE

Piperade BASQUE   Chef Gerald Hirigoyen takes diners on a Basque adventure in this charming, small restaurant. Surrounded by a low wood-beam-lined ceiling, oak floors, and soft sconce lighting, it's a casual affair where diners huddle around white tablecloth–topped tables and indulge in small and large plates of Hirigoyen's superbly flavorful West Coast Basque cuisine. Your edible odyssey starts with small plates—or plates to be shared—like my personal favorites: moist crab meat coddled in a paper-thin crepe accompanied by a sweet and sassy mango and red-pepper salsa; and a bright and simple salad of giant white beans, eggs, chives, and marinated anchovies. Share entrees, too. Indulge in flat-iron steak with braised shallots and french fries or sop up every drop of the sweet and savory red-pepper sauce with the braised seafood and shellfish stew. Save room for orange blossom beignets: Light and airy with a delicate and moist web of dough within and a kiss of orange essence, the beignet is dessert at its finest. There's a community table for drop-in diners and front patio seating during warmer weather.

1015 Battery St. (at Green St.). © 415/391-2555. www.piperade.com. Reservations recommended. Main courses $15–$18. AE, DC, DISC, MC, V. Mon–Fri 11:30am–3pm and 5:30–10:30pm; Sat 5:30–10:30pm; closed Sun. Bus: 10, 12, 30, or 82x.

INEXPENSIVE

Caffè Macaroni 🐞🐞 ITALIAN   You wouldn't know it from the looks (or name) of it, but this tiny, funky restaurant on busy Columbus Avenue is one of the best southern Italian restaurants in the city. It looks as though it can hold only two customers at a time, and if you don't duck your head when entering the upstairs dining room, you might as well ask for one lump or two. Fortunately, the kitchen also packs a wallop, dishing out a large variety of antipasti and excellent pastas. The spinach-and-cheese ravioli with wild-mushroom sauce and the gnocchi are outstanding. The owners and staff are always vivacious and friendly, and young ladies in particular will enjoy the attentions of the charming Italian men manning the counter. If you're still pondering whether you should eat here, consider that most entrees are under $15.

59 Columbus Ave. (at Jackson St.). © 415/956-9737. www.caffemacaroni.com. Reservations accepted on weekdays only. Main courses $9–$18. No credit cards. Mon–Sat 5:30–10pm. Closed last week of Dec–1st week of Jan. Bus: 15 or 41.

L'Osteria del Forno 🐞🐞 ITALIAN   L'Osteria del Forno might be only slightly larger than a walk-in closet, but it's one of the top three authentic Italian restaurants in North Beach. Peer in the window facing Columbus Avenue, and you'll probably see two Italian women with their hair up, sweating from the heat of the brick-lined oven, which cranks out the best focaccia (and focaccia sandwiches) in the city. There's no pomp or circumstance here: Locals come strictly to eat. The menu features a variety of superb pizzas, salads, soups, and fresh pastas, plus a good selection of daily specials (pray for the roast pork braised in milk), which includes a roast of the day, pasta, and ravioli. Small baskets of warm focaccia keep you going until the arrival of the entrees, which should always be accompanied by a glass of Italian red. Good news for folks on the go: You can get pizza by the slice.

519 Columbus Ave. (between Green and Union sts.). © 415/982-1124. Reservations not accepted. Sandwiches $5.50–$6.50; pizzas $10–$17; main courses $6–$14. No credit cards. Sun–Mon and Wed–Thurs 11:30am–10pm; Fri–Sat 11:30am–10:30pm. Bus: 15 or 41.

Pasta Pomodoro 🐞🐞 *Kids* *Value* ITALIAN   If you're looking for a good, cheap meal in North Beach—or anywhere else in town, for that matter—this San Francisco chain can't be beat. There can be a short wait for a table, but after you're seated, you'll be surprised at how promptly you're served. Every dish is fresh and sizable and, best of all, costs a third of what you'd pay elsewhere. Winners include spaghetti *frutti di mare* made with calamari, mussels, scallops, tomato, garlic, and wine; and *genelli pollo,* with roast chicken, sun-dried tomatoes, cream, mushrooms, and Parmesan—both under $8. When I don't feel like cooking, I often stop here for angel-hair pasta with tomato and basil and a decadent spinach salad with candied walnuts and bleu cheese. The tiramisu is huge, delicious, and cheap, too.

655 Union St. (at Columbus Ave.). ℂ 415/399-0300. www.pastapomodoro.com. Reservations not accepted. Main courses $6–$11. AE, MC, V. Sun–Thurs 11am– 10:30pm; Fri–Sat 11am–11pm. Cable car: Powell-Mason line. Bus: 15, 30, 41, or 45. There are 7 other locations, including 2304 Market St., at 16th St. (ℂ 415/558-8123); 3611 California St. (ℂ 415/831-0900); and 816 Irving St., between Ninth and 10th sts. (ℂ 415/566-0900).

Tommaso's ★★ *Kids* ITALIAN   From the street, Tommaso's looks wholly unappealing—a drab, windowless brown facade sandwiched between sex shops. Then why are people always waiting in line to get in? Because everyone knows that Tommaso's, which opened in 1935, bakes one of San Francisco's best traditional-style pizzas. The center of attention in the downstairs dining room is the chef, who continuously tosses huge hunks of garlic and mozzarella onto pizzas before sliding them into the oak-burning brick oven. Nineteen different toppings make pizza the dish of choice, even though Italian classics such as veal Marsala, chicken cacciatore, superb lasagna, and wonderful calzones are also available. Tommaso's also offers half-bottles of house wines, homemade manicotti, and good Italian coffee. If you can overlook the seedy surroundings, this fun, boisterous restaurant is a great place to take the family.

1042 Kearny St. (at Broadway). ℂ 415/398-9696. www.tommasosnorthbeach.com. Reservations not accepted. Pasta and pizza $14–$24; main courses $11–$18. AE, DC, DISC, MC, V. Tues–Sat 5–10:30pm; Sun 4–9:30pm. Closed Dec 15–Jan 15. Bus: 15 or 41.

7 Fisherman's Wharf

For a map of restaurants in this section, see the "Where to Dine Around Town" map on p. 78.

VERY EXPENSIVE

A. Sabella's ★★ *Finds* SEAFOOD   The Sabella family has been serving seafood in San Francisco since the turn of the 20th century and has operated A. Sabella's restaurant on the wharf continuously since 1920, catering heavily to the tourist trade. The menu offers something for everyone—steak, lamb, seafood, chicken, and pasta, all made from scratch with fresh local ingredients. Where A. Sabella's really shines, however, is in the shellfish department. Its 1,000-gallon saltwater tank allows for fresh crab, abalone, and lobster year-round, which means no restaurant in the city can touch A. Sabella's when it comes to feasting on fresh Dungeness crab and abalone out of season. Of course, such luxuries are anything but cheap. But on the bright side, with their kids' menu, you can fill up tots' tummies for a mere $7.50. Added bonuses: The third-floor restaurant overlooks the wharf, and the wine list offers many tasty choices.

Fisherman's Wharf, 2766 Taylor St. (at Jefferson St.), 3rd floor. ✆ **415/771-6775.** www.asabellas.com. Reservations recommended. Most main courses $16–$28. AE, DC, DISC, MC, V. Daily 5–10pm. 2-hr. validated parking at the Wharf Garage, 350 Beach St. Cable car: Powell-Mason and Powell-Hyde lines. Streetcar: F.

Restaurant Gary Danko 🌟🌟🌟 *Finds* FRENCH   James Beard Award–winning chef Gary Danko presides over my top pick for fine dining. Eschewing the white-glove formality of yesteryear's fine dining, Danko offers impeccable cuisine and perfectly orchestrated service in an untraditionally unstuffy environment of wooden paneling and shutters and well-spaced tables. The three- to five-course fixed-price seasonal menu is freestyle, so whether you want a sampling of appetizers or a flight of meat courses, you need only ask. I am a devoted fan of his trademark buttery-smooth glazed oysters with leeks, salsify, and Osetra caviar; seared foie gras, which may be accompanied by peaches, caramelized onions, and *verjus* (a classic French sauce); and adventurous Moroccan spiced squab with *chermoula* (a Moroccan sauce made with cilantro) and orange-cumin carrots. Truthfully, I've never had a dish here that wasn't precious. And wine? The list is stellar, albeit expensive. If after dinner you have the will to pass on the glorious cheese cart or flambéed dessert of the day, a plate of petit fours reminds you that Gary Danko is one sweet and memorable meal. ***Tip:*** If you can't get a reservation and are set on dining here, slip in and grab a seat at the 10-stool first-come, first-served bar where you can also order a la carte.

800 North Point St. (at Hyde St.). ✆ **415/749-2060.** www.garydanko.com. Reservations required. 3- to 5-course fixed-price menu $55–$78. AE, DC, MC, V. Sun–Wed 5:30–9:30pm; Thurs–Sat 5:30–10pm. Valet parking $10. Cable car: Hyde. Bus: 10. Streetcar: F.

Scoma's 🌟 SEAFOOD   A throwback to the dining of yesteryear, Scoma's eschews trendier trout preparations and fancy digs for good old-fashioned seafood served in huge portions amidst a very casual windowed waterfront setting. Gourmands should skip this one. But if your idea of heaven is straightforward seafaring classics like fried calamari, raw oysters, pesto pasta with rock shrimp, and lobster Thermidor with old-time hospitality to match, this is about as good as it gets. Unfortunately, a taste of tradition will cost you big time. Prices are as steep as those at some of the finest restaurants in town. Personally, I'd rather splurge at Gary Danko, Masa's, or A. Sabella's. But many of my out-of-town guests insist we meet at Scoma's, which is fine by me since it's a change of pace from today's chic spots, and the parking's free.

Pier 47 (between Jefferson and Jones sts.). ℂ 415/771-4383. www.scomas.com. Reservations recommended. Most main courses $18–$38. AE, MC, V. Sun–Thurs noon–10pm; Fri–Sat 11:30am–10:30pm; hours change seasonally so call to confirm. Valet parking free. Streetcar: F. Bus: 10 or 47.

EXPENSIVE

Ana Mandara 🐾🐾 VIETNAMESE   Yes, Don Johnson is part owner. But more important, this Fisherman's Wharf favorite serves fine Vietnamese food in an outstandingly beautiful setting. Amid a shuttered room with mood lighting, palm trees, and Vietnamese-inspired decor, diners (mostly tourists) splurge on crispy rolls; lobster with sweet-and-sour sauce and black sticky rice; and wok-charred tournedos of beef tenderloin with sweet onions and peppercress. There is no more expensive Vietnamese dining room in town, but, along with the enjoyable fare, diners pay for the atmosphere, which, if they're in the neighborhood and want something more exotic than the standby seafood dinner, is worth the price.

891 Beach St. (at Polk St.). ℂ 415/771-6800. www.anamandara.com. Reservations recommended. Main courses $17–$29. AE, DISC, MC, V. Mon–Fri 11:30am–2pm; Sun–Thurs 5:30–9:30pm; Fri–Sat 5:30–10:30pm. Valet parking Tues–Sun $9. Bus: 19 or 32. Streetcar: F.

INEXPENSIVE

Frjtz Fries 🐾 BELGIAN   Deep-fried offerings are as abundant as sea lions in the Fisherman's Wharf area, but thankfully this funky-artsy "Belgian fries, crepes, and DJ/Art teahouse" features killer, fat french fries with a barrage of exotic dipping sauces that are head and flippers above the rest. Grab a bag of the addictively cri
fried potatoes—perhaps with chipotle rér
mayo—or swerve toward less lardy options suc
crepe—ranging from Nutella, banana, and whi
rosemary chicken and Swiss cheese—a big, leafy
focaccia sandwich packed with roasted peppers,

mayo, grilled eggplant, and melted Gorgonzola. Wash it down with Belgian ale and rejoin the tourist trample. A second, equally groovy location is in Hayes Valley at 579 Hayes St. (at Laguna St.; ✆ **415/ 864-7654**).

Ghirardelli Square, 900 North Point St. (between Larkin and Polk sts). ✆ **415/928-3886**. www.frjtzfries.com. Reservations not accepted. Fries $3–$4.50; crepes $4.25–$7.50; sandwiches $5.95–$7.25. AE, MC, V. Sun–Thurs 10am–6pm. Fri–Sat 10am–7pm; open later during summer, so call for hours. Bus: 66. Streetcar: F line.

8 The Marina/Pacific Heights/Cow Hollow

For a map of restaurants in this section, see the "Where to Dine Around Town" map on p. 78.

VERY EXPENSIVE

Harris' 🐓🐓 STEAKHOUSE   Every big city has a great steak restaurant, and in San Francisco it's Harris'—a comfortably elegant establishment where the handsome wood-paneled dining room has curving banquettes and stately waiters. Here, the point, of course, is steak, which can be seen hanging in a glass-windowed aging room off Pacific Avenue. They are cut thick—New York–style or T-bone—and are served with a baked potato and seasonal vegetables. You'll also find classic spinach or Caesar salads, and sides of delicious creamed spinach, sautéed shiitake mushrooms, or caramelized onions. Harris' also offers lamb chops, fresh fish, and lobster, and occasionally venison, buffalo, and other seasonal game.

2100 Van Ness Ave. (at Pacific Ave.). ✆ **415/673-1888**. www.harrisrestaurant.com. Reservations recommended. Most main courses $17–$40. AE, DC, DISC, MC, V. Mon–Thurs 5:30–9:30pm; Fri 5:30–10pm; Sat 5–10pm; Sun 5–9:30pm. Valet parking $7. Bus: 12, 47, 49, or 83.

EXPENSIVE

Quince 🐓🐓 CALIFORNIA-ITALIAN   Its discreet location in a quiet residential neighborhood hasn't stopped this tiny and predominantly white-hued restaurant from becoming one of the city's hottest reservations since it opened in late 2003. With only 15 tables, diners are clamoring for a seat in order to savor the pristine nightly changing Italian-inspired menu by Michael Tusk, who mastered the art of pasta while working at the East Bay's famed Chez Panisse and Oliveto restaurants. Regardless, it's worth the effort— especially if you love simple food that honors a few high-quality ingredients. Dining divinity might start with a pillowy spring garlic or white asparagus with a lightly fried egg and brown butter, really hits heavenly notes with the pasta course, be it garganelli with English peas and prosciutto, tagliatelle with veal ragout and fava beans, or artichoke ravioli. Meat and fish selections don't fall short either, with delicately prepared mixed grill plates, tender Alaskan halibut with fava beans, and juicy lamb with fennel and olives. Desserts, though tasty, aren't as celestial, which is just fine since it may leave room for an extra pasta course.

1701 Octavia St. (at Bush St.). (C) **415/775-8500.** www.quincerestaurant.com. Reservations required. Main courses $16–$27. Thurs and Sun 5:30–10pm; Fri–Sat 5:30–10:30pm. Valet parking: $8. Bus: 1, 31, or 38.

MODERATE

A16 🌟🌟 ITALIAN   This sleek spot featuring Neapolitan-style pizza and cuisine from the region of Campania has been so hot since its 2004 opening that on my first visit, tables were filled with reputed chefs and critics. Even without the fanfare, it feels exciting to be at A16, which is named after the motorway that traverses the region. The divided space boasts a full bar up front, a larger dining area and open kitchen in the back, and a wall of wines in between. But its secret weapon is chef Christophe Hille who whips up outstanding appetizers, pizza, and entrees with aplomb. Even if you must have the insanely good braised pork breast with olives, herbs, and caramelized chestnuts to yourself, start by sharing dried fava beans with fennel salad and tuna conserva with braised dandelion greens and crunchy bread crumbs. Shortly after opening, a few items were ho-hum (ricotta and chard involtini, desserts) and service was uneven. But even with its shortcomings, the restaurant still fell under the great category—especially factoring in Shelley Lindgren, who guides diners through the exciting wine list featuring 40 wines by the half-glass, glass, and carafe.

2355 Chestnut St. (between Divisadero and Scott sts.). (C) **415/771-2216.** www.a16sf. com. Reservations recommended. Main courses $8–$10 lunch, $14–$19 dinner. AE, MC, V. Wed–Mon 11:30am–2:30pm; Mon and Wed–Fri 5:30–10:30pm; Sat–Sun 5:30–11pm. Bus: 30 or 30X.

Florio 🌟🌟 FRENCH/ITALIAN   When I'm in the mood for a good meal without hoopla, I head directly to bistrolike Florio. Not only because the staff is friendly; not only because it's almost always painless to get a table or dine at the bar; and not even because the place is accommodating enough to not force quick turnover. The real reason is that I'm addicted to the chicken liver pâté, roasted chicken, steak frites, and virtually every other comfort dish that makes its way to the table. The wines by the glass (and by the bottle) tend to disappoint, but I don't care. I pull up a chair, make myself at home, and enjoy casual and cozy surroundings and consistently satisfying food. I suggest you do the same.

1915 Fillmore St. (between Pine and Bush sts.). © **415/775-4300**. www.floriosf.com. Most main courses $13–$28. AE, MC, V. Sun–Wed 5:30–10pm; Thurs–Sat 5:30–11pm. Bus: 3, 22, 41, or 45.

Greens Restaurant ★★ *Finds* VEGETARIAN

In an old waterfront warehouse, with enormous windows overlooking the bridge, boats, and the bay, this vegetarian restaurant is a pioneer and a legend. Renowned vegetarian cook and executive chef Annie Somerville (author of *Fields of Greens*) cooks with the seasons, using produce from local organic farms. Within the quiet dining room, a weeknight dinner might feature such appetizers as mushroom soup with Asiago cheese and tarragon; or grilled portobello and endive salad. Entrees run the gamut from pizza with wilted escarole, red onions, lemon, Asiago, and Parmesan, to Vietnamese yellow curry or risotto with black trumpet mushrooms, leeks, savory spinach, white-truffle oil, Parmesan Reggiano, and thyme. Those interested in the whole shebang should make reservations for the $46 four-course dinner served on Saturday only. Lunch and brunch are equally fresh and tasty.

The adjacent Greens To Go sells homemade breads, sandwiches, soups, salads, and pastries.

Building A, Fort Mason Center (enter Fort Mason opposite the Safeway at Buchanan and Marina sts.). © **415/771-6222**. Reservations recommended. Main courses $9.50–$14 lunch, $15–$20 dinner; fixed-price dinner $46; Sun brunch $8–$14. DISC, MC, V. Tues–Sat noon–4pm; Sun 10:30am–2pm; Mon–Fri 5:30–9:30pm; Sat 5:30–9pm. Greens To Go Mon–Thurs 8am–8pm; Fri–Sat 8am–5pm; Sun 9am–4pm. Free parking. Bus: 28 or 30.

Isa ★★ FRENCH

Luke Sung, who trained with some of the best French chefs in the city, has captured my and many locals' hearts by creating the kind of menu us foodies dream of: a smattering of small dishes that allow you to try numerous items in one sitting. It's a good thing the menu, considered "French tapas," offers small portions at reasonable prices. After all, it's asking a lot to make a diner choose between sweetbreads and mushroom ragout, seared foie gras with caramelized apples, potato-wrapped sea bass in brown butter, and rack of lamb. Here, a party of two can choose all of these plus one or two more and not be rolled out the door afterward. Adding to the allure is the warm boutique dining environment—60 seats scattered amid a very small dining room in the front, and a tented heated patio out back that sets the mood with a warm yellow glow. Take a peek at the "kitchen," a shoebox of a cooking space, to appreciate Sung's accomplishments that much more. Cocktailers, have your predinner drink elsewhere: Isa serves beer and wine only.

3324 Steiner St. (between Lombard and Chestnut sts.). ☎ **415/567-9588.** Reservations recommended. Main courses $9–$16. MC, V. Mon–Thurs 5:30–10pm; Fri–Sat 5:30–10:30pm. Bus: 22, 28, 30, 30X, 43, or 76.

Pane e Vino 🐾 *Kids* ITALIAN   Pane e Vino recently moved to a space with indoor and outdoor tented dining, and it remains one of San Francisco's favorite ultracasual Italian restaurants. While the rest of the city tries to modernize their manicotti, here food focuses on huge helpings of classics, which are fine for the traditional diner, but not fabulous for the gourmand. That said, prices are reasonable here and the mostly Italian-accented staff is always smooth and efficient under pressure (you'll see). The menu offers a wide selection of appetizers, including a fine carpaccio, *vitello tonnato* (sliced roasted veal and capers in lemony tuna sauce), and the hugely popular chilled artichoke stuffed with bread and tomatoes and served with vinaigrette. The antipasti of mixed grilled vegetables always spurs a fork fight. The broad selection of pastas includes flavorful *pennette alla boscaiola* with porcini mushrooms and pancetta in tomato cream sauce. Other specialties are grilled fish and meat dishes, including chicken breast marinated in lime juice and herbs. Top dessert picks are any of the Italian ice creams, crème caramel, and (but of course) creamy tiramisu.

1715 Union St. (between Gough and Octavia sts.). ☎ 415/346-2111. Reservations highly recommended. Main courses $10–$24. AE, MC, V. Mon–Thurs 11:30am–2:30pm and 5–9:30pm; Fri–Sat 11:30am–10pm; Sun 11:30am–9:30pm. No parking. Bus: 41 or 45.

INEXPENSIVE

Andalé Taqueria 🐾🐾 *Kids* *Value* MEXICAN   Andalé (Spanish for "hurry up") offers incredible high-end fast food for the health-conscious and the just plain hungry. As the long menu explains, this small California chain prides itself on its fresh ingredients and low-cal options. Lard, preservatives, and canned items are eschewed; Andalé favors salad dressings made with double virgin olive oil, whole vegetarian beans (not refried), skinless chicken, salsas and *aguas frescas* made from fresh fruits and veggies, and mesquite-grilled meats. Add the location (on a sunny shopping stretch), sophisticated decor, full bar, and check-me-out patio seating (complete with corner fireplace), and it's no wonder the good-looking, fitness-fanatic Marina District considers this place home. Cafeteria-style service keeps prices low. ***Bargain tips:*** No one can complain about a quarter of a mesquite-roasted chicken with potatoes, salsa, and tortillas for $6.75. If you want to go traditional, stick with the giant burritos or the fantastic $2.95 tacos—a nibbler's dream.

2150 Chestnut St. (between Steiner and Pierce sts.). ℂ 415/749-0506. Reservations not accepted. Most dishes $5.25–$9.50. MC, V. Mon 11am–9pm; Tues–Thurs and Sun 11am–10pm; Fri–Sat 11am–10:30pm. Bus: 22, 28, 30, 30X, 43, 76, or 82X.

Chez Nous 𝒢𝒢 FRENCH   Diners get crammed into the 45-seat dining area of this bright, cheery, small, and bustling cafelike dining room, but the French tapas are so delicious and affordable, no one seems to care. Indeed, this friendly and fast-paced neighborhood haunt has become a blueprint for other restaurants that understand the allure of small plates. But Chez Nous stands out as more than a petite-portion trendsetter. The clincher is that most of its Mediterranean dishes taste so clean and fresh you can't wait to come back and dine here again. Start with the soup, whatever it is; don't skip tasty french fries with *harissa* (Tunisian hot sauce) aioli; savor the lamb chops with lavender sea salt; and save room for their famed dessert, the minicustard-cakelike *canneles de Bordeaux*.

1911 Fillmore St. (between Pine and Bush sts.). ℂ 415/441-8044. Reservations recommended. Main courses $3.50–$12. MC, V. Daily 11:30am–3pm and 5:30–10pm (Fri–Sat until 11pm). Bus: 22, 41, or 45.

La Méditerranée 𝒢 𝒱𝒶𝓁𝓊𝑒 MEDITERRANEAN   With an upscale-cafe ambience and quality food, La Méditerranée has long warranted its reputation as one of the quainter inexpensive restaurants on upper Fillmore. Here you'll find freshly prepared traditional Mediterranean food that's worlds apart from the Euro-eclectic fare many restaurants now call "Mediterranean." Baba ghanouj, tabbouleh, dolmas, and hummus start out the menu. More important, the menu offers one very tasty chicken Cilicia, a phyllo-dough dish that's hand-rolled and baked with cinnamony spices, almonds, chickpeas, and raisins; also good is zesty chicken pomegranate drumsticks on a bed of rice. Both come with green salad, potato salad, or soup for around $9.25. Ground lamb dishes, quiches, and Middle Eastern combo plates round out the very affordable menu, and wine comes by the glass and in half- or full liters. A second location is at 288 Noe St., at Market Street (ℂ 415/431-7210).

2210 Fillmore St. (at Sacramento St.). ℂ 415/921-2956. www.cafelamed.com. Main courses $7–$10 lunch, $8–$10 dinner. AE, MC, V. Sun–Thurs 11am–10pm; Fri–Sat 11am–11pm. Bus: 1, 1BX, 22, or 24.

Mel's Diner 𝒢 𝒦𝒾𝒹𝓈 AMERICAN   Sure, it's contrived, touristy, and nowhere near healthy, but when you get that urge for a chocolate shake and banana cream pie at the stroke of midnight—or when you want to entertain the kids—no other place in the city comes through like Mel's Diner. Modeled after a classic 1950s diner, right down to the jukebox at each table, Mel's harkens back to the halcyon days when cholesterol and fried foods didn't jab your guilty conscience with every greasy, wonderful bite. Too bad the prices don't reflect the '50s; a burger with fries and a Coke costs about $9.50.

There's another Mel's at 3355 Geary St., at Stanyan Street (© **415/ 387-2244**); it's open from 6am to 3am Thursday through Saturday.

2165 Lombard St. (at Fillmore St.). © **415/921-3039.** Main courses $4–$6 breakfast, $6–$8 lunch, $8–$12 dinner. MC, V. Sun–Wed 6am–2am; Thurs 6am–3am; Fri–Sat 24 hr. Bus: 22, 30, or 43.

9 Civic Center

For a map of restaurants in this section, see the "Where to Dine Around Town" map on p. 78.

VERY EXPENSIVE

Jardinière ⋆⋆ CALIFORNIA/FRENCH   Jardinière is a preand postsymphony favorite, and it also happens to be the perfect setting for a cocktail. A culinary dream team runs the sexy dining room: owner-chef Traci Des Jardins and owner-designer Pat Kuleto, who created the swank champagne-inspired decor. On most evenings, the two-story brick structure is abuzz with an older crowd (including ex-mayor Brown, a regular) that sips cocktails at the centerpiece mahogany bar or watches the scene discreetly from the circular balcony. The restaurant's champagne theme extends to twinkling lights and fun ice buckets built into the balcony railing, making the atmosphere conducive to throwing back a few in the best of style—especially when there's live jazz (at 7:30pm nightly).

The daily changing menu is lovely; it might include seared scallops with truffled potatoes and truffle reduction, sautéed petrale sole with Alsatian cabbage and Riesling sauce, or venison with celery root, red wine, braised cabbage, and juniper sauce. But the atmosphere just doesn't have enough warmth for me. Still, anyone in search of a quality meal will not be disappointed. I also have to give kudos to the outstanding cheese selection, great wine list—many by the glass, and over 300 bottles—and Traci and manager Larry Bain's commitment to leading the industry supporting sustainably farmed, wholesome ingredients and environmentally conscious business operations.

300 Grove St. (at Franklin St.). © **415/861-5555.** www.jardiniere.com. Reservations recommended. Main courses $24–$35; 6-course tasting menu $75. AE, DC, DISC, MC, V. Sun–Wed 5–10:30pm; Thurs–Sat 5–11:30pm. Valet parking $10. Bus: 19 or 21.

Finds Hidden Treasures

They're on the way to nowhere, but because they're among the city's most unique, it would be a crime to leave out these destination restaurants. If you're not familiar with the streets of San Francisco, be sure to call first to get directions; otherwise, you'll spend more time driving than dining.

Thanh Long *⑆*, 4101 Judah St. (at 46th Ave.; *©* **415/665-1146**; www.anfamily.com; streetcar: N), is an out-of-the-way Sunset District Vietnamese standout that long after my mom started taking me here as a tot for excellent roasted crab and addictive garlic noodles, has remained a San Francisco secret. Since the owners, the An family, have become rather famous for their aforementioned signature dishes now that they're served in sister restaurants Crustacean in L.A., Vegas, and S.F., suffice it to say the crab's out of the bag. But this location is still far enough on the outskirts of the city to keep it from becoming too overcrowded. The restaurant is more visually pleasing than most Southeast Asian outposts (white tablecloths, tastefully exotic decor), but the extra glitz is reflected in the prices of luxury dishes (main courses run from $15–$40) such as charbroiled tiger prawns with those famed garlic noodles and steamed sea bass with scallions and ginger sauce. On the plus side, unlike the cheaper options around town, there's a full bar here, too, serving fun cocktails such as the Hanoi Sunset—an

MODERATE

Zuni Café *⑆⑆⑆* *Finds* MEDITERRANEAN   Zuni Café embodies the best of San Francisco dining: Its clientele spans young hipsters and gorgeous gays and lesbians as well as the everyday foodie; its cuisine is consistently outstanding; and the atmosphere is electric. Its expanse of windows overlooking Market Street gives the place a sense of space despite the fact that its always packed. For the full effect, stand at the bustling, copper-topped bar and order a glass of wine and a few oysters from the oyster menu (a dozen or so varieties are on hand at all times). Then, because *of course* you made advance reservations, take your seat in the stylish exposed-brick two-level maze of little dining rooms or on the outdoor patio. Then do what we all do: Splurge on chef Judy Rodgers's Mediterranean-influenced intoxicating mixture of Chambord tequila and peach schnapps. Reservations are recommended. Thanh Long is open Sunday and Tuesday through Thursday from 4:30 to 9:30pm, Friday and Saturday from 4:30 to 10:30pm, and is closed on Mondays.

The Ramp ⚓, 855 Terry François St. (at the end of Mariposa St.; ℂ **415/621-2378**; bus: 22 or 48), is an out-of-the-way mecca for seaside snacks, dancing, and drinking that's at its best when the sun is shining. If you're lucky enough to be in San Francisco on one of those rare hot days, head to this bayside hangout. The fare is of the basic pub grub variety—burgers, sandwiches, salads, and soups from $8 to $13—but the rustic boatyard environment and patio seating make this a relaxing place to dine in the sun. In summer, the place really rocks when live bands perform (4:30–7:30pm Sat–Sun Apr–Oct) and when tanned, cocktailing singles prowl the area. It's open for lunch from March to December Monday through Friday from 11am to 3:30pm, brunch Saturday and Sunday from 8:30am to 4pm. The bar is open Monday through Friday from 11am to 8pm, Friday and Saturday from 8:30am to 8pm. From May to October, outdoor barbecue is offered daily from 4 to 7:30pm; the rest of the year, appetizers are featured daily from 5:30 to 8pm.

menu. Although the changing menu always includes meat (such as hanger steak), fish (grilled or braised in the kitchen's brick oven), and pasta (tagliatelle with nettles, applewood-smoked bacon, butter, and Parmesan), it's almost sinful not to order her brick-oven roasted chicken for two with Tuscan-style bread salad. I rarely pass up the polenta with mascarpone and a proper Caesar salad. But then again, the hamburger on grilled rosemary focaccia bread is a strong contender for the city's best. Whatever you decide, be sure to order a stack of shoestring potatoes.

1658 Market St. (at Franklin St.). ℂ **415/552-2522.** Reservations recommended. Main courses $10–$19 lunch, $15–$29 dinner. AE, MC, V. Tues–Sat 11:30am–midnight; Sun 11am–11pm. Valet parking $8. Streetcar: All Market St. streetcars. Bus: 6, 7, 71, or 75.

10 Mission District

For a map of restaurants in this section, see the "Where to Dine Around Town" map on p. 78.

MODERATE

Foreign Cinema ☆☆ MEDITERRANEAN   This place is so chic that it's hard to believe it's a San Francisco restaurant, and it's so well hidden on Mission Street that it eludes me every time I seek the valet. An indoor seat is a lovely place to watch San Francisco's most fashionable. Outdoors (heated, partially covered, but still chilly), the enormous foreign film showing on the side of an adjoining building steals the show. (Although the actual purpose of dining here is not to watch the film, it's still a bummer for those facing away from it.) In 2001, husband-and-wife team John Clark and Gayle Pirie stepped into the kitchen and are now creating a fine Mediterranean menu. Snackers like me find solace in oysters, a devilish *brandade* (fish purée) gratin, and the cheese selections. Heartier eaters can opt for roasted half-chicken with golden chanterelle and red mustard-green risotto; or grilled Meyer Ranch natural rib-eye with Tuscan-style beans and rosemary-fried peppercorn sauce. Truth be told, even if the food weren't good, I'd come here. It's just that cool. By the way, if you have to wait for your table, consider stepping next door to the adjoining bar, Laszlo's.

2534 Mission St. (between 21st and 22nd sts.). ☎ **415/648-7600.** www.foreign cinema.com. Reservations recommended. Main courses $14–$25. AE, MC, V. Sun and Tues–Wed 5:30–10pm; Thurs–Sat 6–11pm; Sat–Sun brunch 11am–5pm. Closed Mon. Valet parking $8. Bus: 14, 14L, or 49.

INEXPENSIVE

Delfina ☆☆ *Value* ITALIAN   Unpretentious warehouse-chic atmosphere, reasonable prices, and chef/co-owner Craig Stoll's ultrafresh seasonal Italian cuisine have made this family-owned restaurant one of the city's most cherished. Stoll, who was one of *Food & Wine*'s Best New Chefs in 2001, changes the menu daily, while his wife Annie works the front of the house (when she's not being a mom). Standards include Niman Ranch flat-iron steak with french fries, and roasted chicken with Yukon Gold mashed potatoes and shiitake mushrooms. The winter menu might include slow-roasted pork shoulder or gnocchi with squash and chestnuts, while spring indulgences can include sand dabs with frisée, fingerling potatoes, and lemon-caper butter, or lamb with polenta and sweet peas. Trust me—order the buttermilk *panna cotta* (custard). *A plus:*

Four tables and counter seating are reserved for walk-in diners. *A downside:* It's impossible to find parking—literally—and there's no valet, so either park illegally (and perhaps get a ticket), come early to scrounge for a parking place, or take a bus or cab. Cocktail alert: Wine and beer only.

3621 18th St. (between Dolores and Guererro sts.). © 415/552-4055. Reservations recommended. Main courses $13–$22. MC, V. Sun–Thurs 5:30–10pm; Fri–Sat 5:30–11pm. Streetcar: J. Bus: 26 or 33.

11 The Castro

Although you see gay and lesbian singles and couples at almost any restaurant in San Francisco, the following spots cater particularly to the gay community—but being gay is certainly not a requirement for enjoying them. For a map of restaurants in this section, see the "Where to Dine Around Town" map on p. 78.

EXPENSIVE

Mecca 🎗🎗 *Finds* AMERICAN   In 1996, Mecca entered the scene in a decadent swirl of chocolate-brown velvet, stainless steel, cement, and brown Naugahyde. It's an industrial-chic supper club that makes you want to order a martini just so you'll match the ambience. The eclectic city clientele (with a heavy dash of same-sex couples) mingles at the oval centerpiece bar. A night here promises a live DJ spinning hot grooves and a fine American meal prepared by chef Stephen Barber and served at tables tucked into several nooks. On the menu are such classics as oysters on the half shell, seared ahi tuna, and wood-oven roasted pork tenderloin. The food is very good, but it's that only-in-San Francisco vibe that makes this place the smokin' hot spot in the Castro.

2029 Market St. (by 14th and Church sts.). © 415/621-7000. www.sfmecca.com. Reservations recommended. Main courses $15–$29. AE, DC, MC, V. Tues–Thurs 5:30–10pm; Fri–Sat 6–11:30pm, bar remains open later; Sun 5–9:30pm. Valet parking $10. Streetcar: F, K, L, or M. Bus: 8, 22, 24, or 37.

INEXPENSIVE

Chow 🎗🎗 *Value* AMERICAN   Chow claims to serve American cuisine, but the management must be thinking of today's America, because the menu is not exactly meatloaf and apple pie. And that's just fine for eclectic and cost-conscious diners. After all, what's not to like about starting with a Cobb salad before moving on to Thai-style noodles with steak, chicken, peanuts, and spicy lime-chile garlic broth, or linguine with clams? Better yet, everything except the fish of the day costs under $15. More traditional are the budget-wise daily sandwich specials, which range from meatball with mozzarella (Sun) to baked chicken with herbed garlic mashed potatoes (Mon); both come with salad, soup, or fries. While the food and prices alone would be a good argument for coming here, beer on tap, a great inexpensive wine selection, and the fun, tavernlike environment clinch the deal. A second location, **Park Chow,** is at 1240 Ninth Ave. (© **415/665-9912**). You can't make reservations unless you've got a party of eight or more, but if you're headed their way, you can call ahead to place your name on the wait list (recommended).

215 Church St. (near Market St.). © **415/552-2469**. Reservations not accepted. Main courses $7–$15. MC, V. Sun–Thurs 11am–11pm; Fri–Sat 11am–midnight. Streetcar: F, J, K, L, or M. Bus: 8 or 37.

12 Haight-Ashbury

For a map of restaurants in this section, see the "Where to Dine Around Town" map on p. 78.

MODERATE

RNM 𝒢𝒢 AMERICAN   Lower Haight is hardly known for glamour, and that's just what makes this ultraswank restaurant such a pleasant surprise. Beyond the full-length sliver mesh curtain is a deliciously glitzy diversion that looks more like it belongs in New York City rather than this funky 'hood. Warmly lit with dark-wood floors and tables, a cool full bar, and lounge mezzanine, it's the perfect setting for an equally appealing Italian- and French-inspired American tapas-style menu by chef Justine Miner who sharpened her culinary skills and knives at San Francisco's Postrio, Café Kati, and Globe. Anticipate tasty appetizers such as ahi tuna tartare with waffle chips, quail egg, and microgreens; charcuterie plate; and caramelized onion and wild-mushroom pizza with fontina cheese and truffle oil and entrees such as porcini-crusted day boat scallops on a purée of artichokes with shiitake mushroom ragout and a salad of mache greens and watermelon radishes with Meyer-lemon vinaigrette; and pan roasted rib-eye steak with pancetta-wrapped red Irish potatoes, wild nettles, Oakville Ranch cabernet butter, and shaved black Himalayan truffles.

598 Haight St. (at Steiner St.). © **415/551-7900**. www.rnmrestaurant.com. Reservations recommended. Small plates and pizza $7–$14; main courses $12–$22. MC, V. Tues–Wed 5–10pm; Thurs–Sat 5–11pm. Closed Sun–Mon. Bus: 7 or 22.

INEXPENSIVE

Cha Cha Cha 𝒢𝒢 𝒱𝒶𝓁𝓊ℯ CARIBBEAN   This is one of my all-time favorite places to get festive, but it's not for everybody. Cha Cha Cha is not a meal, it's an experience. Put your name on the mile-long list, crowd into the minuscule bar, and sip sangria while you wait (try not to spill when you get bumped by all the young, attractive patrons who are also waiting). When you do finally get seated (it usually takes at least an hour), you'll dine in a loud—and I mean *loud*—dining room with Santería altars, banana trees, and plastic tropical tablecloths. The best thing to do is order from the tapas menu and share the dishes family-style. Fried calamari, fried new potatoes, Cajun shrimp, and mussels in saffron broth are all bursting with flavor and accompanied by rich, luscious sauces—whatever you choose, you can't go wrong. This is the kind of place where you take friends in a partying mood, let your hair down, and make an evening of it. If you want all the flavor without the festivities, come during lunch. Their second, larger location, in the Mission District, at 2327 Mission St., between 19th and 20th streets (✆ **415/648-0504**), is open for dinner only and has a full bar.

1801 Haight St. (at Shrader St.). ✆ **415/386-7670.** Reservations not accepted. Tapas $5–$9; main courses $13–$15. MC, V. Daily 11am–4pm; Sun–Thurs 5–11pm; Fri–Sat 5–11:30pm. Streetcar: N. Bus: 6, 7, 66, 71, or 73.

Thep Phanom ✿✿ THAI   Thep Phanom has made the *San Francisco Chronicle's* top 100 Bay Area restaurants for 5 years running. It's the combination of super-fresh ingredients; the perfect lively balance of salty, sweet, hot, and sour flavors; and the attractive and atmospheric surroundings that usually fall short at other ethnic restaurants that make this place extra special. Those who like to play it safe will be more than happy with the likes of pad Thai and coconut-lemongrass soup, but it's advisable to divert from the usual suspects for house specialties such as *Crying tiger* (beef salad with garlic dressing), prawns with eggplant and crisped basil, and *ped swan*—duck with a delicate honey sauce served over spinach. The Haight location usually attracts the young and alternative, but the restaurant's reputation brings in a truly diverse San Francisco crowd. As for the neighborhood: Don't leave anything even remotely valuable in your car.

400 Waller St. (at Fillmore St.). ✆ **415/431-2526.** Reservations recommended. Main courses $7–$12. AE, DC, DISC, MC, V. Daily 5:30–10:30pm. Bus: 6, 7, 22, 66, or 71.

13 Richmond/Sunset Districts

For a map of restaurants in this section, see the "Where to Dine Around Town" map on p. 78.

MODERATE

Beach Chalet Brewery & Restaurant ✿ *Kids* AMERICAN While Cliff House (see below) has historic character worth exploration, this is the most modern ocean-side restaurant, with commanding views of the Pacific Ocean (fog permitting). The Chalet occupies the upper floor of a historic public lounge that originally opened in 1900, was renovated, closed, and was reopened in 1997. Today, the main floor's wonderful restored WPA frescoes and historical displays on the area are enough to lure tourists and locals, but there's nothing historic about the bright and cheery restaurant, which does the trick when you're in the 'hood, but is not a destination in itself. In fact, a great beer selection and live music have been the primary nighttime draws of late.

Dinner is pricey, and the view disappears with the sun, so come for breakfast or lunch when you can eat your hamburger, shrimp nachos, or salmon-stuffed rainbow trout with one of the best vistas around. After dinner, it's a more local thing, especially on select evenings when live bands accompany the cocktails and house-made house-brewed ales and root beer. (Call for schedules.) *Note:* Be careful getting into the parking lot (accessible only from the northbound side of the highway)—it's a quick, sandy turn.

In early 2004, owners Lara and Greg Truppelli added the adjoining **Park Chalet** restaurant. The 3,000-square-foot glass-enclosed extension behind the original landmark building offers more casual fare—with entrees ranging from $10 to $19—such as pizza with radicchio and pancetta and shepherd's pie. Retractable glass walls reveal Golden Gate Park's landmark Dutch windmill and a fireplace warms the room on chillier evenings.

1000 Great Hwy. (at west end of Golden Gate Park, near Fulton St.). © 415/ 386-8439. www.beachchalet.com. Main courses $9.25–$15 lunch, $10–$26 dinner. AE, MC, V. Daily 9am–midnight (however, hours change frequently based on business and seasons, so call ahead). Streetcar: N. Bus: 18, 31, or 38.

Cliff House ℛ (Kids (Finds CALIFORNIA/SEAFOOD

In the old days (we're talking way back), Cliff House was *the* place to go for a romantic night on the town. Nowadays, the aging San Francisco landmark caters mostly to tourists who arrive by the busload to gander at the Sutro Baths remains next door.

But that may not be the case for long. The two restaurants in the main two-story building underwent major renovations over the past 2 years and are debuting as this book goes to press with fresh new looks and menus. (Unfortunately, details are not yet finalized, so sorry if I'm vague.) The new dining room in the Sutro Wing has panoramic views, a heavy seafood influence within its American menu, and is more formal (read: pricey). The Bistro is the more casual spot with a raw bar and takeout counter. Both spots have been refurbished to recall their glory days near the turn of the 20th century and both offer superb ocean views, particularly at sunset, when the fog lets up; unfortunately, in the past, the food has been a distant second to the scenery, but I'm hopeful the new Cliff House will give even locals a reason to head to this tourist attraction. Stay tuned. If you're headed this way, arrive before dusk, request a window seat, order a few appetizers and cocktails, and enjoy the view.

1090 Point Lobos (at Merrie Way). ✆ **415/386-3330.** www.cliffhouse.com. Reservations accepted for Sutro. Sutro main courses $9–$22 lunch, $17–$27 dinner. AE, DC, DISC, MC, V. Call for hours, which have yet to be determined. Bus: 18 or 38.

Kabuto A&S ✿✿ JAPANESE/SUSHI   In a town overflowing with seafood and pretentious taste buds, you'd think it would be easier to find great sushi. The truth is, finding an outstanding sushi restaurant in San Francisco is more challenging than spotting a parking space in Nob Hill. Chopsticking these fish-and-rice delicacies is one of the most joyous and adventurous ways to dine, and Kabuto is one of the best (and most expensive) places to do it. Chef Sachio Kojima, who presides over the small, crowded sushi bar (which moved into an even tinier space across the street from its old location in 2003), constructs each dish with smooth, lightning-fast movements known only to master chefs. If you're big on wasabi, ask for the stronger stuff Kojima serves on request.

5121 Geary Blvd. (at 16th Ave.). ✆ **415/752-5652.** Reservations not accepted. Sushi $3–$10; main courses $11–$18. MC, V. Thurs–Sat and Mon–Tues 11:30am–2:30pm and 5:30–11pm; Sun 11:30am–2:30pm and 5:30–10pm. Bus: 2, 28, or 38.

Straits Café ✿ SINGAPOREAN   Straits Café is what I like to call "adventure dining," because you never quite know what kind of food you're going to get. Burlap palm trees, pastel-painted *trompe l'oeil* houses, faux balconies, and clotheslines strung across the walls evoke a surreal image of a Singaporean village in the Richmond District.

Lunching Near Golden Gate Park

Curiously (and happily), there are no restaurants other than museum cafes in Golden Gate Park, but that doesn't mean your choices are limited to the hot dog cart. The newly chic neighborhood of Inner Sunset boasts a handful of excellent, moderately priced restaurants. Try the bare bones and traditional **Ebisu,** 1283 Ninth Ave., between Lincoln and Irving (✆ **415/566-1770**), which has been a neighborhood favorite for nearly 20 years. It serves some of the city's best sushi, sashimi, and other Japanese fare.

The cuisine, however, is the real thing. Among chef Chris Yeo's spicy Malaysian-Indian-Chinese offerings are *murtabak* (stuffed Indian bread), chile crab, basil chicken, *nonya daging rendang* (beef simmered in lime leaves), *ikan pangang* (fish stuffed with chile paste), and, hottest of all, *sambal udang* (prawns sautéed in chile-shallot sambal sauce). For dessert, try the sago pudding.

3300 Geary Blvd. (at Parker St.). ℭ **415/668-1783.** Reservations recommended. Main courses $14–$22. AE, DC, MC, V. Mon–Thurs noon–2:30pm and 5:30–10pm; Fri–Sat noon–11pm; Sun noon–10pm. Bus: 2, 3, 4, or 38.

INEXPENSIVE

Ton Kiang ★★ *(Kids)* *(Finds)* CHINESE/DIM SUM Ton Kiang is the number one place in the city to have dim sum (served daily). Wait in line (which is out the door 11am–1:30pm), get a table on the first or second floor, and get ready to say yes to dozens of delicacies, which are brought to the table for your approval. From stuffed crab claws, roast Beijing duck, and a gazillion dumpling selections (including scallop and vegetable, shrimp, and beef) to the delicious and hard-to-find *doa miu* (snow pea sprouts flash-sautéed with garlic and peanut oil), shark-fin soup, and a mesmerizing mango pudding, every tray of morsels coming from the kitchen is an absolute delight. Though it's hard to get past the dim sum, which is served all day every day, the full menu of Hakka cuisine is worth investigation as well—fresh and flavorful soups; an array of seafood, beef, and chicken; and clay-pot specialties. This is definitely one of my favorite places to do lunch, and it happens to have an unusually friendly staff.

5821 Geary Blvd. (between 22nd and 23rd aves.). ℭ **415/387-8273.** www. tonkiang.net. Reservations accepted for parties of 8 or more. Dim sum $2–$5.50; main courses $9–$13. AE, MC, V. Daily 10am–10pm. Bus: 38.

5

Exploring San Francisco

San Francisco's parks, museums, tours, and landmarks are favorites for travelers the world over and offer an array of activities to suit every visitor. But no particular activity or place makes the city one of the most popular destinations in the world. It's San Francisco itself—its charm, its atmosphere, its perfect blend of big metropolis with small-town hospitality. No matter what you do while you're here—whether you spend all your time in central areas like Union Square or North Beach, or explore the outer neighborhoods—you're bound to discover the reason classic crooner Tony Bennett—and millions of visitors—leave their hearts in the City by the Bay.

1 Famous San Francisco Sights

Alcatraz Island ★★★ (Kids) Visible from Fisherman's Wharf, Alcatraz Island (aka "The Rock") has seen a checkered history. Juan Manuel Ayala was the first European to discover it in 1775 and named it after the many pelicans that nested on the island. From the 1850s to 1933, when the army vacated the island, it served as a military post, protecting the bay's shoreline. In 1934, the government converted the buildings of the military outpost into a maximum-security prison. Given the sheer cliffs, treacherous tides and currents, and frigid water temperatures, it was believed to be a totally escape-proof prison. Among the famous gangsters who occupied cell blocks A through D were Al Capone, Robert Stroud, the so-called Birdman of Alcatraz (because he was an expert in ornithological diseases), Machine Gun Kelly, and Alvin Karpis. It cost a fortune to keep them imprisoned here because all supplies, including water, had to be shipped in. In 1963, after an apparent escape in which no bodies were recovered, the government closed the prison. In 1969, a group of Native Americans chartered a boat to the island to symbolically reclaim the island for the Indian people. They occupied the island until 1971, the longest occupation of a federal facility by Native Americans to this day, when they were forcibly removed by the U.S. government (see www.nps.gov/alcatraz/indian.html for

Major San Francisco Attractions

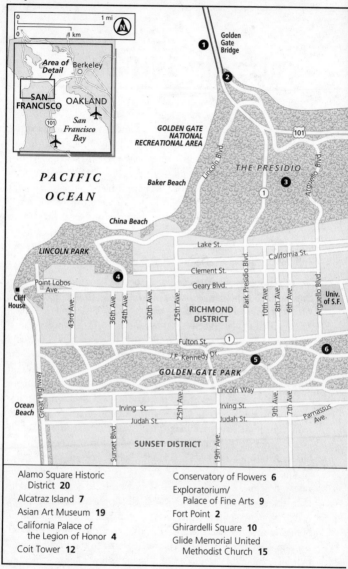

Alamo Square Historic
  District **20**
Alcatraz Island **7**
Asian Art Museum **19**
California Palace of
  the Legion of Honor **4**
Coit Tower **12**

Conservatory of Flowers **6**
Exploratorium/
  Palace of Fine Arts **9**
Fort Point **2**
Ghirardelli Square **10**
Glide Memorial United
  Methodist Church **15**

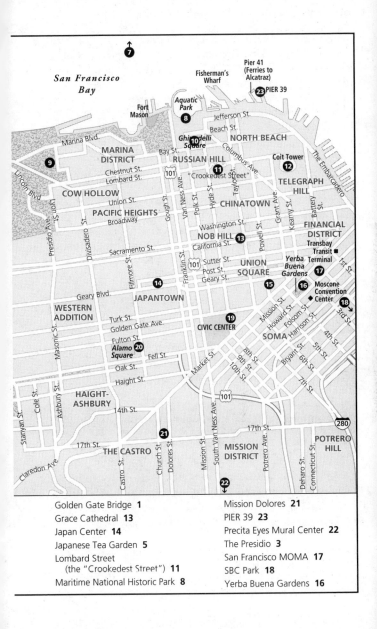

San Francisco Bay

Fisherman's Wharf

Pier 41
(Ferries to
Alcatraz)

23 PIER 39

Fort
Mason

*Aquatic
Park*

8

Jefferson St.

Beach St.

*Ghirardelli
Square*

NORTH BEACH

Bay St.

Columbus Ave.

Coit Tower

12

Marina Blvd.

**MARINA
DISTRICT**

RUSSIAN HILL

Chestnut St.

Lombard St.

11

"Crookedest Street"

TELEGRAPH
HILL

9

COW HOLLOW

Union St.

Gough St.

Van Ness Ave.

Polk St.

Hyde St.

Taylor St.

CHINATOWN

Grant Ave.

Kearny St.

Battery St.

FINANCIAL
DISTRICT

Lincoln Blvd.

Presidio Ave.

PACIFIC HEIGHTS

Broadway

Washington St.

NOB HILL 13

Powell St.

Transbay
Transit
Terminal

Divisadero St.

Fillmore St.

Sacramento St.

California St.

*Yerba
Buena
Gardens*

17

1st St.

Franklin St.

Sutter St.

**UNION
SQUARE**

Post St.

Geary St.

15

16

Moscone
Convention
Center

18

Geary Blvd.

14

JAPANTOWN

Mission St.

Howard St.

Folsom St.

3rd St.

**WESTERN
ADDITION**

Turk St.

Golden Gate Ave.

Fulton St.

CIVIC CENTER 19

SOMA

Harrison St.

4th St.

5th St.

Masonic Ave.

*Alamo
Square* **20**

Fell St.

Oak St.

Market St.

8th St.

9th St.

10th St.

Bryant St.

6th St.

7th St.

**HAIGHT-
ASHBURY**

Haight St.

14th St.

280

Stanyan St.

Cole St.

Ashbury St.

21

17th St.

Church St.

Dolores St.

Mission St.

South Van Ness Ave.

17th St.

Potrero Ave.

**POTRERO
HILL**

Claredon Ave.

THE CASTRO

Castro St.

**MISSION
DISTRICT**

Deharo St.

Connecticut St.

22

more information on the Native American occupation of Alcatraz). The next year the island became part of the Golden Gate National Recreation Area. The wildlife that was driven away during the military and prison years has begun to return—the black-crested night heron and other seabirds are nesting here again—and a new trail passes through the island's nature areas. Tours, including an audio tour of the prison block and a slide show, are given by the park's rangers, who entertain guests with interesting anecdotes.

Allow about 2½ hours for the round-trip boat ride and the tour. Wear comfortable shoes (the National Park Service notes that there are a lot of hills to climb on the tour) and take a heavy sweater or windbreaker, because even when the sun's out, it's cold out there. The excursion is popular and space is limited, so purchase tickets as far in advance as possible. **Blue & Gold Fleet** (℃ **415/705-5555;** www. blueandgoldfleet.com) operates the tour; they accept American Express, MasterCard, and Visa, and there's a $2.25-per-ticket service charge for phone orders. You can also buy tickets in advance from the Blue & Gold ticket office on Pier 41 or online at www.telesales.com. Alcatraz night tours are also available and are a more intimate and wonderfully spooky experience. Check the Blue & Gold Fleet website for updated prices and departure times.

For those who want to get a closer look at Alcatraz without going ashore, two boat-tour operators offer short circumnavigations of the island (see "Self-Guided & Organized Tours," on p. 131, for complete information).

Pier 41, near Fisherman's Wharf. ℃ **415/773-1188** (info only). Admission (includes ferry trip and audio tour) $16 adults with headset, $12 without; $15 seniors 62 and older with headset, $9.75 without; $11 children 5–11 with headset, $8.25 without. Winter daily 9:30am–2:15pm; summer daily 9:30am–4:15pm. Ferries depart 15 and 45 min. after the hour. Arrive at least 20 min. before sailing time.

Cable Cars 𝒜𝒜𝒜 *(Moments* *(Kids*   Although they may not be San Francisco's most practical means of transportation, cable cars are certainly the best loved and are a must-experience when visiting the city. Designated official historic landmarks by the National Park Service in 1964, they clank up and down the city's steep hills like mobile museum pieces, tirelessly hauling thousands of tourists each day to nowhere in particular.

London-born engineer Andrew Hallidie invented San Francisco's cable cars in 1869. He got the idea by serendipity. As the story goes, Hallidie was watching a team of overworked horses haul a heavily laden carriage up a steep San Francisco slope. As he watched, one horse slipped and the car rolled back, dragging the other tired beasts with it. At that moment, Hallidie resolved that he would invent a mechanical contraption to replace such horses, and just 4 years later, in 1873, the first cable car made its maiden run from the top of Clay Street. Promptly ridiculed as "Hallidie's Folly," the cars were slow to gain acceptance. One early onlooker voiced the general opinion by exclaiming, "I don't believe it—the damned thing works!"

Even today, many visitors have difficulty believing that these vehicles, which have no engines, actually work. The cars, each weighing about 6 tons, run along a steel cable, enclosed under the street in a center rail. You can't see the cable unless you peer straight down into the crack, but you'll hear its characteristic clickity-clanking sound whenever you're nearby. The cars move when the gripper (not the driver) pulls back a lever that closes a pincerlike "grip" on the cable. The speed of the car, therefore, is determined by the speed of the cable, which is a constant 9½ mph—never more, never less.

The two types of cable cars in use hold a maximum of 90 and 100 passengers, and the limits are rigidly enforced. The best views are from the outer running boards, where you have to hold on tightly when taking curves.

Hallidie's cable cars have been imitated and used throughout the world, but all have been replaced by more efficient means of transportation. San Francisco planned to do so, too, but the proposal met with so much opposition that the cable cars' perpetuation was actually written into the city charter in 1955. The mandate cannot be revoked without the approval of a majority of the city's voters—a distant and doubtful prospect.

San Francisco's three existing cable car lines form the world's only surviving system of cable cars, which you can experience for yourself should you choose to wait in the endless boarding line (up to a 2-hr. wait in summer). For more information on riding them, see "Getting Around," in chapter 2, p. 20.

Powell-Hyde and Powell-Mason lines begin at the base of Powell and Market sts.; California St. line begins at the foot of Market St. $3 per ride.

Coit Tower ☆☆

In a city known for its great views and vantage points, Coit Tower is one of the best. Located atop Telegraph Hill, just east of North Beach, the round, stone tower offers panoramic views of the city and the bay.

Completed in 1933, the tower is the legacy of Lillie Hitchcock Coit, a wealthy eccentric who left San Francisco a $125,000 bequest "for the purpose of adding beauty to the city I have always loved" and as a memorial to its volunteer firemen. She had been saved from a fire as a child and held the city's firefighters in particularly high esteem.

Inside the base of the tower are impressive murals titled *Life in California* and *1934*, which were completed under the WPA during the New Deal. They are the work of more than 25 artists, many of whom had studied under Mexican muralist Diego Rivera.

The only bummer: The narrow street leading to the tower is often clogged with tourist traffic. If you can, find a parking spot in North Beach and hoof it.

Telegraph Hill. © **415/362-0808.** www.coittower.org. Admission to the top $3.75 adults, $2.50 seniors, $1.50 children 6–12. Daily 10am–6pm. Bus: 39 (Coit).

Fisherman's Wharf *Overrated*   Few cities in America are as adept at wholesaling their historical sites as San Francisco, which has converted Fisherman's Wharf into one of the most popular tourist attractions in the world. Unless you come really early in the morning, you won't find any traces of the traditional waterfront life that once existed here; the only fishing going on around here is for tourists' dollars.

Originally called Meigg's Wharf, this bustling strip of waterfront got its present moniker from generations of fishers who used to base their boats here. Today, the bay has become so polluted with toxins that bright yellow placards warn against eating fish from the waters. A small fleet of fewer than 30 fishing boats still operates from here, but basically Fisherman's Wharf has been converted into one long shopping mall that stretches from Ghirardelli Square at the west end to PIER 39 at the east.

Accommodating a total of 350 boats, two marinas flank PIER 39 and house the Blue & Gold bay sightseeing fleet. In recent years, some 600 California sea lions have taken up residence on the adjacent floating docks. Until they abandon their new playground, which seems more and more unlikely, these playful, noisy creatures (some nights you can hear them all the way from Washington Sq.) are one of the best free attractions on the wharf. Docent-led programs, offered at PIER 39 on weekends from 11am to 5pm, teach visitors about the range, habitat, and adaptability of the California sea lion.

Some people love Fisherman's Wharf; others can't get far enough away from it. Most agree that, for better or for worse, it has to be seen at least once in your lifetime.

www.fishermanswharf.org. Take the Powell-Mason cable car to the last stop and walk to the wharf. By bus, take no. 15, 30, 32, 39, 42, or 82X. By streetcar, take the F-line. If you're arriving by car, park on adjacent streets or on the wharf between Taylor and Jones sts.

Fisherman's Wharf & Vicinity

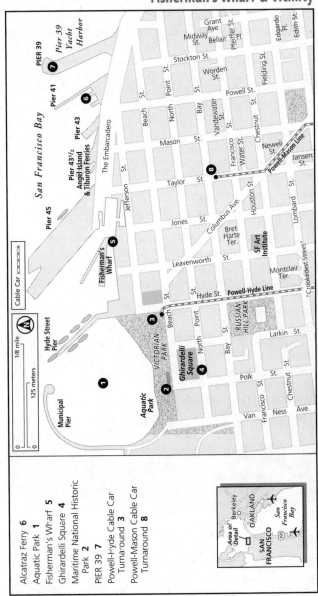

Alcatraz Ferry **6**
Aquatic Park **1**
Fisherman's Wharf **5**
Ghirardelli Square **4**
Maritime National Historic
Park **2**
PIER 39 **7**
Powell-Hyde Cable Car
Turnaround **3**
Powell-Mason Cable Car
Turnaround **8**

Golden Gate Bridge *(stars)* *Kids*   The year 2005 marks the 68th birthday of possibly the most beautiful, and certainly the most photographed, bridge in the world. Often half-veiled by the city's trademark rolling fog, San Francisco's Golden Gate Bridge spans tidal currents, ocean waves, and battering winds to connect the City by the Bay with the Redwood Empire to the north.

With its gracefully swung single span, spidery bracing cables, and zooming twin towers, the bridge looks more like a work of abstract art than one of the 20th century's greatest practical engineering feats. Construction was completed in May 1937 at the then-colossal cost of $35 million.

The 1¼-mile-long steel link (longer if you factor in the approach), which reaches a height of 746 feet above the water, is an awesome bridge to cross. Traffic usually moves quickly, however, so crossing by car won't give you too much time to see the sights. If you drive from the city, park in the lot at the foot of the bridge on the city side and make the crossing by foot. Back in your car, continue to Marin's Vista Point, at the bridge's northern end. Look back, and you'll be rewarded with one of the greatest views of San Francisco.

Millions of pedestrians walk or bike across the bridge each year, gazing up at the tall red towers, out at the vistas of San Francisco and Marin County, and down into the stacks of oceangoing liners. You can walk out onto the span from either end, but be prepared—it's usually windy and cold, and the bridge vibrates. Still, walking even a short distance is one of the best ways to experience the immense scale of the structure.

Hwy. 101 N. www.goldengatebridge.org. $5 cash toll collected when driving south. Bridge-bound Golden Gate Transit buses (© 415/923-2000) depart every 30–60 min. during the day for Marin County, starting from the Transbay Terminal (Mission and First sts.) and stopping at Market and Seventh sts., at the Civic Center, and along Van Ness Ave. and Lombard St.

Lombard Street *(star)* *Overrated*   Known (erroneously) as the "crookedest street in the world," this whimsically winding block of Lombard Street draws thousands of visitors each year (much to the chagrin of neighborhood residents, most of whom would prefer to block off the street to tourists). The angle of the street is so steep that the road has to snake back and forth to make a descent possible. The brick-lined street zigzags around the residences' bright flower gardens, which explode with color during warmer months. This short stretch of Lombard Street is one-way, downhill, and fun to drive. Take the curves slowly and in low gear, and expect a wait during the weekend. Save your film for the bottom where, if you're lucky, you can find a parking space and take a few snapshots of the silly spectacle. You can also take staircases (without curves) up or down on either side of the street. In truth, most locals don't understand what the fuss is all about. I'm guessing the draw is the combination of a classic, unusually steep San Francisco street and a great photo op. *FYI:* Vermont Street, between 20th and 22nd streets in Potrero Hill, is even more crooked, but not nearly as picturesque.

Between Hyde and Leavenworth sts.

PIER 39 *(Overrated*   PIER 39 is a multilevel waterfront complex a few blocks east of Fisherman's Wharf. Constructed on an abandoned cargo pier, it is, ostensibly, a re-creation of a turn-of-the-20th-century street scene, but don't expect a slice of old-time maritime life. This is the busiest mall of the lot and allegedly welcomes 11 million visitors per year. It has more than 100 stores, 11 bay-view restaurants, a two-tiered Venetian carousel, a Hard Rock Cafe, and arcade and aquarium entertainment for the kids. And everything's slated toward helping you part with your travel dollars. It's the place that locals love to hate. That said, it does have a few perks: absolutely beautiful natural surroundings of bay views, fresh sea air, and hundreds of sunbathing sea lions lounging along its neighboring dock.

On the waterfront at The Embarcadero and Beach St. ☎ 415/705-5500. www. pier39.com. Shops open daily 10:30am–8:30pm, with extended weekend hours during summer.

2 Museums

For information on museums in Golden Gate Park, see the "Golden Gate Park" section, beginning on p. 121.

Asian Art Museum ☞   Reopened in its Civic Center home in March 2003, the Asian Art Museum is one of the Western world's largest museums devoted to Asian art. Its collection boasts more than 15,000 art objects, such as world-class sculptures, paintings, bronzes, ceramics, and jade items, spanning 6,000 years of history and regions of south Asia, west Asia, Southeast Asia, the Himalayas, China, Korea, and Japan. Previously in Golden Gate Park, the museum's new home in the city's Beaux Arts–style central library was renovated under Italian architect Gae Aulenti and includes 40,000 square feet of gallery space showcasing 2,500 objects at any given time. Add temporary exhibitions, live demonstrations, learning activities, cafe Asia, and a store, and you've got one very good reason to head to the Civic Center.

200 Larkin St. (between Fulton and McAllister sts.). ℂ **415/581-3500**. www.asian art.org. Admission $10 adults, $7 seniors 65 and over, $6 youths 12–17, free for children under 12, $5 flat rate for all after 5pm Thurs. Free 1st Tues of the month. Tues–Wed and Fri–Sun 10am–5pm; Thurs 10am–9pm. Streetcar: Civic Center. Bus: All Market St. buses.

California Palace of the Legion of Honor 🎭🎭   Designed as a memorial to California's World War I casualties, this neoclassical structure is an exact replica of the Legion of Honor Palace in Paris, right down to the inscription HONNEUR ET PATRIE above the portal.

The Legion of Honor reopened in late 1995, after a 2-year, $35-million renovation and seismic upgrading. The exterior's grassy expanses, cliff-side paths, and incredible view of the Golden Gate and downtown make this an absolute must-visit attraction before you even get in the door. The inside is equally impressive. The museum's permanent collection covers 4,000 years of art and includes paintings, sculpture, and decorative arts from Europe, as well as international tapestries, prints, and drawings. The chronological display of 4,000 years of ancient and European art includes one of the world's finest collections of Rodin's sculptures. The sunlight Legion Café offers indoor and outdoor seating at moderate prices. Plan to spend 2 or 3 hours here.

In Lincoln Park (34th Ave. and Clement St.). ℂ **415/750-3600**, or 415/863-3330 (recorded information). www.thinker.org. Admission $8 adults, $6 seniors 65 and over, $5 youths 12–17, free for children under 12. Fees may be higher for special exhibitions. Free to all on Tues. Tues–Sun 9:30am–5pm. Bus: 18 or 38.

The Exploratorium 🎭🎭 (Kids)   *Scientific American* magazine rated the Exploratorium "the best science museum in the world"—pretty heady stuff for this exciting hands-on science fair. It contains more than 650 permanent exhibits that explore everything from giant-bubble blowing to Einstein's theory of relativity. It's like a mad scientist's penny arcade, an educational fun house, and an experimental laboratory, all rolled into one. Touch a tornado, shape a glowing electrical current, finger-paint using a computer, or take a sensory journey in total darkness in the Tactile Dome ($15 extra)—you could spend all day here and still not see everything. Every exhibit at the Exploratorium is designed to be interactive, educational, safe and, most important, fun. And don't think it's just for kids; parents inevitably end up being the most reluctant to leave. On the way out, be sure to stop in the wonderful gift store, which is chock-full of affordable brain candy.

The museum is in the Marina District at the beautiful **Palace of Fine Arts** 🎭, the only building left standing from the Panama-Pacific

Exposition of 1915. The adjoining park and lagoon—the perfect place for an afternoon picnic—is home to ducks, swans, seagulls, and grouchy geese, so bring bread.

3601 Lyon St., in the Palace of Fine Arts (at Marina Blvd.). ℰ **415/563-7337**, or 415/561-0360 (recorded information). www.exploratorium.edu. Admission $12 adults; $9.50 seniors, youth 13–17, visitors with disabilities, and college students with ID; $8 children 4–12; free for children under 4. Free to all 1st Wed of each month. Groups of 10 or more must make advance reservations. AE, MC, V. Tues–Sun 10am–5pm. Closed Mon except MLK, Jr., Day, Presidents' Day, Memorial Day, and Labor Day. Free parking. Bus: 28, 30, or Golden Gate Transit.

San Francisco Museum of Modern Art (MOMA) ℛ

Swiss architect Mario Botta, in association with Hellmuth, Obata, and Kassabaum, designed this $65-million museum, which has made SoMa one of the more popular areas to visit, for tourists and residents alike. The museum's permanent collection consists of more than 23,000 works, including close to 5,000 paintings and sculptures by artists such as Henri Matisse, Jackson Pollock, and Willem de Kooning. Other artists represented are Diego Rivera, Georgia O'Keeffe, Paul Klee, the Fauvists, and exceptional holdings of Richard Diebenkorn. MOMA was one of the first museums to recognize photography as a major art form; its extensive collection includes more than 12,000 photographs by such notables as Ansel Adams, Alfred Stieglitz, Edward Weston, and Henri Cartier-Bresson. Unfortunately, few works are on display at one time, and for the money the experience can be disappointing—especially compared to the finer museums of New York. Docent-led tours take place daily. Times are posted at the admission desk. Phone for current details of upcoming special events and exhibitions or check MOMA's website.

The **Caffé Museo,** to the right of the museum entrance, offers good-quality soups, sandwiches, and salads. Also, don't miss the **MuseumStore,** with its wonderful array of gifts, books, and trinkets.

151 Third St. (2 blocks south of Market St., across from Yerba Buena Gardens). ℰ **415/357-4000.** www.sfmoma.org. Admission $10 adults, $7 seniors, $6 students over 12 with ID, free for children 12 and under. Half-price for all Thurs 6–8:45pm; free to all 1st Tues of each month. Thurs 11am–8:45pm; Fri–Tues 11am–5:15pm. Closed Wed and major holidays. Streetcar: J, K, L, or M to Montgomery. Bus: 15, 30, or 45.

Yerba Buena Center for the Arts/Yerba Buena Gardens ℛℛ

Finds *Kids* The Yerba Buena Center, which opened in 1993, is the city's cultural facility, similar to New York's Lincoln Center but far more fun on the outside. It stands on top of the northern extension of the underground Moscone Convention Center. The center's two buildings present music, theater, dance, and visual arts. James Stewart Polshek designed the 755-seat theater, and Fumihiko Maki designed the Galleries and Arts Forum, which features three galleries and a space designed especially for dance. Cutting-edge computer art, multimedia shows, traditional exhibitions, and performances occupy the center's high-tech galleries.

More commonly explored is the 5-acre **Yerba Buena Gardens,** a great place to relax in the grass on a sunny day and check out several artworks. The most dramatic outdoor piece is an emotional mixed-media memorial to Martin Luther King, Jr. Created by sculptor Houston Conwill, poet Estella Majozo, and architect Joseph de Pace, it features 12 panels, each inscribed with quotations from King, sheltered behind a 50-foot-high waterfall. For most, this pastoral patch is a brief stopover to the surrounding attractions (see below). New to the gardens in 2004 are seasonal free **outdoor festivals** held on varied dates from May through October. It's definitely worth discovering whether you can catch one of these, as performances include dance, music, poetry, and more by the San Francisco Ballet, Opera, and Symphony and others; see www.ybgf.org for details.

On the periphery of Yerba Buena Gardens are a number of worthy individually operated excursions. In the Children's Center, **Zeum** (𝒞 415/777-2800) includes a cafe, interactive cultural center, bowling lanes, ice-skating rink, fabulous 1906 carousel, and interactive play and learning garden. Sony's **Metreon Entertainment Center** (𝒞 415/369-6000; www.metreon.com) is a 350,000-square-foot complex housing great movie theaters, an IMAX theater, a bountiful gourmet food court, interactive attractions (including one that features Maurice Sendak's *Where the Wild Things Are* and surprisingly exciting virtual bowling), and shops. As part of the plan to develop this area as the city's cultural hub, the **California Historical Society** opened at 678 Mission St. in 1995 and is home to a research library and a publicly accessible California photography and fine arts collection.

701 Mission St. 𝒞 **415/978-ARTS** (box office). www.yerbabuenaarts.org. Admission $6 adults, $3 seniors and students. Free to all 1st Tues of each month. Free for seniors and students with ID every Thurs. Tues–Sun 11am–5pm; 1st Thurs of each month 11am–8pm. Streetcar: Powell or Montgomery. Bus: 5, 9, 14, 15, 30, or 45.

3 Neighborhoods Worth a Visit

To really get to know San Francisco, break out of the downtown and Fisherman's Wharf areas to explore the ethnically and culturally diverse neighborhoods. Walk the streets, browse the shops, grab a bite at a local restaurant—you'll find that San Francisco's beauty and charm are around every corner, not just at the popular tourist destinations.

Note: For information on Fisherman's Wharf, see its entry under "Famous San Francisco Sights," on p. 105. For information on San Francisco neighborhoods and districts that aren't discussed here, see "Neighborhoods in Brief," in chapter 2, beginning on p. 17.

NOB HILL

When the cable car started operating in 1873, this hill became the city's exclusive residential area. Newly wealthy residents who had struck it rich in the gold rush and were known as the "Big Four" and the "Comstock Bonanza kings" built their mansions here, but they were all destroyed by the earthquake and fire in 1906. The only two surviving buildings are the Flood Mansion, which serves today as the **Pacific Union Club,** and the **Fairmont Hotel,** which was under construction when the earthquake struck. Today, the burned-out sites of former mansions hold the city's luxury hotels—the **Mark Hopkins,** the **Stanford Court,** the **Fairmont,** and the **Huntington**—as well as spectacular **Grace Cathedral,** which stands on the Crocker mansion site. Nob Hill is worth a visit if only to stroll around **Huntington Park,** attend a Sunday service at the cathedral, or ooh and aah your way around the Fairmont's spectacular lobby.

SOUTH OF MARKET (SoMa)

From Market Street to Townsend Street and The Embarcadero to Division Street, SoMa has become the city's newest cultural and multimedia center. The process started when alternative clubs began opening in the old warehouses in the area nearly a decade ago. A wave of entrepreneurs followed, seeking to start new businesses in what was once an extremely low-rent area compared to the neighboring Financial District. Today, gentrification and high rents hold sway, spurred by a building boom that started with the **Moscone Convention Center** and continued with the **Center for the Arts at Yerba Buena Gardens,** the **San Francisco Museum of Modern Art,** the **Four Seasons Hotel,** and the **Metreon.** Other institutions, businesses, and museums move into the area on an ongoing basis. A substantial portion of the city's nightlife takes place in ware spaces throughout the district.

NORTH BEACH ✦✦✦

In the late 1800s, an enormous influx of Ita North Beach firmly established this aromatic

"Little Italy." Dozens of Italian restaurants and coffeehouses continue to flourish in what is still the center of the city's Italian community. Walk down **Columbus Avenue** on any given morning, and you're bound to be bombarded by the wonderful aromas of roasting coffee and savory pasta sauces. Although there are some interesting shops and bookstores in the area, it's the dozens of eclectic little cafes, delis, bakeries, and coffee shops that give North Beach its Italian-bohemian character.

CHINATOWN 🕿🕿

The first of the Chinese immigrants came to San Francisco in the early 1800s to work as servants. By 1851, 25,000 Chinese people were working in California, and most had settled in San Francisco's Chinatown. Fleeing famine and the Opium Wars, they had come seeking the good fortune promised by the "Gold Mountain" of California, and hoped to return with wealth to their families in China. For the majority, the reality of life in California did not live up to the promise. First employed as workers in the gold mines during the gold rush, they later built the railroads, working as little more than slaves and facing constant prejudice. Yet the community, segregated in the Chinatown ghetto, thrived. Growing prejudice led to the Chinese Exclusion Act of 1882, which halted all Chinese immigration for 10 years and severely limited it thereafter (the Chinese Exclusion Act was not repealed until 1943). Chinese people were also denied the opportunity to buy homes outside the Chinatown ghetto until the 1950s.

Today, San Francisco has one of the largest communities of Chinese people in the United States. More than 80,000 people live in Chinatown, but the majority of Chinese people have moved out into newer areas like the Richmond and Sunset districts. Although frequented by tourists, the area continues to cater to Chinese shoppers, who crowd the vegetable and herb markets, restaurants, and shops. Tradition runs deep here, and if you're lucky, through an open window you might hear women mixing mah-jongg tiles as they play +h   game.

enue and Bush Street marks the entry to
e neighborhood is Portsmouth Square,
ng board games or just sitting quietly.
where the Chinese celebratory colors
much in evidence, you'll find three
Buddhist and Taoist) at no. 146, Tien
nd Norras (Buddhist) at no. 109. If
you do not disturb those in prayer.

A block west of Grant Avenue, **Stockton Street,** from 1000 to 1200, is the community's main shopping street, lined with grocers, fishmongers, tea sellers, herbalists, noodle parlors, and restaurants. Here, too, is the Buddhist Kong Chow Temple, at no. 855, above the Chinatown post office. Explore at your leisure.

JAPANTOWN

More than 12,000 citizens of Japanese descent (1.4% of the city's population) live in San Francisco, or Soko, as the Japanese who first emigrated here often called it. Initially, they settled in Chinatown and south of Market along Stevenson and Jessie streets from Fourth to Seventh streets. After the earthquake in 1906, SoMa became a light industrial and warehouse area, and the largest Japanese concentration took root in the Western Addition between Van Ness Avenue and Fillmore Street, the site of today's Japantown. By 1940, it covered 30 blocks.

In 1913, the Alien Land Law was passed, depriving Japanese Americans of the right to buy land. From 1924 to 1952, the United States banned Japanese immigration. During World War II, the U.S. government froze Japanese bank accounts, interned community leaders, and removed 112,000 Japanese Americans—two-thirds of them citizens—to camps in California, Utah, and Idaho. Japantown was emptied of Japanese people, and war workers took their place. Upon their release in 1945, the Japanese found their old neighborhood occupied. Most of them resettled in the Richmond and Sunset districts; some did return to Japantown, but it had shrunk to a mere 6 or so blocks. Among the community's notable sights are the **Buddhist Church of San Francisco,** 1881 Pine St. (at Octavia St.); the **Konko Church of San Francisco,** 1909 Bush St. (at Laguna St.); the **Sokoji-Soto Zen Buddhist Temple,** 1691 Laguna St. (at Sutter St.); **Nihonmachi Mall,** 1700 block of Buchanan Street between Sutter and Post streets, which contains two steel fountains by Ruth Asawa; and the **Japan Center,** an Asian-oriented shopping mall occupying 3 square blocks bounded by Post, Geary, Laguna, and Fillmore streets. At its center stands the five-tiered **Peace Pagoda,** designed by world-famous Japanese architect Yoshiro Taniguchi "to convey the friendship and goodwill of the Japanese to the people of the United States." Surrounding the pagoda, in a network of arcades, squares, and bridges, are dozens of shops and showrooms featuring everything from TVs and tansu chests to pearls, bonsai (dwarf trees), and kimonos. When it opened in 1968, the complex seemed as modern as a jumbo jet. Today, the concrete structure is less impressive, but it still holds some interest-ing surprises. **Kabuki Springs & Spa** is the center's most famous tenant. The Japan Center houses numerous restaurants, teahouses, and shops, a multiplex movie theater, and the Asian-inspired 14-story **Radisson Miyako Hotel** (p. 62).

There is often live entertainment in this neighborhood on summer weekends, including Japanese music and dance performances, tea cer-emonies, flower-arranging demonstrations, martial-arts presentations, and other cultural events. The Japan Center (*©* **415/922-6776**) is open daily from 10am to midnight, although most shops close much earlier. To get there, take bus no. 2, 3, or 4 (exit at Buchanan and Sut-ter sts.) or no. 22 or 38 (exit at the northeast corner of Geary Blvd. and Fillmore St.).

HAIGHT-ASHBURY

Few of San Francisco's neighborhoods are as varied—or as famous—as Haight-Ashbury. Walk along Haight Street, and you'll encounter everything from drug-dazed drifters begging for change to an armada of the city's funky-trendy shops, clubs, and cafes. Turn any-where off Haight, and instantly you're among the clean-cut, young urban professionals who can afford the steep rents in this hip 'hood. The result is an interesting mix of well-to-do and we'll-screw-you aging flower children, former Dead-heads, homeless people, and throngs of tourists who try not to stare as they wander through this most human of zoos. Some find it depressing, others find it fasci-nating, but everyone agrees that it ain't what it was in the free-lovin' psychedelic Summer of Love. Is it still worth a visit? Not if you are here for a day or two, but it's certainly worth an excursion on longer trips, if only to enjoy a cone of Cherry Garcia at the now-famous Ben & Jerry's Ice Cream Store on the corner of Haight and Ashbury streets, and then to wander and gawk at the area's intentional freaks.

THE CASTRO

Castro Street, between Market and 18th streets, is the center of the city's gay community as well as a lovely neighborhood teeming with shops, restaurants, bars, and other institutions that cater to the area's colorful residents. Among the landmarks are **Harvey Milk Plaza** and the **Castro Theatre,** a 1930s movie palace with a Wurlitzer. The gay community began to move here in the late 1960s and early 1970s from a neighborhood called Polk Gulch, which still has a number of gay-oriented bars and stores. Castro is one of the liveli-est streets in the city and the perfect place to shop for gifts and revel in free-spiritedness.

THE MISSION DISTRICT

Once inhabited almost entirely by Irish immigrants, the Mission District is now the center of the city's Latino community as well as a mecca for young, hip residents. It's an oblong area stretching roughly from 14th to 30th streets between Potrero Avenue on the east and Dolores on the west. In the outer areas, many of the city's finest Victorians still stand, although many seem strangely out of place in the mostly lower-income neighborhoods. The heart of the community lies along 24th Street between Van Ness and Potrero, where dozens of excellent ethnic restaurants, bakeries, bars, and specialty stores attract people from all over the city. The area surrounding 16th Street and Valencia is a hotbed for impressive—and often impressively cheap—restaurants and bars catering to the city's hip crowd. The Mission District at night doesn't feel like the safest place (although in terms of creepiness, the Tenderloin, a few blocks off Union Square, beats the Mission by far), and walking around the area should be done with caution, but it's usually quite safe during the day and is highly recommended.

For an even better insight into the community, go to the **Precita Eyes Mural Arts Center,** 2981 24th St., between Harrison and Alabama streets (© **415/285-2287**), and take one of the 1½- to 2-hour tours conducted on Saturday and Sunday at 11am and 1:30pm. The 11am tour costs $10 for adults, $8 for students with ID, $5 for seniors, and $2 for children under 18; the 1:30pm tour, which is half an hour longer and includes a slide show, costs $12 for adults, $8 for students with ID, $5 for seniors, and $2 for children under 18. You'll see 60 murals in an 8-block walk. Every year during Mural Awareness Month (usually May), tours are given daily. All but the Saturday-morning tour (call for starting place) leave from the center's 24th Street location (© **415/285-2287**). Other signs of cultural life in the neighborhood are progressive theaters such as Theater Rhinoceros and Theater Artaud.

At 16th Street and Dolores is the Mission San Francisco de Assisi, better known as **Mission Dolores** (p. 130). It's the city's oldest surviving building and the district's namesake.

4 Golden Gate Park ✶✶✶

Everybody loves **Golden Gate Park**—people, dogs, birds, frogs, turtles, bison, trees, bushes, and flowers. Literally, everything feels unified here in San Francisco's enormous arboreal front yard, but this great city landmark wasn't always a favorite place to convene. It was conceived in the 1860s and 1870s and took its current shape in the 1880s and 1890s, thanks to the skill and effort of John McLaren, a Scot who arrived in 1887 and began landscaping the park. Totaling 1,017 acres, the park is a narrow strip that stretches inland from the Pacific coast. No one had thought about the challenge the sand dunes and wind would present to any landscape artist. McLaren developed a new strain of grass called "sea bent," which he had planted to hold the sandy soil along the Firth of Forth, and he used it to anchor the soil here, too. He also built the two windmills that stand on the western edge of the park to pump water for irrigation. Every year the ocean eroded the western fringe of the park, and ultimately he solved this problem, too. It took him 40 years to build a natural wall, putting out bundles of sticks that the tides covered with sand. Under his brilliant eye, the park took shape.

Today's Golden Gate Park is a truly magical place. Spend 1 sunny day stretched out on the grass along JFK Drive, have a good read in the Shakespeare Garden, or stroll around Stow Lake, and you, too, will understand the allure. It's an interactive botanical symphony, and everyone is invited to play in the orchestra.

The park consists of hundreds of gardens and attractions connected by wooded paths and paved roads. While many worthy sites are clearly visible, there are infinite hidden treasures, so pick up information at **McLaren Lodge and Park Headquarters** (at Stanyan St. and Fell St.; ℂ **415/831-2700**) if you want to find the more hidden spots. It's open daily and offers park maps for $3. Of the dozens of special gardens in the park, most recognized are **McLaren Memorial Rhododendron Dell, The Rose Garden, Strybing Arboretum,** and, at the western edge of the park, a springtime array of thousands of tulips and daffodils around the **Dutch windmill.**

In addition to the highlights described in this section, the park contains lots of recreational facilities: tennis courts; baseball, soccer, and polo fields; a golf course; riding stables; and fly-casting pools. The Strawberry Hill boathouse handles boat rentals.

For further information, call the San Francisco Visitor Information Center at ℂ **415/283-0177.** Enter the park at Kezar Drive, an extension of Fell Street; bus riders can take no. 5, 6, 7, 16AX, 16BX, 66, or 71.

PARK HIGHLIGHTS
CONSERVATORY OF FLOWERS 🐾🐾 Built in 1879, this glorious Victorian glass structure is the oldest public conservatory in the western hemisphere. After a bad storm in 1995 and delayed renovations, the conservatory was closed and visitors were only able

Golden Gate Park

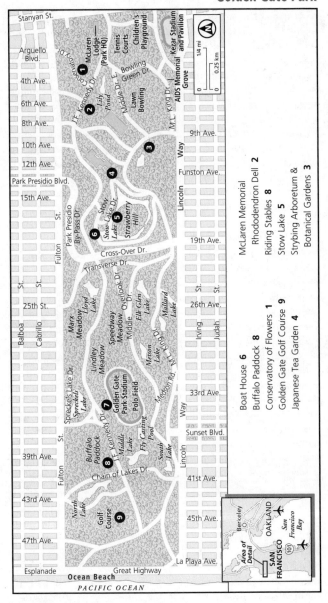

McLaren Memorial
Rhododendron Dell **2**
Riding Stables **8**
Stow Lake **5**
Strybing Arboretum &
Botanical Gardens **3**

Boat House **6**
Buffalo Paddock **8**
Conservatory of Flowers **1**
Golden Gate Golf Course **9**
Japanese Tea Garden **4**

to imagine what wondrous displays existed within the striking glass assemblage. Thankfully, a $25-million renovation, including a $4-million exhibit upgrade, was completed in 2003, and now you can check out the rare tropical flora of the Congo, Philippines, and beyond within the stunning structure. It doesn't take long to visit, but make a point of staying a while; outside there are good sunny spots for people-watching as well as paths leading to impressive gardens begging to be explored. If you're around during summer and fall, don't miss the Dahlia Garden to the right of the entrance in the center of what was once a carriage roundabout—it's an explosion of colorful Dr. Seuss–like blooms. The conservatory is open Tuesday through Sunday from 9am to 4:30pm; closed Mondays. Admission is $5 for adults; $3 for children 12 to 17 years of age, seniors, and students with ID; and free to all the first Tuesday of the month. For more information, visit www.conservatoryofflowers. org or call © **415/666-7001.**

JAPANESE TEA GARDEN   John McLaren, the man who began landscaping Golden Gate Park, hired Makoto Hagiwara, a wealthy Japanese landscape designer, to further develop this garden originally created for the 1894 Midwinter Exposition. It's a quiet place with cherry trees, shrubs, and bonsai crisscrossed by winding paths and high-arched bridges over pools of water. Focal points and places for contemplation include the massive bronze Buddha (cast in Japan in 1790 and donated by the Gump family), the Buddhist wooden pagoda, and the Wishing Bridge, which, reflected in the water, looks as though it completes a circle. The garden is open daily November through February from 8:30am to 5pm (teahouse 10am–4:30pm), March through October from 8:30am to 6pm (teahouse 10am–5:30pm). For **information** on admission, call © **415/752-4227.** For the **teahouse,** call © **415/752-1171.**

STRAWBERRY HILL/STOW LAKE   Rent a paddleboat or rowboat and cruise around the circular lake as painters create still lifes, joggers pass along the grassy shoreline, ducks waddle around waiting to be fed, and turtles bathe on rocks and logs. Strawberry Hill, the 430-foot-high artificial island and highest point in the park that lies at the center of Stow Lake, is a perfect picnic spot; it boasts a bird's-eye view of San Francisco and the bay. It also has a waterfall and peace pagoda. For the **boathouse,** call © **415/752-0347.** Boat rentals are available daily from 10am to 4pm, weather permitting; four-passenger rowboats go for $13 per hour, and four-person paddleboats run $17 per hour; fees are cash-only.

STRYBING ARBORETUM & BOTANICAL GARDENS   Six thousand plant species grow here, among them some ancient plants in a special "primitive garden," rare species, and a grove of California redwoods. Docent tours begin at 1:30pm daily, with an additional 10:30am tour on weekends. Strybing is open Monday through Friday from 8am to 4:30pm, and Saturday and Sunday from 10am to 5pm. For more information, call (C) **415/661-1316** or visit www.strybing.org.

5 The Presidio & Golden Gate National Recreation Area

THE PRESIDIO

In October 1994, the Presidio passed from the U.S. Army to the National Park Service and became one of a handful of urban national parks that combines historical, architectural, and natural elements in one giant arboreal expanse. (It also contains a previously private golf course and a home for George Lucas's production company.) The 1,480-acre area incorporates a variety of terrain—coastal scrub, dunes, and prairie grasslands—that shelter many rare plants and more than 150 species of birds, some of which nest here.

This military outpost has a 220-year history, from its founding in September 1776 by the Spanish under José Joaquin Moraga to its closure in 1994. From 1822 to 1846, the property was in Mexican hands.

During the war with Mexico, U.S. forces occupied the fort, and in 1848, when California became part of the Union, it was formally transferred to the United States. When San Francisco suddenly became an important urban area during the gold rush, the U.S. government installed battalions of soldiers and built Fort Point to protect the entry to the harbor. It expanded the post during the Civil War and during the Indian Wars of the 1870s and 1880s. By the 1890s, the Presidio was no longer a frontier post but a major base for U.S. expansion into the Pacific. During the war with Spain in 1898, thousands of troops camped here in tent cities awaiting shipment to the Philippines, and the Army General Hospital treated the sick and wounded. By 1905, 12 coastal defense batteries were built along the headlands. In 1914, troops under the command of Gen. John Pershing left here to pursue Pancho Villa and his men. The Presidio expanded during the 1920s, when Crissy Army Airfield (the first airfield on the West Coast) was established, but the major action was seen during World War II, after the attack on Pearl Harbor. Soldiers dug foxholes along nearby beaches, and the Presidio became the headquarters for the Western

Golden Gate National Recreation Area

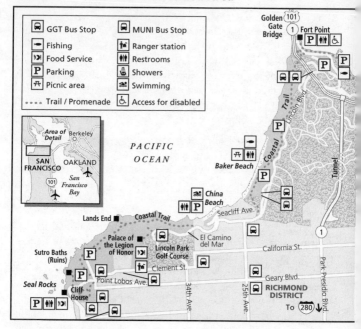

Defense Command. Some 1.75 million men were shipped out from nearby Fort Mason to fight in the Pacific; many returned to the Presidio's hospital, whose capacity peaked 1 year at 72,000 patients. In the 1950s, the Presidio served as the headquarters for the Sixth U.S. Army and a missile defense post, but its role slowly shrank. In 1972, it was included in new legislation establishing the Golden Gate National Recreation Area; in 1989, the Pentagon decided to close the post and transfer it to the National Park Service.

Today, the area encompasses more than 350 historic buildings, a scenic golf course, a national cemetery, and a variety of terrain and natural habitats. The National Park Service offers walking and biking tours around the Presidio; reservations are suggested. For more information, call the **Presidio Visitors Center** at ℂ **415/561-4323.** Take bus no. 28, 45, 76, or 82X to get there.

GOLDEN GATE NATIONAL RECREATION AREA

The largest urban park in the world, GGNRA makes New York's Central Park look like a putting green, covering three counties along 28 miles of stunning, condo-free shoreline. Run by the National

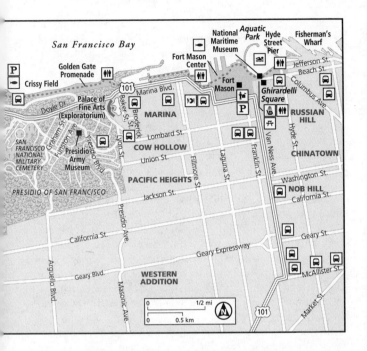

Park Service, the Recreation Area wraps around the northern and western edges of the city, and just about all of it is open to the public with no access fees. The Muni bus system provides transportation to the more popular sites, including Aquatic Park, Cliff House, Fort Mason, and Ocean Beach. For more information, contact the **National Park Service** (© **415/561-4700**). For more detailed information on particular sites, see the "Getting Outside" section, later in this chapter.

Here is a brief rundown of the salient features of the park's peninsula section, starting at the northern section and moving westward around the coastline:

Aquatic Park, adjacent to the Hyde Street Pier, has a small swimming beach, although it's not that appealing (and darned cold). Far more entertaining is a visit to the ship-shaped museum across the lawn that's part of the San Francisco Maritime National Historical Park.

Fort Mason Center, from Bay Street to the shoreline, consists of several buildings and piers used during World War II. Today they hold a variety of museums, theaters, shops, and organizations, and

Greens vegetarian restaurant (p. 92), which affords views of the Golden Gate Bridge. For information about Fort Mason events, call ✆ **415/441-3400.** The park headquarters is also at Fort Mason.

Farther west along the bay at the northern end of Laguna Street is **Marina Green,** a favorite local spot for kite-flying, jogging, and walking along the Promenade. The St. Francis Yacht Club is also here.

Next comes the 3½-mile paved **Golden Gate Promenade** ⟨, San Francisco's best and most scenic biking, jogging, and walking path. It runs along the shore past **Crissy Field** (be sure to stop and watch the gonzo windsurfers and kites surfers, who catch major wind here, and admire the newly restored marshlands) and ends at Fort Point under the Golden Gate Bridge.

Fort Point ⟨ (✆ **415/556-1693**) was built in 1853 to 1861 to protect the narrow entrance to the harbor. It was designed to house 500 soldiers manning 126 muzzle-loading cannons. By 1900, the fort's soldiers and obsolete guns had been removed, but the formidable brick edifice remains. Fort Point is open Friday through Sunday only (temporary, due to bridge retrofit, and most likely through 2007) 10am to 5pm, and guided tours and cannon demonstrations are given at the site once or twice a day on open days, depending on the time of year.

Lincoln Boulevard sweeps around the western edge of the bay to **Baker Beach,** where the waves roll ashore—a fine spot for sunbathing, walking, or fishing. Hikers can follow the **Coastal Trail** from Fort Point along this part of the coastline all the way to Lands End.

A short distance from Baker Beach, **China Beach** is a small cove where swimming is permitted. Changing rooms, showers, a sun deck, and restrooms are available.

A little farther around the coast is **Lands End** ⟨, looking out to Pyramid Rock. A lower and an upper trail offer hiking amid windswept cypresses and pines on the cliffs above the Pacific.

Still farther along the coast lie **Point Lobos,** the **Sutro Baths,** and **Cliff House** ⟨. Cliff House (www.cliffhouse.com), which is completing renovations on its restaurants while still serving basic drinks and selling trinkets as this book goes to press, has been serving refreshments to visitors since 1863 and providing views of Seal Rocks, home to a colony of sea lions and many marine birds. (Alas, my favorite attraction here, the Musée Mécanique, an arcade featuring antique games, has moved to temporary digs at Pier 45; call ✆ **415/346-2000** or visit http://museemecanique.citysearch.com for details, as nobody yet knows where its permanent home will be.) Northeast of Cliff House, only traces of the Sutro Baths remain, since the swimming facility, a major summer attraction that could accommodate up to 24,000 people, burned down in 1966.

A little farther inland at the western end of California Street is **Lincoln Park,** which contains a golf course and the spectacular California Palace of the Legion of Honor museum (p. 114).

At the southern end of Ocean Beach, 4 miles down the coast, is another area of the park around Fort Funston, where there's an easy loop trail across the cliffs (ranger office © **415/239-2366**). Here you can watch hang gliders take advantage of the high cliffs and strong winds.

Farther south along Route 280, **Sweeney Ridge,** accessible only by car, affords sweeping views of the coastline from the many trails that crisscross its 1,000 acres. From here the expedition led by Don Gaspar de Portolá first saw San Francisco Bay in 1769. It's in Pacifica; take Sneath Lane off Route 35 (Skyline Blvd.) in San Bruno.

The GGNRA extends into Marin County, where it encompasses the Marin Headlands, Muir Woods National Monument, and the Olema Valley behind the Point Reyes National Seashore.

6 Religious Buildings Worth Checking Out

Glide Memorial United Methodist Church ⊛ *(Moments)*   There would be nothing special about this Tenderloin-area church if it weren't for its exhilarating lively sermons and accompanying gospel choir. Reverend Cecil Williams's enthusiastic and uplifting preaching and singing with homeless and poor people of the neighborhood attracted nationwide fame over the past 30-plus years. In 1994, during the pastor's 30th-anniversary celebration, singers Angela Bofill and Bobby McFerrin joined comedian Robin Williams, author Maya Angelou, and talk-show queen Oprah Winfrey to honor him publicly. Cecil Williams now shares pastor duties with Douglas Fitch, alternating presiding over the nondogmatic, fun Sunday services in front of a diverse audience that crosses all socioeconomic boundaries. Go for an uplifting experience and some hand-clapping gospel choir music.

330 Ellis St. (west of Union Square). © **415/674-6000.** www.glide.org. Services Sun at 9 and 11am. Streetcar: Powell. Bus: 27. BART: Powell.

Grace Cathedral   Although this Nob Hill cathedral, designed by architect Lewis P. Hobart, appears to be made of stone, it is in fact constructed of reinforced concrete, beaten to achieve a stonelike effect. Construction began on the site of the Crocker mansion in 1928 but was not completed until 1964. Among the more interesting features of the building are its stained-glass windows, particularly those by the French Loire studios and Charles Counick, depicting such modern figures as Thurgood Marshall, Robert Frost, and Albert Einstein; the replicas of Ghiberti's bronze *Doors of Paradise* at the east end; the series of religious murals completed in the 1940s by Polish artist John de Rosen; and the 44-bell carillon. Along with its magical ambience, Grace lifts spirits with services, musical performances, and its weekly Forum (Sun 9:30–10:30am except summer and major holidays), where guests lead discussions about spirituality in modern times.

1100 California St. (between Taylor and Jones sts.). ✆ 415/749-6300. www.grace catherdral.org.

Mission Dolores   San Francisco's oldest standing structure, the Mission San Francisco de Assisi (aka Mission Dolores), has withstood the test of time, as well as two major earthquakes, relatively intact. In 1776, at the behest of Franciscan missionary Junípero Serra, Father Francisco Palou came to the Bay Area to found the sixth in a series of missions that dotted the California coastline. From these humble beginnings grew what was to become the city of San Francisco. The mission's small, simple chapel, built solidly by Native Americans who were converted to Christianity, is a curious mixture of native construction methods and Spanish-colonial style. A statue of Father Serra stands in the mission garden, although the portrait looks somewhat more contemplative, and less energetic, than he must have been in real life. A 45-minute audio tour costs $5; otherwise, admission is $3 for adults and $2 for children.

16th St. (at Dolores St.). ✆ 415/621-8203. $3 adults, $2 children. May–Oct daily 9am–4:30pm; Nov–Apr daily 9am–4pm; Good Friday 9am–noon. Closed Thanksgiving and Dec 25. Streetcar: J. Bus: 14, 26, or 33 to Church and 16th sts.

7 Architectural Highlights

ALAMO SQUARE HISTORIC DISTRICT   San Francisco's collection of Victorian houses, known as **Painted Ladies,** is one of the city's most famous assets. Most of the 14,000 extant structures date from the second half of the 19th century and are private residences. Spread throughout the city, many have been beautifully restored and ornately painted. The small area bordered by Divisadero Street on the west, Golden Gate Avenue on the north, Webster Street on the east, and Fell Street on the south—about 10 blocks west of the Civic Center—has one of the city's greatest concentrations of Painted Ladies. One of the most famous views of San Francisco—seen on postcards and posters all around the city—depicts sharp-edged

Financial District skyscrapers behind a row of Victorians. This fantastic juxtaposition can be seen from Alamo Square, in the center of the historic district, at Fulton and Steiner streets.

CITY HALL & CIVIC CENTER   Built between 1913 and 1915, City Hall, located in the Civic Center District, is part of this "City Beautiful" complex done in the Beaux Arts style. The dome rises to a height of 308 feet on the exterior and is ornamented with oculi and topped by a lantern. The interior rotunda soars 112 feet and is finished in oak, marble, and limestone, with a monumental marble staircase leading to the second floor. No doubt you saw it on TV during early 2004, when much of the hoopla surrounding the short-lived and controversial gay marriage proceedings was depicted on the front steps. (Remember Rosie O'Donnell emerging from this very building after getting married to her girlfriend?)

8 Self-Guided & Organized Tours

THE 49-MILE SCENIC DRIVE

The self-guided, 49-mile drive is one easy way to orient yourself and to grasp the beauty of San Francisco and its extraordinary location. Beginning in the city, it follows a rough circle around the bay and passes virtually all the best-known sights, from Chinatown to the Golden Gate Bridge, Ocean Beach, Seal Rocks, Golden Gate Park, and Twin Peaks. Originally designed for the benefit of visitors to San Francisco's 1939 and 1940 Golden Gate International Exposition, the route is marked by blue-and-white seagull signs. Although it makes an excellent half-day tour, this miniexcursion can easily take longer if you decide, for example, to stop to walk across the Golden Gate Bridge or to have tea in Golden Gate Park's Japanese Tea Garden.

The San Francisco **Visitor Information Center,** at Powell and Market streets (p. 13), distributes free route maps, which are handy since a few of the Scenic Drive marker signs are missing. Try to avoid the downtown area during the weekday rush hours from 7 to 9am and 4 to 6pm.

BOAT TOURS

One of the best ways to look at San Francisco is from a boat bobbing on the bay. There are several cruises to choose from, and many of them start from Fisherman's Wharf.

Blue & Gold Fleet, PIER 39, Fisherman's Wharf (© 415/773-1188; www.blueandgoldfleet.com), tours the bay year-round in a sleek, 350-passenger sightseeing boat, complete with food and beverage facilities. The fully narrated, 1¼-hour cruise passes beneath the Golden Gate Bridge and comes within yards of Alcatraz Island. Don a jacket, bring the camera, and make sure it's a clear day for the best bay cruise. Frequent daily departures from PIER 39's West Marina begin at 10am during summer and 11am in winter. Tickets cost $20 for adults, $16 for seniors over 62 and juniors 12 to 17, and $12 for children 5 to 11; children under 5 are admitted free. There's a $2.25 charge for ordering tickets by phone; discounts are available online at www.telesails.com.

The **Red & White Fleet,** Pier 43½ (© **415/447-0597;** www. redandwhite.com), offers daily "Bay Cruises" tours that leave from Pier 43½. The tour boats cruise beneath the Golden Gate Bridge and past the Marin Headlands, Sausalito, Tiburon, Angel Island, and Alcatraz and are narrated in various languages. Prices are $20 for adults, $16 for seniors and teens 12 to 18, and $12 for children 5 to 11. Discounts are available through online purchase.

BUS TOURS

Gray Line (© **888/428-6937** or 415/434-8687; www.sfsightseeing. com) is San Francisco's largest bus-tour operator. It offers several itineraries daily. Free pickup and return are available between centrally located hotels and departure locations. Reservations are required for most tours, which are available in several foreign languages, including French, German, Spanish, Italian, Japanese, and Korean.

9 Getting Outside

Half the fun in San Francisco takes place outdoors. If you're not in the mood to trek it, there are other things to do that allow you to enjoy the surroundings.

BEACHES   For beach information, call the San Francisco Visitor Information Center at © **415/283-0177.** Most days it's too chilly to hang out at the beach, but when the fog evaporates and the wind dies down, one of the best ways to spend the day is ocean side in the city. On any truly hot day, thousands flock to the beach to worship the sun, build sandcastles, and throw the ball around. Without a wet suit, swimming is a fiercely cold endeavor and is not recommended. Only two beaches are considered safe for swimming: **Aquatic Park,** adjacent to the Hyde Park Pier, and **China Beach,** a small cove on the western edge of the South Bay. But dip at your own risk—there are no lifeguards on duty. Also on the South Bay, **Baker Beach** is ideal for picnicking, sunning, walking, or fishing against the backdrop of the

Golden Gate (though pollution makes your catch not necessarily worthy of eating).

Ocean Beach, at the end of Golden Gate Park, on the western-most side of the city, is San Francisco's largest beach—4 miles long. Just offshore, at the northern end of the beach, in front of Cliff House, are the jagged Seal Rocks, inhabited by various shorebirds and a large colony of barking sea lions (bring binoculars for a close-up view). To the left, Kelly's Cove is one of the more challenging surf spots in town. Ocean Beach is ideal for strolling or sunning, but don't swim here—tides are tricky, and each year bathers drown in the rough surf.

Stop by Ocean Beach bus terminal at the corner of Cabrillo and La Playa to learn about San Francisco's playful history in local artist Ray Beldner's whimsically historical sculpture garden. Then hike up the hill to explore Cliff House and the ruins of the Sutro Baths. These baths, able to accommodate 24,000 bathers, were lost to fire in 1966.

BIKING   The San Francisco Parks and Recreation Department maintains two city-designated bike routes. One winds 7½ miles through Golden Gate Park to Lake Merced; the other traverses the city, starting in the south, and continues over the Golden Gate Bridge. These routes are not dedicated to bicyclists, who must exercise caution to avoid crashing into pedestrians. Helmets are recommended for adults and required by law for kids under 18. A bike map is available from the San Francisco Visitor Information Center, at Powell and Mason streets (see "Visitor Information," in chapter 2), and from bicycle shops all around town.

Ocean Beach has a public walk- and bikeway that stretches along 5 waterfront blocks of the Great Highway between Noriega and Santiago streets. It's an easy ride from Cliff House or Golden Gate Park.

Avenue Cyclery, 756 Stanyan St., at Waller Street, in the Haight (© 415/387-3155), rents bikes for $5 per hour or $25 per day. It's open daily, April through September from 10am to 7pm and October through March from 10am to 6pm.

BOATING   At the **Golden Gate Park Boat House** (© 415/752-0347) on Stow Lake, the park's largest body of water, you can rent a rowboat or pedal boat by the hour and steer over to Strawberry Hill, a large, round island in the middle of the lake, for lunch. There's usually a line on weekends. The boathouse is open daily from 10am to 4pm, weather permitting.

Cass Marina, 1702 Bridgeway, Sausalito (© **800/472-4595** or 415/332-6789; www.cassmarina.com), is a certified sailing school that rents sailboats measuring 22 to 101 feet. Sail to the Golden Gate Bridge on your own or with a licensed skipper. In addition, large sailing yachts leave from San Francisco and Sausalito on a regularly scheduled basis. Call or check the website for schedules, prices, and availability of sailboats. The marina is open Wednesday through Monday from 9am to sunset.

CITY STAIR CLIMBING   Many health clubs have stair-climbing machines and step classes, but in San Francisco, you need only go outside. The following city stair climbs will give you not only a good workout, but great sightseeing, too.

Filbert Street Steps, between Sansome Street and Telegraph Hill, are a particular challenge. Scaling the sheer eastern face of Telegraph Hill, this 377-step climb winds through verdant flower gardens and charming 19th-century cottages. Napier Lane, a narrow, wooden plank walkway, leads to Montgomery Street. Turn right and follow the path to the end of the cul-de-sac, where another stairway continues to Telegraph's panoramic summit.

The **Lyon Street Steps,** between Green Street and Broadway, were built in 1916. This historic stairway street contains four steep sets of stairs totaling 288 steps. Begin at Green Street and climb all the way up, past manicured hedges and flower gardens, to an iron gate that opens into the Presidio. A block east, on Baker Street, another set of 369 steps descends to Green Street.

GOLF   San Francisco has a few beautiful golf courses. One of the most lavish is the **Presidio Golf Course** (© **415/561-4664;** www.presidiogolf.com). Greens fees are $42 Monday through Thursday, $52 on Friday, and $72 on Saturday and Sunday; rates decrease later in the day. Carts are $16. There are also two decent municipal courses in town.

The 9-hole **Golden Gate Park Course,** 47th Avenue and Fulton Street (© **415/751-8987;** www.goldengateparkgolf.com), charges greens fees of $13 per person Monday through Thursday, $17 Friday through Sunday. The 1,357-yard course is par 27. All holes are par 3, tightly set, and well trapped with small greens. The course is a little weathered in spots, but it's casual, fun, and inexpensive. It's open daily at 6:30am.

The 18-hole **Lincoln Park Golf Course,** 34th Avenue and Clement Street (© **415/221-9911**), charges greens fees of $31 per person Monday through Thursday, $35 Friday through Sunday, with rates decreasing after 2pm. It's San Francisco's prettiest municipal course, with terrific views and fairways lined with Monterey cypress and pine trees. The 5,181-yard layout plays to par 68, and the 17th hole has a glistening ocean view. This is the oldest course in the city and one of the oldest in the West. It's open daily at daybreak.

A good place for a tune-up is the **Mission Bay Golf Center,** Sixth Street at Channel Street (*©* **415/431-7888**). San Francisco's most popular driving range is an impeccably maintained 7-acre facility that consists of a double-decker steel and concrete arc containing 66 covered practice bays. The grass landing area extends 300 yards, has nine target greens, and is lit for evening use. There's a putting green and a chipping and bunker practice area. The center is open Monday from 11:30am to 11pm, Tuesday through Sunday from 7am to 11pm. A bucket of balls costs $8, and the last bucket is sold at 10pm. To get there from downtown San Francisco, take Seventh Street south to Channel Street and turn right.

HANDBALL   The city's best handball courts are in Golden Gate Park, opposite Seventh Avenue, south of Middle Drive East. Courts are available free, on a first-come, first-served basis.

PARKS   In addition to **Golden Gate Park** and the **Golden Gate National Recreation Area** (p. 121 and 126 respectively), San Francisco boasts more than 2,000 acres of parkland, most of which is perfect for picnicking or throwing around a Frisbee.

Smaller city parks include **Buena Vista Park** (Haight St. between Baker and Central sts.), which affords fine views of the Golden Gate Bridge and the area around it and is also a favored lounging ground for gay lovers; **Ina Coolbrith Park** (Taylor St. between Vallejo and Green sts.), offering views of the Bay Bridge and Alcatraz; and **Sigmund Stern Grove** (19th Ave. and Sloat Blvd.) in the Sunset District, which is the site of a famous free summer music festival.

One of my personal favorites is **Lincoln Park,** a 270-acre green on the northwestern side of the city at Clement Street and 34th Avenue. The California Palace of the Legion of Honor is here (p. 114), as is a scenic 18-hole municipal golf course (see "Golf," above). But the best things about this park are the 200-foot cliffs that overlook the Golden Gate Bridge and San Francisco Bay. To get to the park, take bus no. 38 from Union Square to 33rd and Geary streets, then walk a few blocks.

RUNNING   The **Bay to Breakers Foot Race** *⚡* (*©* **415/359-2800;** www.baytobreakers.com) is an annual 7.5-mile run from downtown to Ocean Beach. About 80,000 entrants take part in it, one of San Francisco's trademark events. Costumed participants and hordes of spectators add to the fun. The event, sponsored by the *San Francisco Examiner* and Albertson's supermarket chain, is held on the third Sunday of May.

The *San Francisco Chronicle* **Marathon** takes place annually in the middle of July. For more information, call ℂ **415/284-9653** or visit www.chroniclemarathon.com.

Great **jogging paths** include the entire expanse of Golden Gate Park, the shoreline along the Marina, and The Embarcadero.

SKATING (CONVENTIONAL & IN-LINE)   Although people skate in Golden Gate Park all week long, Sunday is best because that's when John F. Kennedy Drive between Kezar Drive and Transverse Road is closed to automobiles. A smooth "skate pad" is on your right, just past the Conservatory. Another hot skating, biking, and walking spot is the recently renovated **Embarcadero Promenade,** which stretches from the new SBC Park (Townsend St. and The Embarcadero) to Fisherman's Wharf. **Skates on Haight,** 1818 Haight St. (ℂ **415/752-8376**), 1 block from the park, is the best place to rent in-line or conventional skates. The cost of $6 per hour, $24 per day, includes protective wrist guards and kneepads. A major credit card and ID deposit are required. The shop is open daily from 10am to 6pm.

TENNIS   The **San Francisco Parks and Recreation Department** (ℂ **415/753-7001**) maintains more than 100 courts throughout the city. Almost all are available free, on a first-come, first-served basis. The exceptions are the 21 courts in **Golden Gate Park,** which cost $4 to $8 depending on the day and whether you're a resident or visitor, and can be yours for 90 minutes max. Courts must be reserved for weekend play by calling ℂ **415/831-6301** on Wednesday from 4 to 6pm, Thursday and Friday from 9am to 5pm. For midweek reservations, call ℂ **415/753-7001.**

WALKING & HIKING   The **Golden Gate National Recreation Area** offers plenty of opportunities. One incredible walk (or bike ride) is along the Golden Gate Promenade, from Aquatic Park to the Golden Gate Bridge. The 3.5-mile paved trail heads along the northern edge of the Presidio out to Fort Point, passing the marina, Crissy Fields' new restored wetlands, a small beach, and plenty of athletic locals. You can also hike the Coastal Trail all the way from the Fort Point area to Cliff House. The park service maintains several other trails in the city. For more information or to pick up a map of the Golden Gate National Recreation Area, stop by the park service headquarters at Fort Mason at the north end of Laguna Street (© **415/561-4700**).

Although most people drive to this spectacular vantage point, a more rejuvenating way to experience **Twin Peaks** is to walk up from the back roads of U. C. Medical Center (off Parnassus) or from either of the two roads that lead to the top (off Woodside or Clarendon aves.). The best time to trek is early morning, when the city is quiet, the air is crisp, and sightseers haven't crowded the parking lot. Keep an eye out for cars, however, because there's no real hiking trail, and be sure to walk beyond the lot and up to the highest vantage point.

10 Spectator Sports

The Bay Area's sports scene includes several major professional franchises. Check the local newspapers' sports sections for daily listings of local events.

MAJOR LEAGUE BASEBALL

The **San Francisco Giants** ✦ play at the new and absolutely stunning **SBC Park,** Third and King streets (© **415/972-2000;** www.sfgiants.com), in the China Basin section of SoMa. From April to October, 40,930 fans root for the National League Giants. The unobstructed bay vistas take in bobbing boats beyond the outfield at the recently completed $225-million "SBC Park." Tickets are hard to come by; you can try to track them down through **Tickets.com** (© **510/762-2277;** www.tickets.com). Special express bus service is available from Market Street on game days; call **Muni** (© **415/673-6864**) for pickup points and schedule information.

The American League's **Oakland Athletics** play across the bay at the Networks Associates Coliseum, at the Hegenberger Road exit from I-880, Oakland (© **510/430-8020**). The stadium holds close to 50,000 spectators and is accessible through BART's Coliseum station. Tickets are available from the Coliseum Box Office or by phone through **Tickets.com** (© **510/762-2277;** www.tickets.com).

PRO BASKETBALL

The **Golden State Warriors** of the NBA play at the Networks Associates Coliseum, at the Hegenberger Road exit from I-880, Oakland (© **510/986-2200;** www.nba.com/warriors). The Warriors play in The Arena at Oakland, a 19,200-seat facility. The season runs November through April, and most games start at 7:30pm. Tickets are available at the arena and by phone through **Tickets.com** (© **510/762-2277**).

PRO FOOTBALL

The **San Francisco 49ers** (www.sf49ers.com) play at 3Com/Candlestick Park, Giants Drive and Gilman Avenue ((© **415/468-2249**), on Sundays August through December; kickoff is usually at 1pm. Tickets sell out early in the season but are available at higher prices through ticket agents beforehand and from "scalpers" (illegal ticket-sellers who are usually at the gates). Ask your hotel concierge for the best way to track down tickets. Special express bus service is available from Market Street on game days; call **Muni** ((© **415/673-6864**) for pickup points and schedule information.

The 49ers' archenemies, the **Oakland Raiders** (www.ofma.com), play at the Network Associates Stadium, off the 880 freeway (Nimitz). Call © **800/949-2626** for ticket information.

COLLEGE FOOTBALL

The **University of California Golden Bears** play at California Memorial Stadium, 61 Harmon Gym, University of California, Berkeley ((© **800/GO-BEARS** or 510/642-3277; wwwcalbears.com), on the university campus across the bay. Tickets are usually available at game time. Phone for schedules and information.

6

Shopping

Like its population, San Francisco's shopping is both worldly and intimate. Every persuasion, style, era, and fetish is represented, not in big, tacky shopping malls, but in hundreds of quaint, dramatically different boutiques scattered throughout the city. Whether you're looking for Chanel or Chinese herbal medicine, San Francisco's got it. Just pick a neighborhood and break out your credit cards—you're sure to end up with at least a few take-home treasures.

1 The Shopping Scene

MAJOR SHOPPING AREAS

San Francisco has many shopping areas, but the following places are where you'll find most of the action.

UNION SQUARE & ENVIRONS San Francisco's most congested and popular shopping mecca is centered on Union Square and bordered by Bush, Taylor, Market, and Montgomery streets. Most of the big department stores and many high-end specialty shops are here. Be sure to venture to Grant Avenue, Post and Sutter streets, and Maiden Lane. This area is a hub for public transportation; all Market Street and several other buses run here, as do the Powell-Hyde and Powell-Mason cable car lines. You can also take the Muni streetcar to the Powell Street station.

CHINATOWN When you pass through the gate to Chinatown on Grant Avenue, say good-bye to the world of fashion and hello to a swarm of cheap tourist shops selling everything from linen and jade to plastic toys and $2 slippers. But that's not all Chinatown has to offer. The real gems are tucked away on side streets or are small, one-person shops selling Chinese herbs, original art, and jewelry. Grant Avenue is the area's main thoroughfare, and the side streets between Bush Street and Columbus Avenue are full of restaurants, markets, and eclectic shops. Stockton Street is best for grocery shopping (including live fowl and fish). Walking is best, because traffic through this area is slow at best and parking is next to impossible.

Most stores in Chinatown are open daily from 10am to 10pm. Take bus no. 1, 9X, 15, 30, 41, or 45.

UNION STREET Union Street, from Fillmore Street to Van Ness Avenue, caters to the upper-middle-class crowd. It's a great place to stroll, window-shop the plethora of boutiques, try the cafes and restaurants, and watch the beautiful people parade by. Take bus no. 22, 41, or 45.

CHESTNUT STREET Parallel and a few blocks north, Chestnut is a younger version of Union Street. It holds endless shopping and dining choices, and an ever-tanned, superfit population of post-graduate singles who hang around cafes and scope each other out. Take bus no. 22, 28, 30, 41, 43, or 76.

FILLMORE STREET Some of the best shopping in town is packed into 5 blocks of Fillmore Street in Pacific Heights. From Jackson to Sutter streets, Fillmore is the perfect place to grab a bite and peruse the high-priced boutiques, crafts shops, and incredible housewares stores. (Don't miss Zinc Details; p. 148.) Take bus no. 1, 2, 3, 4, 12, 22, or 24.

HAIGHT STREET Green hair, spiked hair, no hair, or mohair—even the hippies look conservative next to Haight Street's dramatic fashion freaks. The shopping in the 6 blocks of upper Haight Street between Central Avenue and Stanyan Street reflects its clientele. It offers everything from incense and European and American street styles to furniture and antique clothing. Bus nos. 6, 7, 66, and 71 run the length of Haight Street. The Muni streetcar N line stops at Waller Street and Cole Street.

SOMA Although this area isn't suitable for strolling, you'll find almost all the discount shopping in warehouse spaces south of Market.

Tips **Just the Facts: Hours & Taxes**

Store hours are generally Monday through Saturday from 10am to 6pm and Sunday from noon to 5pm. Most department stores stay open later, as do shops around Fisherman's Wharf, the most heavily visited (by tourists) area.

Sales tax in San Francisco is 8.5%, which is added on at the register for all goods and services purchased. If you live out of state and buy an expensive item, you might want to have the store ship it home for you. You'll have to pay for shipping, but you'll escape paying the sales tax.

You can pick up a discount-shopping guide at most major hotels. Many bus lines pass through this area.

HAYES VALLEY   It's not the prettiest area in town, with some of the shadier housing projects a few blocks away. But while most neighborhoods cater to more conservative or trendy shoppers, lower Hayes Street, between Octavia and Gough streets, celebrates anything vintage, chic, artistic, or downright funky. With new shops opening frequently, it's definitely the most interesting new shopping area in town, with furniture and glass stores, thrift shops, trendy shoe stores, and men's and women's clothiers. You can find lots of great antiques shops south on Octavia and on nearby Market Street. Take bus no. 16AX, 16BX, or 21.

FISHERMAN'S WHARF & ENVIRONS *(Overrated*   The tourist-oriented malls along Jefferson Street include hundreds of shops, restaurants, and attractions. Among them are Ghirardelli Square, PIER 39, The Cannery, and The Anchorage.

2 Shopping A to Z

ANTIQUES

Jackson Square, a historic district just north of the Financial District's Embarcadero Center, is the place to go for the top names in fine furniture and fine art. You can find a number of Asian-art dealers here. More than a dozen dealers on the 2 blocks between Columbus and Sansome streets specialize in European furnishings from the 17th to the 19th centuries. Most shops here are open Monday through Friday from 9am to 5pm and Saturday from 11am to 4pm.

ART

The San Francisco Gallery Guide, a comprehensive, bimonthly publication listing the city's current shows, is available free by mail. Send a self-addressed, stamped envelope to San Francisco Bay Area Gallery Guide, 1369 Fulton St., San Francisco, CA 94117 (© **415/ 921-1600**); or pick one up at the San Francisco Visitor Information Center at 900 Market St. Most of the city's major art galleries are clustered downtown in the Union Square area.

BOOKS

In addition to the listings below, there's a **Barnes & Noble** superstore at 2550 Taylor St., between Bay and North Point streets, near Fisherman's Wharf (© **415/292-6762**) and a four-storied **Borders** at 400 Post St., at Union Square (© **415/399-1633**).

San Francisco Shopping

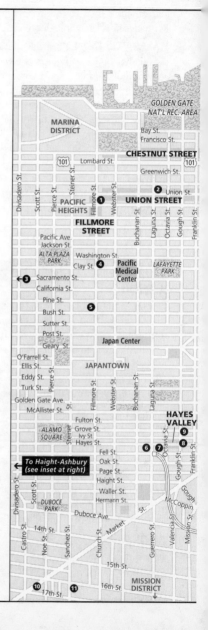

Municipal Pier

Aquatic Park

FISHERMAN'S WHARF & ENVIRONS

Pier 45   Pier 43½   Pier 43   Pier 41   Pier 39

Ghirardelli Square

RUSSIAN HILL

North Point St.
Bay St.
Francisco St.
Chestnut St.
Lombard St.
Greenwich St.
Filbert St.
Union St.
Green St.
Vallejo St.
Broadway

Jefferson St.
Beach St.

NORTH BEACH

Columbus Ave.

WASHINGTON SQUARE

TELEGRAPH HILL

Pier 35
Pier 33
Pier 31
Pier 27

Pier 23
Pier 19
Pier 17
Pier 15
Pier 9
Pier 7
Pier 5
Pier 3
Pier 1

Embarcadero

Tunnel

NOB HILL

Pacific Ave.
Jackson St.
Washington St.
Clay St.
Sacramento St.
California St.
Pine St.
Bush St.
Sutter St.
Post St.

CHINATOWN

Kearny St.
Sansome St.
Battery St.
Davis St.
Front St.
Drumm St.

Justin Herman Plaza

■ **Ferry Building (World Trade Center)**

Van Ness Ave.
Polk St.
Larkin St.
Hyde St.
Leavenworth St.
Jones St.
Taylor St.
Mason St.
Powell St.
Stockton St.
Grant Ave.
Montgomery St.

FINANCIAL DISTRICT

San Francisco-Oakland Bay Bridge

Steuart St.
Spear St.
Main St.
Beale St.
Fremont St.
1st St.

TENDER-LOIN

Geary St.
O'Farrell St.
Ellis St.
Eddy St.
Turk St.
Golden Gate Ave.
McAllister St.

CIVIC CENTER

UNION SQUARE & ENVIRONS

Union Square

Market St.

YERBA BUENA GARDENS

Moscone Convention Center

SOMA

2nd St.
Delancey St.
SOUTH PARK

Mission St.
Howard St.
Folsom St.
Harrison St.

5th St.
6th St.
7th St.
8th St.
9th St.
10th St.
11th St.
12th St.
15th St.

Brannan St.
Bryant St.
Townsend St.
King St.
Berry St.
Channel St.
Division St.
Alameda St.

3rd St.
4th St.
Illinois St.

SBC Park

Van Ness Ave.

Haight-Ashbury

Conservatory Dr.
Fulton St.
Grove St.
Hayes St.
Fell St.

McLaren Lodge

John F. Kennedy Dr.

GOLDEN GATE PARK

PANHANDLE

Oak St.
Page St.
Waller St.
Beulah St.
Frederick St.
Carl St.
Parnassus Ave.

Stanyan St.
Shrader St.
Cole St.
Clayton St.
Belvedere St.
Downey St.
Ashbury St.
Masonic Ave.
Delmar St.

HAIGHT STREET

Kezar Dr.

Pavilion

Kezar Stadium

0   1/4 mi
0   0.25 km

City Lights Booksellers & Publishers *(Finds)* Brooding literary types browse this famous bookstore owned by Lawrence Ferlinghetti, the renowned Beat Generation poet. The three-level bookshop prides itself on a comprehensive collection of art, poetry, and political paperbacks, as well as more mainstream books. Open daily until midnight. 261 Columbus Ave. (at Broadway). © 415/362-8193. www.citylights.com.

A Clean, Well-Lighted Place for Books *(Finds)* Voted best bookstore by the *San Francisco Bay Guardian,* this independent store has good new fiction and nonfiction sections, and specializes in music, art, mystery, and cookbooks. The store is well known for its author readings and events. For a calendar of events, call or check the website. 601 Van Ness Ave. (between Turk St. and Golden Gate Ave.). © 415/441-6670. www.bookstore.com.

CHINA, SILVER & GLASS

Gump's *(Finds)* Founded over a century ago, Gump's offers gifts and treasures ranging from Asian antiquities to contemporary art glass and exquisite jade and pearl jewelry. Many items are made specifically for the store. Gump's also has one of the city's most revered holiday window displays. Closed Sunday. 135 Post St. (between Kearny St. and Grant Ave.). © 415/982-1616. www.gumps.com.

DEPARTMENT STORES (DOWNTOWN)

Macy's The seven-story Macy's West features contemporary fashions for women, juniors, and children, plus jewelry, fragrances, cosmetics, and accessories. The sixth floor offers a "hospitality suite" where visitors can leave their coats and packages, grab a cup of coffee, or find out more about the city from the concierge. The top floors contain home furnishings, and the Cellar sells kitchenware and gourmet foods. You'll even find a Boudin Cafe (though the food is not as good compared to their food at other locations) and a Wolfgang Puck Cafe on the premises. Across the street, Macy's East has five floors of men's fashions, the largest Men's Polo by Ralph Lauren shop in the country, and the Fresh Choice cafe. Stockton and O'Farrell sts., Union Square. © 415/397-3333.

Neiman Marcus Some call this Texas-based chain "Needless Mark-ups." But those who can afford the best of everything can't deny that the men's and women's clothes, precious gems, and conservative formalwear are some of the most glamorous in town. The Rotunda Restaurant, on the top floor, is a beautiful, relaxing place for lunch and afternoon tea. 150 Stockton St. (between Geary and O'Farrell sts.), Union Square. ✆ 415/362-3900.

Nordstrom Renowned for its personalized service, this is the largest branch of the Seattle-based fashion department-store chain. Nordstrom occupies the top five floors of the San Francisco Shopping Centre and is the mall's primary anchor. Equally devoted to women's and men's fashions, the store has one of the best shoe selections in the city and thousands of suits in stock. The City Centre Grill, on the fourth floor, has a panoramic view and is ideal for an inexpensive lunch or light snack. Nordstrom Spa, on the fifth floor, is the perfect place to relax after a hectic day of bargain hunting. In the San Francisco Shopping Centre, 865 Market St. (between 4th and 5th sts.). ✆ 415/243-8500.

DISCOUNT SHOPPING

Jeremy's *(Value* This boutique is a serious mecca for fashion hounds thanks to the wide array of top designer fashions, from shoes to suits, at rock-bottom prices. There are no cheap knockoffs here, just good men's and women's clothes and accessories that the owner scoops up from major retailers who are either updating their merchandise or discarding returns. 2 S. Park (between Bryant and Brannan sts. at Second St.). ✆ 415/882-4929.

FASHION

See also "Vintage Clothing," later in this chapter.

UNISEX

Gucci America Donning Gucci's golden Gs is not a cheap endeavor. But if you've got the cash, you'll find all the latest lines of shoes, leather goods, scarves, and pricey accessories here, such as a $9,000 handmade crocodile bag. 200 Stockton St. (between Geary and Post sts.). ✆ 415/392-2808.

MAC *(Finds* No, we're not talking cosmetics. The more-modern-than-corporate stock at this hip and hidden shop just combined its men's and women's fashion meccas in a new space next door to pastry pit stop Citizen Cake. Drop in for imported tailored suits and women's separates in new and intriguing fabrics as well as gorgeous ties, vibrant sweaters, and a few choice home accouterments. Lines include London's Paul Smith, Belgium's SO, New York's John Bartlett, and local sweater sweetheart Laurie B. The best part? Prices are more reasonable than many of the trendy clothing stores in the area. 387 Grove St. (at Gough St.). ✆ 415/863-3011.

Niketown Here it's not "I can," but "I can spend." At least that's what the kings of sportswear were banking on when they opened this megastore in 1997. As you'd expect, inside the doors it's Nike's world, offering everything the merchandising team could create. 278 Post St. (at Stockton St.). ✆ **415/392-6453.**

Wilkes Bashford *(Finds)* Wilkes Bashford is one of the most expensive and best-known clothing stores in the city. In its 3-plus decades in business, the boutique has garnered a reputation for stocking only the finest clothes in the world (Willie Brown, former mayor of San Francisco, does his suit shopping here). Most fashions come from Italy and France; they include women's designer sportswear and couture and men's Kiton and Brioni suits (at $2,500 and up, they're considered the most expensive suits in the world). Closed Sunday. 375 Sutter St. (at Stockton St.). ✆ **415/986-4380.**

MEN'S FASHIONS

Brooks Brothers In San Francisco, this bulwark of tradition is 1 block east of Union Square. Brooks Brothers introduced the button-down collar and single-handedly changed the standard of the well-dressed businessman. The multilevel shop also sells traditional casual wear, including sportswear, sweaters, and shirts. 150 Post St. (at Grant Ave.). ✆ **415/397-4500.**

Cable Car Clothiers Dapper men head to this beautiful landmark building for traditional attire, such as three-button suits with natural shoulders, Aquascutum coats, McGeorge sweaters, and Atkinson ties. Closed Sunday. 441 Sutter St. (between Stockton and Powell sts.). ✆ **415/397-4740.**

WOMEN'S FASHIONS

Ab Fits Duck into this North Beach destination for jeans to fit all shapes, styles, and sizes as well as smart and sassy contemporary wear for gals on the go. The snuggly-fitting stock ranges from Levi's, Earl, Edwin, and Seven to chic wear from the likes of Rozae Nichols, Nanette Lepore, and James Perse. 1519 Grant Ave. (at Union and Filbert sts.). ✆ **415/982-5726.**

The Chanel Boutique Ever fashionable and expensive, Chanel is appropriately located on Maiden Lane, the quaint downtown side street where the most exclusive stores and spas cluster. You'll find here what you'd expect from Chanel: clothing, accessories, scents, cosmetics, and jewelry. 155 Maiden Lane (between Stockton St. and Grant Ave.). ✆ **415/981-1550.**

Métier *(Finds)* Some savvy shoppers consider this the best women's clothing shop in town. Within its walls you'll find classic, sophisticated, and expensive creations. Offerings include European ready-to-wear lines and designers; fashions by Italian designers Anna Molinari and Alberto Biani; and a distinguished collection of antique-style, high-end jewelry from L.A.'s Kathie Waterman as well as ultrapopular custom-designed poetry jewelry by Jeanine Payer. Closed Sunday. 355 Sutter St. (between Stockton and Grant sts.). ✆ **415/989-5395.**

FOOD

Joseph Schmidt Confections *(Finds)* Here, chocolate takes the shape of exquisite sculptural masterpieces—such as long-stemmed tulips and heart-shaped boxes—that are so beautiful, you'll be hesitant to bite the head off your adorable panda bear. Once you do, however, you'll know why this is the most popular—and reasonably priced—chocolatier in town. 3489 16th St. (at Sanchez St.). ✆ **800/861-8682** or 415/861-8682. www.jsc.com.

Ten Ren Tea Co. *(Finds)* At the Ten Ren Tea Co. shop, you will be offered a steaming cup of tea when you walk in the door. In addition to a selection of almost 50 traditional and herbal teas, the company stocks related paraphernalia, such as pots, cups, and infusers. If you can't make up your mind, take home a mail-order form. The shop is open daily from 9am to 9pm. 949 Grant Ave. (between Washington and Jackson sts.). ✆ **415/362-0656.**

GIFTS

Cost Plus Imports At the Fisherman's Wharf cable car turntable, Cost Plus is a vast warehouse crammed to the rafters with Chinese baskets, Indian camel bells, Malaysian batik scarves, and innumerable other items from Algeria to Zanzibar. More than 20,000 items from 40 nations, imported directly from their country of origin, pack this well-priced warehouse. There's also a decent wine shop here. It's open Monday through Saturday from 10am to 9pm and Sunday from 10am to 8pm. 2552 Taylor St. (between North Point and Bay sts.). ✆ **415/928-6200.**

SFMOMA MuseumStore *(Finds)* With an array of artistic cards, books, jewelry, housewares, knickknacks, and creative tokens of San Francisco, it's virtually impossible not to find something here you'll consider a must-have. (Check out the Fog Dome!) Aside from being one of the locals' favorite shops, it offers far more tasteful mementos than most Fisherman's Wharf options. You can also check them out online at www.sfmoma.org. 151 Third St. (2 blocks south of Market St., across from Yerba Buena Gardens). ℂ 415/357-4035. www.sfmoma.org.

HOUSEWARES/FURNISHINGS

Alabaster *(Finds*   Any interior designer who knows Biedermeier from Bauhaus knows that this Hayes Valley shop sets local home accessories trends with its predominantly off-white collection of must-haves. 597 Hayes St. (at Laguna St.). ℂ 415/558-0482.

Biordi Art Imports *(Finds*   Whether you want to decorate your dinner table, color your kitchen, or liven up the living room, Biordi's Italian majolica pottery is the most exquisite and unusual way to do it. The owner has been importing these hand-painted collectibles for 54 years, and every piece is a showstopper. Call for a catalog. They'll ship anywhere. Closed Sunday. 412 Columbus Ave. (at Vallejo St.). ℂ 415/392-8096. www.biordi.com.

Propeller   This airy skylight-lit shop is a must-stop for lovers of the latest in übermodern furniture and home accessories. Owner/designer Lorn Dittfeld handpicks pieces by emerging designers from as far away as Sweden, Italy, and Canada, as well as a plethora of national newbies. Drop in to lounge on the hippest sofas; grab pretty and practical gifts like ultracool magnetic spice racks; or adorn your home with Bev Hisey's architectural candlesticks and graphic pillows, diamond-cut wood tables by William Earle, or hand-tufted graphic rugs by Angela Adams. The shop's closed Monday except by appointment. 555 Hayes St. (between Laguna and Octavia sts.). ℂ 415/701-7767. www.propeller-sf.com.

The Wok Shop   This shop has every conceivable implement for Chinese cooking, including woks, brushes, cleavers, circular chopping blocks, dishes, oyster knives, bamboo steamers, and strainers. It also sells a wide range of kitchen utensils, baskets, handmade linens from China, and aprons. 718 Grant Ave. (at Clay St.). ℂ 415/989-3797 or 888/780-7171 for mail order. www.wokshop.com.

Zinc Details *(Finds*   One of my favorite stores in the city, Zinc Details has received accolades everywhere from *Elle Decor Japan* to *Metropolitan Home* for its amazing collection of locally handcrafted glass vases, pendant lights, ceramics, and furniture. Most pieces are true works of art created specifically for the store. 1905 Fillmore St. (between Bush and Pine sts.). ℂ 415/776-2100. www.zincdetails.com.

JEWELRY

De Vera Galleries *(Finds*   Don't come here unless you've got money to spend. Designer Federico de Vera's unique rough-stone jewelry collection, art glass, and vintage knickknacks are too beautiful to pass up and too expensive to be a painless purchase. Still, if you're looking for a keepsake, you'll find it here. 29 Maiden Lane (at Kearny St.). *C* **415/788-0828.** www.deveraobjects.com.

Dianne's Old & New Estates   Buy yourself a bauble and treat yourself to a trinket at this shop featuring top-of-the-line antique jewelry—pendants, diamond rings, necklaces, bracelets, and natural pearls. For a special gift, check out the collection of platinum wedding and engagement rings and vintage watches. Don't worry if you can't afford it now—the shop offers 1-year interest-free layaway. Closed on Wednesday. 2181A Union St. (at Fillmore St.). *C* **888/346-7525** or 415/346-7525.

Pearl & Jade Empire   The Pearl & Jade Empire has been importing jewelry from all over the world since 1957. It specializes in unusual pearls and jade and offers restringing on the premises as well as boasting a collection of amber from the Baltic Sea. 427 Post St. (between Powell and Mason sts.). *C* **415/362-0606.** www.pearlempire.com.

Union Street Goldsmith   A showcase for Bay Area goldsmiths, this exquisite shop sells a contemporary collection of fine custom-designed jewelry in platinum and all karats of gold. Many pieces emphasize colored stones. 1909 Union St. (at Laguna St.). *C* **415/776-8048.** www.unionstreetgoldsmith.com.

MUSIC

Recycled Records *(Finds*   Easily one of the best used-record stores in the city, this loud shop in the Haight has a good selection of promotional CDs and cases of used "classic" rock LPs. Sheet music, tour programs, and old *TV Guide*s are for sale, too. It's open late daily; hours vary, so call ahead. 1377 Haight St. (between Central and Masonic sts.). *C* **415/626-4075.**

Streetlight Records   Overstuffed with used music in all three formats, this place is best known for its records and excellent CD collection. Rock music is cheap, and the money-back guarantee guards against defects. There's a second location at 2350 Market St., between Castro and Noe streets (*C* **415/282-8000**). 3979 24th St. (between Noe and Sanchez sts.). *C* **415/282-3550.**

Virgin Megastore   With thousands of CDs, including an impressive collection of imports, videos, DVDs, a multimedia department, a cafe, and related books, this enormous Union Square store can make any music-lover blow his or her entire vacation fund. It's open Sunday through Thursday from 10am to 10pm and Friday

and Saturday from 10am to midnight. 2 Stockton St. (at Market St.).
© 415/397-4525.

SHOES

Birkenstock   This relaxed store is known for its earthy form-fitting sandals, clogs, and lace-ups. 42 Stockton St. (between Market and O'Farrell sts.). © 415/989-2475.

Bulo   If you have a fetish for foot fashions, you must check out Bulo, which carries nothing but imported Italian shoes. The selection is small but styles run the gamut, from casual to dressy, reserved to wildly funky. New shipments come in every 3 to 4 weeks, so the selection is ever-changing, eternally hip, and, unfortunately, ever-expensive, with many pairs going for close to $200. Men's store: 437A Hayes St. (at Gough St.). © 415/864-3244. Women's store: across the street, at 418 Hayes St. (© 415/255-4939).

Gimme Shoes   The staff is funky-fashion snobby, the prices are steep, and the European shoes and accessories are utterly chic. Additional locations are 416 Hayes St. (© **415/864-0691**) and 50 Grant Ave. (© **415/434-9242**). 2358 Fillmore St. (at Washington St.). © 415/441-3040.

TOYS

The Chinatown Kite Shop   This shop's playful assortment of flying objects includes attractive fish kites, windsocks, hand-painted Chinese paper kites, wood-and-paper biplanes, pentagonal kites, and do-it-yourself kite kits, all of which make great souvenirs or decorations. Computer-designed stunt kites have two or four control lines to manipulate loops and dives. Open daily from 10am to 9pm. 717 Grant Ave. (between Clay and Sacramento sts.). © 415/391-8217.

The Disney Store   Capitalizing on the world's love for The Mouse and his friends, this store offers everything Disney-oriented you could possibly want—from clothes and toys to high-end commissioned art from the Disney gallery. Those looking for a simple token can fork over $5 for a souvenir, while more serious collectors can throw down $4,500 for a Yamagata Disney lithograph. The store is open Monday through Friday from 10am to 7pm, Saturday from 10am to 8pm, Sunday from 11am to 7pm. Hours are extended during the holiday season; call for details. 400 Post St. (at Powell St.). © 415/391-6866.

VINTAGE CLOTHING

Aardvark's   One of San Francisco's largest secondhand clothing dealers, Aardvark's has seemingly endless racks of shirts, pants, dresses, skirts, and hats from the past 30 years. It's open daily from 11am to 7pm. 1501 Haight St. (at Ashbury St.). © 415/621-3141.

Buffalo Exchange   This large storefront on upper Haight Street is crammed with racks of antique and new fashions from the 1960s, 1970s, and 1980s. It stocks everything from suits and dresses to neckties, hats, handbags, and jewelry. Buffalo Exchange anticipates some of the hottest new street fashions. A second shop is at 1800 Polk St., at Washington St. (© **415/346-5726**). 1555 Haight St. (between Clayton and Ashbury sts.). © 415/431-7733.

Good Byes *(Finds)*   One the best new- and used-clothes stores in San Francisco, Good Byes carries only high-quality clothing and accessories, including an exceptional selection of men's fashions at unbelievably low prices (for example, $350 preowned shoes for $35). Women's wear is in a separate boutique across the street. 3464 Sacramento St. and 3483 Sacramento St. (between Laurel and Walnut sts.). © 415/346-6388.

La Rosa   On a street packed with vintage-clothing shops, this is one of the more upscale options. It features a selection of high-quality, dry-cleaned secondhand goods. Formal suits and dresses are its specialty, but you'll also find sport coats, slacks, and shoes. The more moderately priced sister store, **Held Over,** is located at 1543 Haight St., near Ashbury (© **415/864-0818**). 1711 Haight St. (at Cole St.). © 415/668-3744.

WINE

Wine Club San Francisco *(Value)*   The Wine Club is a discount warehouse that offers bargain prices on more than 1,200 domestic and foreign wines. Bottles cost between $4 and $1,100. 953 Harrison St. (between Fifth and Sixth sts.). © 415/512-9086.

7

San Francisco After Dark

For a city with fewer than a million inhabitants, San Francisco boasts an impressive after-dark scene. Dozens of piano bars and top-notch lounges augment a lively dance-club culture, and skyscraper lounges offer dazzling city views. The city's arts scene is also extraordinary: The opera is justifiably world renowned, the ballet is on its toes, the Asian Art Museum has settled into its new Civic Center digs, and theaters are high in both quantity and quality. In short, there's always something going on, so get out there.

For up-to-date nightlife information, turn to the *San Francisco Weekly* (www.sfweekly.com) and the *San Francisco Bay Guardian* (www.sfbg.com), both of which run comprehensive listings. They are available free at bars and restaurants and from street-corner boxes all around the city. *Where* (www.wheresf.com), a free tourist-oriented monthly, also lists programs and performance times; it's available in most of the city's finer hotels. The Sunday edition of the *San Francisco Chronicle* features a "Datebook" section, printed on pink paper, with information on and listings of the week's events. If you have Internet access, it's a good idea to check out www.citysearch.com for the latest in bars, clubs, and events. And if you want to secure seats at a hot-ticket event, either buy well in advance or contact the concierge of your hotel and see if they can't swing something for you.

TIX Bay Area (© 415/433-7827; www.tixbayarea.org) sells half-price tickets to theater, dance, and music performances on the day of the show only; tickets for Sunday and Monday events, if available, are sold on Saturday and Sunday. TIX Bay Area also sells advance, full-price tickets for most performance halls, sporting events, concerts, and clubs. A service charge, ranging from $2 to $5, is levied on each ticket. Only cash and traveler's checks are accepted for half-price tickets; Visa and MasterCard are accepted for full-price tickets. TIX, located on Powell Street between Geary and Post streets, is open Tuesday through Thursday from 11am to 6pm, Friday and Saturday from 11am to 7pm, and Sunday from 11am to 3pm.

You can also get tickets to most theater and dance events through **City Box Office,** 180 Redwood St., Suite 100, between Golden

Gate and McAllister streets off Van Ness Avenue (✆ **415/392-4400;** www.cityboxoffice.com). MasterCard and Visa are accepted.

Tickets.com (✆ **415/478-2277** or 510/762-2277; www.tickets.com) sells computer-generated tickets (with a hefty service charge of $3–$15 convenience fee per ticket!) to concerts, sporting events, plays, and special events. Call for the local office nearest you. **Ticketmaster** (✆ **415/421-TIXS;** www.ticketmaster.com) also offers advance ticket purchases (also with a service charge).

For information on local theater, check out www.bayareatheatre.org.

For information on major league baseball, pro basketball, pro and college football, and horse racing, see the "Spectator Sports" section of chapter 5, beginning on p. 137.

And don't forget that this isn't New York: Bars close at 2am, so get an early start if you want a full night on the town in San Francisco.

1 The Performing Arts

Special concerts and performances take place in San Francisco year-round. **San Francisco Performances,** 500 Sutter St., Suite 710 (✆ **415/398-6449;** www.performances.org), has brought acclaimed artists to the Bay Area for 25 years. Shows run the gamut from chamber music to dance to jazz. Performances are in several venues, including the Performing Arts Center, Herbst Theater, and the Center for the Performing Arts at Yerba Buena Center. The season runs from late September to May. Tickets cost from $12 to $60 and are available through **City Box Office** (✆ **415/392-4400**).

CLASSICAL MUSIC

Philharmonia Baroque Orchestra   Acclaimed by the *New York Times* as "the country's leading early music orchestra," Philharmonia Baroque performs in San Francisco and all around the Bay Area. The season lasts September through April. Performing in Herbst Theater, 401 Van Ness Ave. ✆ **415/392-4400** (box office) or 415/252-1288 (administrative offices). www.philharmonia.org. Tickets $28–$62.

San Francisco Symphony   Founded in 1911, the internationally respected San Francisco Symphony has long been an important part of the city's cultural life under such legendary conductors as Pierre Monteux and Seiji Ozawa. In 1995, Michael Tilson Thomas took over from Herbert Blomstedt; he has led the orchestra to new heights and crafted an exciting repertoire of classical and modern music. The season runs September through June. Summer symphony activities include a Composer Festival and a Summer in the City series. Tickets are very hard to come by, but if you're desperate,

San Francisco After Dark

you can usually pick up a few outside the hall the night of the concert. Performing at Davies Symphony Hall, 201 Van Ness Ave. (at Grove St.). 📞 415/864-6000 (box office). www.sfsymphony.org. Tickets $12–$97.

OPERA

In addition to San Francisco's major opera company, you might check out the amusing **Pocket Opera,** 469 Bryant St. (📞 **415/972-8930;** www.pocketopera.org). From mid-February to mid-July, the comic company stages farcical performances of well-known operas in English. The staging is intimate and informal, without lavish costumes and sets. The cast ranges from 3 to 16 players, supported by a chamber orchestra. The rich repertoire includes such works as *Don Giovanni* and *The Barber of Seville.* Performances are on Saturday and Sunday. Call the box office for complete information, location (which varies), and show times. Tickets cost from $15 (students) to $30.

San Francisco Opera The San Francisco Opera was the second municipal opera in the United States and is one of the city's cultural icons. Brilliantly balanced casts may feature celebrated stars like Frederica Von Stade and Plácido Domingo, along with promising newcomers and regular members, in productions that range from traditional to avant-garde. All productions have English supertitles. The season starts in September and lasts just 14 weeks. Performances are held most evenings, except Monday, with matinees on Sundays. Tickets go on sale as early as June for subscribers and August for the general public, and the best seats sell out quickly. Unless Domingo is in town, some less coveted seats are usually available until curtain time. War Memorial Opera House, 301 Van Ness Ave. (at Grove St.). 📞 **415/864-3330** (box office). www.sfopera.com. Tickets $25–$195; standing room $15–$30.

THEATER

American Conservatory Theater (A.C.T.) *Finds* The Tony Award–winning American Conservatory Theater made its debut in 1967 and quickly established itself as the city's premier resident theater group and one of the nation's best. The A.C.T. season runs September through July and features both classic and experimental works. A.C.T. recently returned to its home, the fabulous **Geary Theater** (1910), a national historic landmark, after the theater sustained severe damage in the 1989 earthquake and closed for renovations. Now it is fully refurbished and modernized to such an extent that it's regarded as one of America's finest performance spaces. Performing at the Geary Theater, 415 Geary St. (at Mason St.). 📞 **415/749-2ACT.** www.act-sf.org. Tickets $19–$68.

Tips Dinner Party

Hungry for dinner and a damned good time? It ain't cheap, but Teatro ZinZanni is a delightfully rollicking ride of food, whimsy, drama, and song within a stunningly elegant 1926 tent on The Embarcadero. Part musical theater and part comedy show, the 3½-hour dinner theater includes a surprisingly decent five-course meal served by dozens of performers who weave both the audience and astounding physical acts (think Cirque du Soleil) into their wacky and playful world. Anyone in need of a night of giggles should definitely book a table here. Shows are held Wednesday through Sunday and tickets are $99 to $125 including dinner. The tent is located at Pier 29 on The Embarcadero at Battery Street. Call © **415/438-2668** or see www.teatrozinzanni.org for more details.

DANCE

In addition to the local companies, top traveling troupes like the Joffrey Ballet and the American Ballet Theatre make regular appearances. Primary modern dance spaces include the **Cowell Theater,** at Fort Mason Center, Marina Boulevard at Buchanan Street (© **415/441-3400**), and the **ODC Theatre,** 3153 17th St., at Shotwell Street in the Mission District (© **415/863-9834**). Check the local papers for schedules or contact the theater box offices for more information.

San Francisco Ballet   Founded in 1933, the San Francisco Ballet is the oldest professional ballet company in the United States and is regarded as one of the country's finest. It performs an eclectic repertoire of full-length, neoclassical, and contemporary ballets. Even the *New York Times* proclaimed, "The San Francisco Ballet under Helgi Tomasson's leadership is one of the spectacular success stories of the arts in America." The 2005 Repertory Season runs February through May; the company performs *The Nutcracker* each December. The San Francisco Ballet Orchestra accompanies all performances. War Memorial Opera House, 301 Van Ness Ave. (at Grove St.). © **415/865-2000** for tickets and information. www.sfballet.org. Tickets $10–$165.

2 Comedy & Cabaret

Bay Area Theatresports (BATS) *Finds*   Combining improvisation with competition, BATS operates an improvisational tournament, in which four-actor teams compete against each other, taking on hilarious challenges from the audience. Judges flash scorecards goodnaturedly or honk a horn for scenes that just aren't working. Shows are on Thursday through Sunday only. Phone for reservations. Performing at Center for Improvisational Theatre at the Fort Mason Center, Building B, 3rd floor. ✆ 415/474-8935. www.improv.org. Tickets $8–$15.

Beach Blanket Babylon *(Moments* A San Francisco tradition, *Beach Blanket Babylon* evolved from Steve Silver's Rent-a-Freak service—a group of party-givers extraordinaire who hired themselves out as a "cast of characters" complete with fabulous costumes and sets, props, and gags. After their act caught on, it moved into the Savoy-Tivoli, a North Beach bar. By 1974, the audience had grown too large for the facility, and *Beach Blanket* has been at the 400-seat Club Fugazi ever since. The show is a comedic musical send-up that is best known for outrageous costumes and oversize headdresses. It's been playing for 31 years, and almost every performance sells out. The show is updated often enough that locals still attend. Those under 21 are welcome at a Sunday matinee at 3pm, when no alcohol is served; photo ID is required for evening performances. Write for weekend tickets at least 3 weeks in advance, or get them through TIX Bay Area (✆ **415/433-7827**). *Note:* There are only 44 tickets per show with assigned seating. All other tickets are within specific sections depending on price, but seating is first-come, first-seated within that section. Performances are Wednesday and Thursday at 8pm, Friday and Saturday at 7 and 10pm, and Sunday at 3 and 7pm. At Club Fugazi, Beach Blanket Babylon Blvd., 678 Green St. (between Powell St. and Columbus Ave.). ✆ **415/421-4222**. www.beachblanketbabylon.com. Tickets $20–$55.

Cobb's Comedy Club   Cobb's features such national headliners as Joe Rogan, Brian Regan, and Jake Johannsen. There is comedy every night except Monday, including a 15-comedian All-Pro Wednesday showcase (a 3-hr. marathon). Cobb's is open to those 18 and over, and occasionally to kids 16 and 17 when accompanied by a parent or legal guardian (call ahead). Shows are held Tuesday through Thursday and Sunday at 8pm, Friday and Saturday at 8 and 10pm. 915 Columbus Ave. (at Lombard St.). ✆ **415/928-4320**. www.cobbscomedy club.com. Cover $15–$35. 2-beverage minimum.

Punch Line Comedy Club   Adjacent to The Embarcadero One office building, this is the largest comedy nightclub in the city. Three-person shows with top national and local talent are featured here Tuesday through Saturday. Showcase night is Sunday, when 15 comics take the mic. There's an all-star showcase or a special event on Monday. Shows are Tuesday through Thursday and Sunday at 9pm, Friday and Saturday at 9 and 11pm. 444 Battery St. (between Washington and Clay sts.), plaza level. ℂ 415/397-4337 or 415/397-7573 for recorded information. www.punchlinecomedyclub.com. Cover $5 Sun–Mon; $8–$15 Tues–Sat. 2-drink minimum.

3 The Club & Music Scene

The greatest legacy from the 1960s is the city's continued tradition of live entertainment and music, which explains the great variety of clubs and music enjoyed by San Francisco. The hippest dance places are South of Market Street (SoMa), in former warehouses; the artsy bohemian scene centers are in the Mission; and the most popular cafe culture is still in North Beach.

Note: The club and music scene is always changing, often outdating recommendations before the ink can dry on a page. Most of the venues below are promoted as different clubs on various nights of the week, each with its own look, sound, and style. Discount passes and club announcements are often available at clothing stores and other shops along upper Haight Street.

Drink prices at most bars, clubs, and cafes range from about $3.50 to $9, unless otherwise noted.

ROCK & BLUES CLUBS

In addition to the following listings, see "Dance Clubs," below, for (usually) live, danceable rock.

The Boom Boom Room *(Finds)*   The late John Lee Hooker and his partner Alex Andreas bought this Western Addition club several years back and used Hooker's star power to pull in some of the best blues bands in the country (even the Stones showed up for an unannounced

---

Tips **Dial-a-Scene**

The local newspapers won't direct you to the city's underground club scene, nor will they advise you which of the dozens of clubs are truly hot. To get dialed in, do what the locals do—turn to the **Be-At Line** (ℂ 415/626-4087) for its daily recorded update on the town's most hoppin' hip-hop, acid-jazz, and house clubs. The far more commercial **Club Line** (ℂ 415/339-8686; www.sfclubs.com) offers up-to-date schedules for the city's larger dance venues.

---

jam session). It's a dark and small and cramped and steamy joint—just like a blues bar should be—that hosts blues and boogie bands 7 nights a week until 2am. If you're going to The Fillmore (see below) to see a band, stop by here first for a drink and come back after your show for more great music. The neighborhood's a bit rough, so be sure to park in the underground lot across the street. 1601 Fillmore St. (at Geary Blvd.). ✆ 415/673-8000. www.boomboomblues.com. Cover varies from free to $15.

The Fillmore *Finds* Reopened after years of neglect, the Fillmore, made famous by promoter Bill Graham in the 1960s, is attracting big names again. Check listings in papers, or call the theater for information on upcoming events. And if you make it to a show, check out the fabulous collection of vintage concert posters chronicling the hall's history. 1805 Geary Blvd. (at Fillmore St.). ✆ 415/346-6000. www.thefillmore.com. Tickets $17–$35.

The Saloon An authentic gold rush survivor, this North Beach dive is the oldest bar in the city. Popular with both bikers and daytime pinstripers, it schedules live blues nightly. 1232 Grant Ave. (at Columbus St.). ✆ 415/989-7666. Cover $4–$5 Fri–Sat.

JAZZ & LATIN CLUBS

Cafe du Nord *Finds* Although it's been around since 1907, this basement supper club is rightfully self-proclaimed as the place for a "slightly lurid indie pop scene set in a beautiful old speakeasy." With a younger generation now appreciating the music—swing, jazz, alternative, pop, you name it—the place is often packed from the 40-foot mahogany bar to the back room, where the focus is on live performances. *Note:* If Lavay Smith and Her Red Hot Skillet Lickers or Ledisi are in the house, definitely don't miss them. 2170 Market St. (at Sanchez St.). ✆ 415/861-5016. www.cafedunord.com. Cover $5–$15.

Jazz at Pearl's This is one of the best jazz venues in the city. The live jams last until 1:30am nightly. Ribs and chicken are served, too; they run from $5 to $20. 256 Columbus Ave. (at Broadway). ✆ 415/291-8255. www.jazzatpearls.com. 2-drink minimum.

DANCE CLUBS

Although a lot of clubs allow dancing, the following are the places to go if all you want to do is shake your groove thang.

Nickie's Bar-be-cue Don't show up here for dinner—the only hot thing you'll find is the small, crowded dance floor. But don't let that stop you from checking it out—Nickie's is a sure thing. Here the old-school hits are in full force, casually dressed young dancers

Tips Local Talent

Want to see the best of local jazz, cabaret, or blues performers? Check the *San Francisco Chronicle*'s Sunday "Datebook" to see if the following artists are in the house. Better yet, buy their CDs and take San Francisco's music scene home with you:

- **Faith Winthrop,** a veteran cabaret diva with a velvet voice and heartfelt delivery.
- **Ledisi,** a young local blues singer with a penchant for scatting and smoky, deep, soulful self-written tunes.
- **Jacqui Naylor,** a seductive young talent with a love for standards and reinventing a phrase with her own modern twist.
- **Lavay Smith & Her Red Hot Skillet Lickers**—swing hasn't swung this hard since it was invented.

lose all their inhibitions, and the crowd consists of all types of friendly San Franciscans. This place is perpetually hot, so dress accordingly; you can always cool down with a pint from the wine-and-beer bar. Keep in mind that lower Haight is on the periphery of a shady neighborhood, so don't make your car look tempting, and stay alert as you walk through the area. Closed on Sundays. 460 Haight St. (between Fillmore and Webster sts.). ✆ **415/621-6508.** www.nickies. com. Cover $3–$5.

Paradise Lounge   Labyrinthine Paradise features three dance floors simultaneously vibrating to different beats. Smaller, auxiliary spaces host different events (poetry readings are fairly common) and include a pool room with a half-dozen tables. The crowd ranges from everyday party people to grungy-alternative types. Open Friday and Saturday only. 1501 Folsom St. (at 11th St.). ✆ **415/861-6906.** www.paradiselounge.com. Cover $3–$15.

Ten 15   Get decked out and plan on a late night if you're headed to this enormous party warehouse. Three levels, a full-color laser system, and a gigantic dance floor make for an extensive variety of dancing venues, complete with a 20- and 30-something gyrating mass who live for the DJs' pounding house, disco, and acid-jazz music. Each night is a different club that attracts its own crowd, ranging from yuppie to hip-hop. A recent $1.5-million renovation added 6,000 square feet of dance floor and a VIP area. Call ahead for a complete schedule of events. 1015 Folsom St. (at Sixth St.). ✆ **415/ 431-1200.** www.1015.com. Cover $5–$15.

SUPPER CLUBS

If you can eat dinner, listen to live music, and dance (or at least wiggle in your chair) in the same room, it's a supper club—those are our criteria here.

Harry Denton's Starlight Room *(Moments*   Come to this celestial high-rise cocktail lounge and nightclub, where tourists and locals watch the sunset at dusk and boogie down to live swing and big-band or DJs' tunes after dark. The room is classic 1930s San Francisco, with red-velvet banquettes, chandeliers, and fabulous views. But what really attracts flocks of all ages is a night of Harry Denton–style fun, which usually includes plenty of drinking and unrestrained dancing. The full bar stocks a decent collection of single-malt Scotches and champagnes, and you can snack from the pricey Starlight appetizer menu (make a reservation to guarantee a table and you'll also have a place to rest your weary dancing-dogs). Early evening is more relaxed, but come the weekend, this place gets loose. *Tip:* Come dressed for success (no jeans or sneakers), or you'll be turned away at the door. Atop the Sir Francis Drake hotel, 450 Powell St., 21st floor. (℅ 415/395-8595. www.harrydenton.com. Cover $10 Wed after 7pm; $5 Thurs after 8pm; $10 Fri after 8pm; $15 Sat after 8pm.

Julie's Supper Club   Julie's is a longtime standby for cocktails and late dining in a groovy setting. The vibe in both rooms is very 1950s cartoon, with a space-age Jetsons appeal and good-looking singles on the prowl. The food is hit-or-miss, but the atmosphere is definitely a winner—casual and playful—and it comes with a little interesting history: This building is one location where the Symbionese Liberation Army held Patty Hearst hostage in the 1970s. Menu items range from $6 to $20 and happy hour, Tuesday through Friday from 5pm to 7:30pm, includes free snacks. 1123 Folsom St. (at Seventh St.). (℅ 415/861-0707. www.juliessupperclub.com.

DESTINATION BARS WITH DJ GROOVES

Bambuddha Lounge *(Finds*   The hottest place for the young and the trendy to feast, flirt, or just be fabulous is this restaurant/bar adjoining the funky-cool Phoenix Hotel. With a 20-foot reclining Buddha on the roof, ultramodern San Francisco–meets–Southeast Asian decor (including waterfalls in the dining room and outdoor poolside cocktail lounge and *salas,* Balinese-style outdoor lounge areas), very affordable and above-average Pan-Asian cuisine served late into the eve and topping out at $15, and a state-of-the-art sound system streaming ambient, down-tempo, hip-hop, funk, and house music, this is the "it" joint of the moment. 601 Eddy St. (at Polk St.). ☎ 415/885-5088. www.bambuddhalounge.com.

The Bliss Bar   Surprisingly trendy for sleepy family-oriented Noe Valley, this small, stylish, and friendly bar is a great place to stop for a varied mix of locals, colorful cocktail concoctions, and a DJ spinning at the front window from 4 to 11pm 4 nights per week (call for days). If it's open, take your cocktail into the too-cool back Blue Room. And if you're on a budget, stop by from 4:30 to 7pm when martinis, lemon drops, cosmos, watermelon cosmos, and apple martinis are $3. 4026 24th St. (between Noe and Castro sts.) ☎ 415/826-6200. www.blissbar.sf.com.

The Monkey Club   Casual and tucked away in a quiet section of the Mission, this hip locals bar (think 20s through 30s) is an ever fun and rather red spot to kick it on plush and comfy couches backed by giant picture windows; nibble on decent and inexpensive appetizers; and down stiff drinks while a DJ spins grooving house, jazz, and world music Wednesday through Sunday. 2730 21st St. (at Bryant St.). ☎ 415/ 647-6546.

Wish Bar   Flirtation, fun, and a very attractive staff await at this somewhat mellow, narrow bar in the popular night crawler area around 11th and Folsom streets. Swathed in burgundy and black with exposed cinderblock walls and cement floors, all's aglow a la candlelight and red-shaded sconces. With a bar in the front, DJ spinning housey lounge music in the back, and seating—including cushy leather couches—in between, it's often packed with a surprisingly diverse (albeit youthful) crowd and ever filled with eye candy. 1539 Folsom St. (between 11th and 12th sts.). ☎ 415/278-9474.

A RETRO CLUB

Club Deluxe *Finds*   Before the recent 1940s trend hit the city, Deluxe and its fedora-wearing clientele had been celebrating the bygone era for years. Fortunately, even with all the retro hype, the vibe here hasn't changed. Expect an eclectic mix of throwbacks and generic San Franciscans in the intimate bar and adjoining lounge, and live jazz or swing most nights. Although many regulars dress the part, there's no attitude here, so come as you like. 1511 Haight St. (at Ashbury St.). ☎ 415/552-6949. Cover $3–$10.

4 The Bar Scene

Finding your idea of a comfortable bar has a lot to do with picking a neighborhood filled with your kind of people and investigating that area. There are hundreds of bars throughout San Francisco, and although many are obscurely located and can't be classified by their neighborhood, the following is a general description of what you'll find, and where:

- **Chestnut and Union Street** bars attract a postcollegiate crowd.
- Young alternatives frequent **Mission District** haunts.
- **Upper Haight** caters to eclectic neighborhood cocktailers.
- **Lower Haight** is skate- and snowboarder grungy.
- Tourists mix with theatergoers and thirsty businesspeople in **downtown** pubs.
- **North Beach** serves all types.
- **The Castro** caters to gay locals and tourists.
- **SoMa** offers an eclectic mix.

The following is a list of a few of San Francisco's most interesting bars. Unless otherwise noted, these bars do not have cover charges.

Li Po Cocktail Lounge *Finds*   A dim, divey, slightly spooky Chinese bar that was once an opium den, Li Po's alluring character stems from its mishmash clutter of dusty Asian furnishings and mementos, including an unbelievably huge ancient rice-paper lantern hanging from the ceiling and a glittery golden shrine to Buddha behind the bar. The bartenders love to creep out patrons with tales of opium junkies haunting the joint. 916 Grant Ave. (between Washington and Jackson sts.). © 415/982-0072.

Perry's   If you read *Tales of the City*, you already know that this bar and restaurant has a colorful history as a pickup place for Pacific Heights and Marina singles. Although the times are not as wild today, locals still come to casually check out the happenings at the dark mahogany bar. A separate dining room offers breakfast, lunch, dinner, and weekend brunch. It's a good place for hamburgers, simple fish dishes, and pasta. Menu items range from $6 to $22. 1944 Union St. (at Laguna St.). © 415/922-9022.

Tips **Smoke Signals**

California forbids smoking in bars, restaurants, hotel lobbies, and public areas of any kind. Some bars break the rules. Others ask their guests to step outside. Either way, don't count on lighting up inside any public place. Establishment owners are quick to enforce the rule because they can be fined if patrons disobey.

The Red Room   Ultramodern, small, and deliciously dim, this lounge reflects no other color but ruby red. It's a sexy place to sip the latest cocktail. In the Commodore Hotel, 827 Sutter St. (at Jones St.). ℭ 415/346-7666.

Spec's *Finds*   The location of Spec's—Saroyan Place, a tiny alley at 250 Columbus Ave.—makes it less of a walk-in bar and more of a lively local hangout. Its funky decor—maritime flags hang from the ceiling; posters, photos, and oddities line the exposed-brick walls—gives it a character that intrigues every visitor. A "museum," displayed under glass, contains memorabilia and items brought back by seamen who drop in between voyages. The clientele is funky enough to keep you preoccupied while you drink a beer. 12 Saroyan Place (at 250 Columbus Ave.). ℭ 415/421-4112.

Toronado   Lower Haight isn't exactly a charming street, but there's plenty of nightlife here, catering to an artistic/grungy/skateboarding 20-something crowd. While Toronado definitely draws in the young'uns, its 40-plus microbrews on tap and 60 bottled beers also entice a more eclectic clientele in search of beer heaven. The brooding atmosphere matches the surroundings: an aluminum bar, a few tall tables, dark lighting, and a back room packed with tables and chairs. A DJ picks up the pace on Friday and Saturday nights. 547 Haight St. (at Fillmore St.). ℭ 415/863-2276. www.toronado.com.

Tosca *Finds*   Open daily from 5pm to 2am, Tosca is a low-key and large popular watering hole for local politicos, writers, media types, incognito visiting celebrities such as Johnny Depp or Nicholas Cage, and similar cognoscenti of unassuming classic characters. Equipped with dim lights, red leather booths, and high ceilings, it's everything you'd expect an old North Beach legend to be. 242 Columbus Ave. (between Broadway and Pacific Ave.). ℭ 415/986-9651.

Vesuvio   Situated along Jack Kerouac Alley, across from the famed City Lights bookstore, this renowned literary beatnik hangout is packed to the second-floor rafters with neighborhood writers, artists, songsters, wannabes, and everyone else ranging from longshoremen and cab drivers to businesspeople, all of whom come for the laid-back atmosphere. The convivial space is two stories of cocktail tables, complemented by a changing exhibition of local art. In addition to drinks, Vesuvio features an espresso machine. No credit cards. 255 Columbus Ave. (at Broadway). ℭ 415/362-3370. www.vesuvio.com.

BREWPUBS

Gordon Biersch Brewery Restaurant   Gordon Biersch Brewery is San Francisco's largest brew restaurant, serving decent food and tasty beer to an attractive crowd of mingling professionals. There are always several beers to choose from, ranging from light to dark. Menu items run $9.50 to $20. (See p. 80 for more information.) 2 Harrison St. (on The Embarcadero). ✆ 415/243-8246. www.gordonbiersch.com.

San Francisco Brewing Company   Surprisingly low key for an alehouse, this cozy brewpub serves its creations with burgers, fries, grilled chicken breast, and the like. The bar is one of the city's few remaining old saloons (ca. 1907), aglow with stained-glass windows, tile floors, skylit ceiling, beveled glass, and mahogany bar. A massive overhead fan runs the full length of the bar—a bizarre contraption crafted from brass and palm fronds. The handmade copper brew kettle is visible from the street. Most evenings the place is packed with everyday folks enjoying music or comedy, darts, chess, backgammon, cards, dice and, of course, beer. Menu items range from $3.70—curiously, for edamame (soybeans)—to $20 for a full rack of baby back ribs with all the fixings. The happy-hour special, an 8½-ounce microbrew beer for a dollar (or a pint for $2.50), is offered daily from 4 to 6pm and midnight to 1am. 155 Columbus Ave. (at Pacific St.). ✆ 415/434-3344. www.sfbrewing.com.

COCKTAILS WITH A VIEW

See p. 162 for a full review of **Harry Denton's Starlight Room.** Unless otherwise noted, the below establishments have no cover charge.

Carnelian Room   On the 52nd floor of the Bank of America Building, the Carnelian Room offers uninterrupted views of the city. From a window-front table you feel as though you can reach out, pluck up the TransAmerica Pyramid, and stir your martini with it. In addition to cocktails, the restaurant serves a three-course meal ($39 per person). Jackets are required and ties for men are optional, but encouraged. *Note:* The restaurant has one of the most extensive wine lists in the city—1,600 selections, to be exact. 555 California St., in the Bank of America Building (between Kearny and Montgomery sts.). ✆ 415/ 433-7500. www.carnelianroom.com.

Cityscape   When you sit under the glass roof and sip a drink here, it's as though you're sitting out under the stars and enjoying views of the bay. Dinner, focusing on steak and seafood, is available, and there's dancing to a DJ's picks nightly from 10pm. The mirrored

Finds   Midnight (or Midday) Mochas

If you happen to be wandering around North Beach past your bedtime and need your caffeine fix, seek out these two cafes. They offer not only excellent espresso, but also a glimpse back at the days of the beatniks, when nothing was as crucial as a strong cup of coffee, a good smoke, and a stimulating environment.

Doing the North Beach thing is little more than hanging out in a sophisticated but relaxed atmosphere over a well-made cappuccino. You can do it at **Caffè Greco**, 423 Columbus Ave., between Green and Vallejo streets (© **415/397-6261**), and grab a bite, too—until midnight. The affordable cafe fare includes beer and wine as well as a good selection of coffees, focaccia sandwiches, and desserts (try the gelato or homemade tiramisu).

Caffè Trieste, 601 Vallejo St., at Grant Avenue (© **415/392-6739**; www.cafetriste.com), is one of San Francisco's most beloved cafes—very down-home Italian, with only espresso drinks and pastries at indoor and outdoor seating. Opera is always on the jukebox, unless it's Saturday afternoon, when the family and their friends literally break out in arias during an operatic performance from 2 to 6pm. Another perk: They offer access to free Wi-Fi with purchase, but you'll have to bring your own laptop. Check 'em out until 10:30pm Sunday through Thursday and 11:30pm on Friday and Saturday.

columns and floor-to-ceiling draperies help create an elegant and romantic ambience here. *FYI:* they also offer a live champagne brunch on Sundays from 10am to 2pm. Hilton San Francisco, Tower I, 333 O'Farrell St. (at Mason St.), 46th floor. © 415/923-5002. Cover $10 Sat night.

Equinox   Though locals don't frequent this Fi-Di (Financial District) place, it's very popular with tourists. The hook? The 17-story Hyatt's rooftop restaurant has a revolving floor that gives each table a 360-degree panoramic view of the city every 45 minutes. In addition to cocktails, the Equinox serves dinner daily. In the Hyatt Regency Hotel, 5 Embarcadero Center. © 415/788-1234.

Top of the Mark *Moments*   This is one of the most famous cocktail lounges in the world, and for good reason—the spectacular glass-walled room features an unparalleled 19th-floor view. During World War II, Pacific-bound servicemen toasted their good-byes to the States here. While less dramatic today than they were back then, evenings spent here are still sentimental, thanks to the romantic atmosphere. Live entertainment (think swing band) Friday and Saturday starts at 8:30pm. Drinks range from $7 to $10. A $49 three-course fixed-price sunset dinner is served Friday and Saturday at 7:30pm. Sunday brunch, served from 10am to 2pm, costs $49 for adults and includes a glass of champagne; for children 5 to 14, the brunch is $25. In the Mark Hopkins Inter-Continental, 1 Nob Hill (California and Mason sts.). ℂ 415/616-6916. Cover $5–$10.

A SPORTS BAR

Greens Sports Bar   If you think San Francisco sports fans aren't as enthusiastic as those on the East Coast, try to get a seat at Green's during a 49ers game. It's a classic old sports bar, with lots of polished dark wood and windows that open onto Polk Street, but it's loaded with modern appliances (including two large-screen televisions and 18 smaller ones) and modern partyers (read: dot.comers and the mid-20s and -30s set). With 18 beers on tap, a pool table, and a happy hour Monday through Friday from 4 to 7pm, there are reasons to cheer here even when the home team's got a day off. 2239 Polk St. (at Green St.). ℂ 415/775-4287.

WINE & CHAMPAGNE BARS

The Bubble Lounge   Toasting the town is a nightly event at this two-level champagne bar. With 300 champagnes, about 30 by the glass, brick walls, couches, and velvet curtains, there's plenty of pop in this fizzy lounge. 714 Montgomery St. (at Columbus Ave.). ℂ 415/434-4204. www.bubblelounge.com.

Hayes and Vine   You'll find 1,200 wines (with more than 50 by the glass) from around the world at this unpretentious wine bar staffed by true cognoscenti of fine wine. (It's a good thing, too, because you have probably never heard of 90% of these wines.) Be sure to ask about taking a "flight," which allows you to try several different wines for a fixed price. Cheese, breads, antipasti, charcuterie, and desserts are also served. 377 Hayes St. (at Gough St.). ℂ 415/626-5301. www.hayesandvine.com.

London Wine Bar   This British-style wine bar and store is a popular after-work hangout for Financial District suits. It's more of a place to drink and chat, however, than one in which to admire fine wines. Usually 50 wines, mostly from California, are open at any given time and 800 are available by the bottle. It's a great venue for sampling local Napa Valley wines before you buy. 415 Sansome St. (between Sacramento and Clay sts.). ✆ 415/788-4811. www.londonwinebar.com.

5 Gay & Lesbian Bars & Clubs

Just like straight establishments, gay and lesbian bars and clubs target varied clienteles. Whether you're into leather or Lycra, business or bondage, in San Francisco, there's gay nightlife just for you.

Check the free weeklies, the *San Francisco Bay Guardian* and *San Francisco Weekly*, for listings of events and happenings around town. The *Bay Area Reporter* is a gay paper with comprehensive listings, including a weekly community calendar. All these papers are free and distributed weekly on Wednesday or Thursday. They can be found stacked at the corners of 18th and Castro streets and Ninth and Harrison streets, as well as in bars, bookshops, and other stores around town. There are also a number of gay and lesbian guides to San Francisco. See "Gay & Lesbian Travelers," in chapter 1, beginning on p. 8, for further details and helpful information. Also check out the rather homely, but very informative site titled "Queer Things to Do in the San Francisco Bay Area" at www.io.com/~larrybob/sanfran.html for a plethora of gay happenings.

Listed below are some of the city's most established mainstream gay hangouts.

The Café *(Finds* When this place first got jumping, it was the only predominantly lesbian dance club on Saturday nights in the city. Once the guys found out how much fun the girls were having, however, they joined the party. Today, it's a happening mixed gay and lesbian scene with three bars, a pool table, a steamy, free-spirited dance floor, and a small, heated patio where smoking and schmoozing is allowed. A perk: They open at 3pm daily. 2367 Market St. (at Castro St.). ✆ 415/861-3846. www.cafesf.com.

The Endup It's a different nightclub every night of the week, but regardless of who's throwing the party, the place is always jumping to the tunes blasted by DJs. There are two pool tables, a fireplace, an outdoor patio and, on the dance floor, a mob of gyrating souls. Some nights are straight, so call ahead. 401 Sixth St. (at Harrison St.). ✆ 415/357-0827. www.theendup.com. Cover free to $10.

Metro This bar provides the gay community with high-energy dance music and the best view of the Castro District from its large balcony. The bar seems to attract people of all ages who enjoy the friendliness of the bartenders and the highly charged, cruising atmosphere. There's a Chinese restaurant on the premises if you get hungry. 3600 16th St. (at Market St.). ✆ **415/703-9750.** www.metrocitybarsf.com.

The Stud   The Stud, which has been around for more than 30 years, is one of the most successful gay establishments in town. The interior has an antiques-shop look and a miniature train circling the bar and dance floor. Music is a balanced mix of old and new, and nights vary from cabaret to oldies to disco. Call in advance for the evening's offerings. Drink prices range from $3 to $13. Happy hour runs daily until 9pm with $1 draft beers. 399 Ninth St. (at Harrison St.). ✆ **415/863-6623** or event info line ✆ **415/252-STUD.** Cover $3–$10. www.studsf.com.

Twin Peaks Tavern   Right at the intersection of Castro, 17th, and Market streets is one of the Castro's most famous (at 40 years old) gay hangouts. It caters to an older crowd and claims to be the first gay bar in America. Because of its relatively small size and desirable location, the place becomes fairly crowded and convivial by 8pm, earlier than many neighboring bars. 401 Castro St. (at 17th and Market sts.). ✆ **415/864-9470.**

6 Film

The **San Francisco International Film Festival** (✆ **415/931-FILM;** www.sffs.org), held in April, is one of America's oldest film festivals. Entries include new films by beginning and established directors. Call or surf ahead for a schedule or information, and check out their website for more information on purchasing tickets, which are relatively inexpensive.

If you're not here in time for the festival, don't despair. The classic, independent, and mainstream cinemas in San Francisco are every bit as good as the city's other cultural offerings.

REPERTORY CINEMAS

Castro Theatre *Finds*   Built in 1922, the beautiful Castro Theatre is known for its screenings of classics and for its Wurlitzer organ, which is played before each show. There's a different feature almost nightly, and more often than not it's a double feature. Bargain matinees are usually offered on Wednesday, Saturday, Sunday, and holidays. Phone for schedules, prices, and show times. 429 Castro St. (near Market St.). ✆ **415/621-6120.** www.thecastrotheatre.com.

Red Vic   The worker-owned Red Vic movie collective originated in the neighboring Victorian building that gave it its name. The theater specializes in independent releases and contemporary cult hits and situates its patrons among an array of couches. Prices are $7 for adults ($5 for matinees) and $4 for seniors and kids 12 and under. Tickets go on sale 20 minutes before each show. Phone for schedules and show times. 1727 Haight St. (between Cole and Shrader sts.). © 415/ 668-3994. www.redvicmoviehouse.com.

Roxie   The Roxie consistently screens the best new alternative films anywhere. The low-budget contemporary features are largely devoid of Hollywood candy coating; many are West Coast premieres. Films change weekly and sometimes more often. Phone for schedules, prices, and show times. 3117 16th St. (at Valencia St.). © 415/ 863-1087. www.roxie.com.

Index

See also Accommodations and Restaurant indexes below.

ACCOMMODATIONS

RESTAURANTS

FROMMER'S® COMPLETE TRAVEL GUIDES

FROMMER'S® DOLLAR-A-DAY GUIDES

FROMMER'S® PORTABLE GUIDES

FROMMER'S® NATIONAL PARK GUIDES

Algonquin Provincial Park
Banff & Jasper
Family Vacations in the National
  Parks

Grand Canyon
National Parks of the American
  West
Rocky Mountain

Yellowstone & Grand Teton
Yosemite & Sequoia/Kings
  Canyon
Zion & Bryce Canyon

FROMMER'S® MEMORABLE WALKS

Chicago
London

New York
Paris

San Francisco

FROMMER'S® WITH KIDS GUIDES

Chicago
Las Vegas
New York City

Ottawa
San Francisco
Toronto

Vancouver
Walt Disney World® & Orlando
Washington, D.C.

SUZY GERSHMAN'S BORN TO SHOP GUIDES

Born to Shop: France
Born to Shop: Hong Kong,
  Shanghai & Beijing

Born to Shop: Italy
Born to Shop: London

Born to Shop: New York
Born to Shop: Paris

FROMMER'S® IRREVERENT GUIDES

Amsterdam
Boston
Chicago
Las Vegas
London

Los Angeles
Manhattan
New Orleans
Paris
Rome

San Francisco
Seattle & Portland
Vancouver
Walt Disney World®
Washington, D.C.

FROMMER'S® BEST-LOVED DRIVING TOURS

Austria
Britain
California
France

Germany
Ireland
Italy
New England

Northern Italy
Scotland
Spain
Tuscany & Umbria

THE UNOFFICIAL GUIDES®

Beyond Disney
California with Kids
Central Italy
Chicago
Cruises
Disneyland®
England
Florida
Florida with Kids
Inside Disney

Hawaii
Las Vegas
London
Maui
Mexico's Best Beach Resorts
Mini Las Vegas
Mini Mickey
New Orleans
New York City
Paris

San Francisco
Skiing & Snowboarding in the
  West
South Florida including Miami &
  the Keys
Walt Disney World®
Walt Disney World® for
  Grown-ups
Walt Disney World® with Kids
Washington, D.C.

SPECIAL-INTEREST TITLES

Athens Past & Present
Cities Ranked & Rated
Frommer's Best Day Trips from London
Frommer's Best RV & Tent Campgrounds
  in the U.S.A.
Frommer's Caribbean Hideaways
Frommer's China: The 50 Most Memorable Trips
Frommer's Exploring America by RV
Frommer's Gay & Lesbian Europe
Frommer's NYC Free & Dirt Cheap

Frommer's Road Atlas Europe
Frommer's Road Atlas France
Frommer's Road Atlas Ireland
Frommer's Wonderful Weekends from
  New York City
The New York Times' Guide to Unforgettable
  Weekends
Retirement Places Rated
Rome Past & Present

Travel Tip: He who finds the best hotel deal has more to spend on facials involving knobbly vegetables.

Hello, the Roaming Gnome here. I've been nabbed from the garden and taken round the world. The people who took me are so terribly clever. They find the best offerings on Travelocity. For very little cha-ching. And that means I get to be pampered and exfoliated till I'm pink as a bunny's doodah.

*** travelocity®

1-888-TRAVELOCITY / travelocity.com / America Online Keyword: Travel

Travel Tip: Make sure there's customer service for any change of plans — involving friendly natives, for example.

One can plan and plan, but if you don't book with the right people you can't seize le moment and canoodle with the poodle named Pansy. I, for one, am all for fraternizing with the locals. Better yet, if I need to extend my stay and my gnome nappers are willing, it can all be arranged through the 800 number at, oh look, how convenient, the lovely company coat of arms.

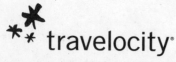

travelocity®

1-888-TRAVELOCITY / travelocity.com / America Online Keyword: Travel